Praise for *Green Living*

"This book continues *E/The Environmental Magazine*'s great tradition of providing readers with practical tips for living healthier, more eco-friendly lives. The authors clearly lay out the steps we all can take to ensure a better world for ourselves and future generations. I encourage everyone to open it immediately and find at least one green action to take right away."

—Alisa Gravitz, executive director, Co-op America

"*Green Living* is the most thorough guide to the sustainable lifestyle I've seen. If you're looking for timely advice on everything from pesticide-free food to hybrid cars, your search has ended."

—Ed Begley Jr., actor and environmental activist

"If every American picked just one thing to do from this great book, we would be well on our way to a better, cleaner, safer world."

—Laurie David, television producer, activist, trustee, Natural Resources Defense Council

GREEN LIVING

The *E Magazine* Handbook
for Living Lightly on the Earth

BY THE EDITORS OF

E/THE ENVIRONMENTAL MAGAZINE

A PLUME BOOK

PLUME
Published by Penguin Group
Penguin Group (USA) Inc., 375 Hudson Street, New York, New York 10014, U.S.A.
Penguin Group (Canada), 10 Alcorn Avenue, Toronto, Ontario, Canada M4V 3B2
(a division of Pearson Penguin Canada Inc.)
Penguin Books Ltd., 80 Strand, London WC2R 0RL, England
Penguin Ireland, 25 St. Stephen's Green, Dublin 2, Ireland (a division of Penguin Books Ltd.)
Penguin Group (Australia), 250 Camberwell Road, Camberwell, Victoria 3124, Australia
(a division of Pearson Australia Group Pty. Ltd.)
Penguin Books India Pvt. Ltd., 11 Community Centre, Panchsheel Park, New Delhi – 110 017, India
Penguin Books (NZ), cnr Airborne and Rosedale Roads, Albany, Auckland, New Zealand
(a division of Pearson New Zealand Ltd.)
Penguin Books (South Africa) (Pty.) Ltd., 24 Sturdee Avenue, Rosebank, Johannesburg 2196, South Africa

Penguin Books Ltd., Registered Offices: 80 Strand, London WC2R 0RL, England

First published by Plume, a member of Penguin Group (USA) Inc.

First Printing, June 2005
10   9   8   7

Ⓟ REGISTERED TRADEMARK—MARCA REGISTRADA

CIP data is available.
ISBN 978-0-452-28574-3

Printed in the United States of America
Set in Legacy Serif
Designed by Joseph Rutt

PUBLISHER'S NOTE
This publication is designed to provide accurate and authoritative information about living an environmentally conscious lifestyle. However, neither the publisher nor any of the authors is engaged in rendering legal, accounting, financial, investment, medical, nutritional, architectural, engineering, travel, or other professional services. Nothing in this book is intended as a substitute for consulting with a professional. All matters regarding your health and your children's health require medical advice and supervision. The information contained in this book cannot replace sound judgment and good decision-making in any context.

The recipes in this book are to be followed exactly as written. Neither any author nor the publisher is responsible for any adverse reactions to recipes.

The authors have made every effort to provide addresses, Internet addresses, and telephone numbers that were accurate at the time of writing. Neither the publisher nor any author assumes responsibility for errors or for changes in such information.

The scanning, uploading, and distribution of this book via the Internet or via any other means without the permission of the publisher is illegal and punishable by law. Please purchase only authorized electronic editions, and do not participate in or encourage electronic piracy of copyrighted materials. Your support of the author's rights is appreciated.

BOOKS ARE AVAILABLE AT QUANTITY DISCOUNTS WHEN USED TO PROMOTE PRODUCTS OR SERVICES. FOR INFORMATION PLEASE WRITE TO PREMIUM MARKETING DIVISION, PENGUIN GROUP (USA) INC., 375 HUDSON STREET, NEW YORK, NEW YORK 10014.

For the loyal readers of *E/The Environmental Magazine,*
who have supported our work since 1990.

Acknowledgments

The comprehensive guide you hold in your hands has many fingerprints on it. We don't profess to know everything there is to know about living lightly on the Earth, but we get by, as our Beatle-loving publisher might say, with a little help from our friends. And these friends include the many collaborators who wrote sections of the book (their names are at the end) or who gave us useful advice when we were putting it together. *Green Living* would never have been written without the initial encouragement of former Plume editor Ryan Harbage, whose idea it was. Our editor at Plume, Jake Klisivitch, helped shape and slim down a bulky manuscript and provided Icelandic music CDs to keep us motivated. And, as always, we owe a huge debt of gratitude to our agent, Sabine Hrechdakian, who is tough and tender in equal measures, and always at the right times.

Contents

"How you imagine the world determines how you live in it."
—David Suzuki

Preface

We all think of ourselves as environmentalists, even if our biggest gesture on behalf of the planet is taking the recycling out once a week. Overwhelmingly, we support clean air, clean water, and healthy forests, even if it means cracking down on the corporate sector and doing a little belt-tightening ourselves.

According to a recent Gallup Poll, Americans by large majorities not only support the environmental movement in general, but actually take action in support of their beliefs. For instance, 90 percent recycle, 83 percent have made concrete steps to reduce energy use, and 83 percent are trying to use less water. That same 83 percent has consciously avoided environmentally harmful products, and 73 percent have bought environmentally beneficial products. In 2004, 62 percent of Americans said they worry "a great deal" about the environment.

Forty percent of the American people have contributed money to an environmental group, 31 percent have signed petitions, and 20 percent have attended meetings. An incredible 13 percent have gone much further and contacted a business to complain about its products or policies because they harm the environment. As Gallup describes it, "Thirty years after its founding, most Americans view the environmental movement positively. Large majorities of the public agree with its goals, see it as doing more good than harm, and trust it to protect our nation's environment, while significant minorities claim participation in its activities and organizations."

Yet Americans aren't always able to grasp the impact of their personal choices; some 44 percent of those surveyed agreed with the statement, "What I do does *not* impact the health of natural habitats." The truth is that Americans, with just 4.5 percent of the world's population, consume

33 percent of its materials. The "ecological footprint" of the average American consumer (the land needed to provide the materials supporting his or her lifestyle) is thirty acres, while the average Italian can get by on less than fifteen acres! Even though most of us are interested in the environment, we lack the basic knowledge and information on how to make informed green lifestyle decisions.

That's where *E/The Environmental Magazine* comes in. Founded in 1990, the mission of the bimonthly newsstand publication is to deliver to the public user-friendly information about often complex subjects. We figure that most people don't have the time to read peer-reviewed scientific journals, and even if they did they'd have trouble coping with the insider language and technical terms.

In 1996, *E* launched its "Green Living" section, with articles on travel, health, the home, investing, consumer products, and "eating right" in every issue. Our "EarthTalk" feature gives readers a chance to write in with environmental questions. This "back of the book" journalism has become a very popular part of the magazine because it hits our readers right where they live. Rather than the big issues of climate change, rainforest deforestation, and overpopulation, it's about the carpet on your floor, the car in your driveway, and the food on your table.

This book grew out of *E*'s "Green Living" reporting, and we've made it as thorough and comprehensive as we can. As in the magazine itself, there are extensive resource listings in all of the chapters so you can follow up your reading by taking action. So while this is a consumer guide, it's also a manual for getting involved in the environmental movement.

We hope you enjoy the book, and that it plays a part in "greening up" your life. Please visit us on the Web at www.emagazine.com for the latest green information.

Jim Motavalli
Editor of *E/The Environmental Magazine*

chapter one

The Passionate Palate
Smart Food Choices

Photo by Gail Mooney/Masterfile

When federal scientist Jim Bohnsack is in the mood for seafood, he asks the restaurant server: Do you have turtle-safe shrimp?

Some look at him as if he landed from Mars. Others understand and, if all goes well, present him with a heaping plate of hot boiled shrimp caught with nets that don't ensnare and kill sea turtles, thanks to turtle escape hatches. Shrimp fishing trawlers are a major killer of turtles. Yet, foreign fleets, unlike U.S.-based ships, don't use Turtle-Excluder Devices.

Bohnsack has good reason to be sensitive about what he eats. He researches snapper, grouper, and other popular dinner-plate fish for a living for the NOAA Fisheries, and what he and scientists around the world are discovering about fish isn't reassuring.

More than 90 percent of the world's swordfish, marlin, giant tuna, and other large predatory fishes have been caught by far-roaming industrial fishing fleets—making a collapse of those stocks possible, according to a newsmaking study published in the journal *Nature* in 2003. At Biscayne National Park south of Miami, scientist Jerry Ault dove twenty-eight times in 2002 before he saw his first grouper or snapper large enough to reproduce.

"I was really in shock," says Ault, of University of Miami's Rosenstiel School of Marine and Atmospheric Science, who was co-leading an underwater census of fish in the Florida Keys with Bohnsack. "What it's really saying to you is I'm having trouble finding reproductive fish out there. That is *really* scary for the future."

Plummeting fisheries help illustrate the quandary facing health-conscious Earthwise consumers in aisle after supermarket aisle. The choices at the seafood counter—some easy on the Earth, many others destructive—are so dizzying that several conservation groups have issued little cheat sheets in the form of wallet-sized cards. And even *they* aren't necessarily complete.

At the meat and poultry counter, most packages are silent about hormones, antibiotics, and feed that may include ground-up animals or animal waste. Five thousand people die each year from food poisoning, often due to meat and poultry; beyond that, 76 million cases of food-borne illness sicken people each year, according to Consumer Federation of America. Hamburger raises the specter of an *E. coli* outbreak, which, while still rare, can produce lingering doubts for a shopper. "As few as two or three bacteria are enough to cause human illness, which is really scary," microbiologist Dr. Glenn Morris Jr. of University of Maryland, told the PBS television documentary program *Frontline*. Pressed further, he said two or three *E. coli* bacteria can be "enough to kill someone."

Even the produce section can give you pause, as many fruits and vegetables grow with the aid of synthetic fertilizers, pesticides, and in some cases even sewage sludge. Some grow with the help of fertilizers that legally contain lead, arsenic, and cadmium from "recycled" toxic waste. Fertilizer is so poorly regulated that industry, power-plant, and mining wastes can be mixed with plant food, according to Duff Wilson, an investigative reporter with the *New York Times* and author of *Fateful Harvest: The True Story of a Small Town, a Global Industry, and a Toxic Secret*. Wilson discovered forty-six states have no limits on—or public disclosure about—arsenic, beryllium, cadmium, lead, mercury, and dioxins that lace some fertilizers.

CHOICES AT THE CHECKOUT

And if all that's not enough, consider the baffling decisions facing you in the supermarket interior. Six out of ten processed foods you could choose to drop into your cart contain genetically modified ingredients, such as corn altered to contain its own pesticide (*Bacillus thuringiensis*) in every cell. Some other corn and 81 percent of all soybeans grown in the United States are engineered for another purpose—to thrive after being doused with a chemical weed-killer.

Check the Codes

While at the produce counter, you can tell whether a zucchini or a Hawaiian-grown papaya are genetically engineered or organic by employing this little-known strategy: Look at the code printed on the tiny sticker stuck on the produce. If the PLU code begins with the number 9, it's organic. Conventionally grown fruits and vegetables bear a code beginning with 4. If the code begins with an 8, the produce is genetically engineered—making this the only genetic engineering label in the United States. While this numbering system is handy for ensuring that you picked up organic fruit instead of the conventional variety, it's unlikely that you'll pick up a piece of genetically engineered produce. Very few varieties are sold.

Coca-Cola. Sprite. Pepsi. Hershey's bars. M&Ms. Campbell's soups. Progresso soups. Cereals by the big-name companies: Kellogg's, Post, Quaker, and General Mills. Even Harvest Burgers by Morningstar and black bean burgers from Natural Touch. They're among hundreds of products found to contain genetically modified organisms, according to tests conducted for the True Food Shopping List originated by Greenpeace and now managed by the Genetic Engineering Action Network—an umbrella organization of activists, scientists, and academics who work to address the potential risks poised by genetic manipulation. Yet, labels don't say—and Congress doesn't require them to say—anything about genetically engineered ingredients.

All of this has driven discriminating consumers into the arms of the burgeoning organic foods industry. But even there, consumers have to be careful. Not all "organic" labels are created equal. Only "certified organic" items are certified to be 100 percent organic. Those labeled "made with organic ingredients" are something less—they're 70 to 94 percent organic.

While organic food remains a solid choice for green consumers, there is a growing belief that another strategy makes even more sense while providing more fresh-from-the-farm flavor: Buy local food. Support local produce, local farms, local distinction. Especially when you shop at a farmers' market, your fruits and vegetables stand a good chance of having been grown with minimal pesticide, if any. You get a chance to shake hands with the people who raised your produce, and your conversations and purchases may influence how they grow crops next year.

With local produce, you're also going easy on global warming: The food traveled twenty miles from the field to your kitchen, not two thousand miles. A "transcontinental strawberry," as writer Michael Pollan termed it in the *New York Times Magazine*, provides five calories of food energy but "takes 435 calories of fossil-fuel energy to deliver to my door." A careful

The Case Against Meat

Consider:

- You'd save more water by not eating a single pound of California beef than you would by not showering for an entire year, wrote John Robbins in his book *The Food Revolution*.

- Producing a single hamburger patty uses enough fuel to drive twenty miles. It also causes the loss of five times its weight in topsoil.

- More than a third of all raw materials and fossil fuels consumed in the United States are used in animal production.

- Because of deforestation to create grazing land, each vegetarian saves an acre of trees per year.

- It takes 4.8 pounds of grain (fed to cattle) to produce one pound of beef.

- A pound of wheat can be grown with sixty pounds of water, whereas a pound of meat requires 2,500 to 6,000 pounds, according to authors Paul and Anne Ehrlich.

- Harvard nutritionist Jean Mayer estimates that reducing meat production by just 10 percent in the United States would free enough grain to feed 60 million people.

- While it is true that many animals graze on land that would be unsuitable for cultivation, it's also true that the demand for meat has taken millions of productive acres away from farm inventories. The cost of that is incalculable. As *Diet for a Small Planet* author Frances Moore Lappé writes, imagine sitting down to an eight-ounce steak. "Then imagine the room filled with forty-five to fifty people with empty bowls in front of them. For the 'feed cost' of your steak, each of their bowls could be filled with a full cup of cooked cereal grains."

- Energy-intensive U.S. factory farms generated 1.4 billion tons of animal waste in 1996, which, the EPA reports, pollutes American waterways more than all other industrial sources combined. Meat production has also been linked to severe erosion of billions of acres of once-productive farmland and to the destruction of rainforests.

- There are 20 billion head of livestock taking up space on the Earth, more than triple the number of people.

consumer, Pollan has taken to buying food and unpasteurized milk from area farmers, even if they're not certified organic.

Fans of local and organic foods are adamant: They want healthy, sustainably produced, *flavorful* food—like the juice-dripping-down-the-chin peaches of their childhood and sun-ripened sugary tomatoes that taste like they were plucked off the vine moments ago.

SLOW DOWN!

Enough with tasteless tomatoes and enough with homogenous fast food. Bring on the opposite, or "Slow Food," as the movement founded in Italy by Carlo Petrini in 1986 is called. Now spread into the United States, the movement gives a voice to small-scale producers and encourages a market for foods left endangered by industrial standardization or environmental damage. Louisiana heritage strawberries number among the foods promoted by the Slow Food Foundation's Ark of Taste project, as is a corn variety that seemed destined for extinction—Tuscarora White Corn, given by Iroquois Indians to George Washington and his starving troops at Valley Forge. Others have intensely local identities, such as the Delaware chicken; Vermont's mild-taste Gilfeather turnip; the Crane melons, developed by the Crane family of California's Sonoma County; and Washington's native Olympia oyster, originally walloped by pulp-mill pollution and overharvesting. It now has dwindled to almost token status in Puget Sound due to local producers' preference to grow hardier Asian oysters.

To Patrick Martins, president of Slow Food USA, slow food is sustainable food. "It is about living well," he said in 2001, "and eating with a mission."

That mission can be manifold, for few things stir passions as much as food. Some people buy local food to keep small farmers afloat and head off hated urban sprawl and its accompanying traffic jams. Steadfast vegetarians—about 3 percent of American adults—always avoid meat for intensely personal reasons, including religion, health, concerns about pollution from factory farms, or disgust over how animals are raised. Vegans, for similar reasons, go even further to also avoid dairy products, eggs, honey, or any animal products (including silk, cosmetics, and wool). "Ethical omnivores" are just as passionate about their choice to eat meat and dairy products *only* if animals are raised humanely.

Virtually all chickens these days are factory raised, with as many as six egg-laying hens living in a wire-floored cage the size of an album cover. Beef cattle have an average of fourteen square feet in their crowded feedlots. Morley Safer reported on the television program *60 Minutes* that today's factory pig is no "Babe": "[They] see no sun in their limited lives, with no hay to lie on, no mud to roll in. The sows live in tiny cages, so narrow they cannot even turn around. They live over metal grates, and their waste is pushed through slats beneath them and flushed into huge pits."

Eating, in short, is more than a necessity for life. It has also long been a ritual celebrated with birthday cakes, $20,000 wedding receptions, Easter hams, Passover seders, Hindu holiday samosas, Mother's Day brunches, Chinese New Year feasts, Cinco de Mayo celebrations, Thanksgiving turkeys.

But increasingly, eating also is a method of voting.

"Every time we pull out our wallet to buy something, we are casting a vote for the kind of society and economy we want. Whether we fully realize it or not, we vote with our dollars every single day, either for or against sustainability, for or against health, for or against justice," asserts Ronnie Cummins, national director of the Organic Consumers Association in Little Marais, Minnesota. "There's only one reason for buying organic food, clothing, and other products; for supporting Fair Trade; and giving preference to independently owned local and regional businesses—because it's the best way to live.

"One of the most encouraging social and political phenomena in the United States and the global North is that more and more consumers are challenging the status quo and starting to put their money where their values lie."

Spend $10 at a farmers' market, for instance, and that money encourages small regional farmers to grow carpets of lettuce and waist-high sweet corn on land that otherwise might sprout housing subdivisions. Spend $10 on organic shade-grown coffee, and that purchase helps ensure the winter homes of Baltimore Orioles and other songbirds.

But spend $10 on an Atlantic swordfish steak, and it'll have an entirely different effect. Allen Susser of Chef Allen's restaurant in Miami stopped serving swordfish some years ago because filets now come from fish that average ninety pounds—down from 400 pounds a century ago. Ninety pounds sounds big for a fish, until you hear that females can't reproduce until they weigh at least 150 pounds. If fish are caught before they reproduce, where will future swordfish come from? "The swordfish used to be a big, humongous fish," Susser says. "To see that adult population be whittled down like that . . . really sends the message home. So I'm not serving swordfish."

Susser votes with his food dollars.

CURRENT EVENTS/LEGISLATIVE/POLITICAL

When the natural grocery chain Whole Foods Market opened its foodie paradise with a 248-seat café and sushi bar in the Time Warner Center in February 2004, it instantly became Manhattan's biggest supermarket and symbolized a phenomenon. Organic foods represent the fastest-growing food market—for good reason. Rising 21 percent yearly and projected to reach $30.7 billion by 2007, according to the market analysis firm Datamonitor, the industry may be a small fraction of the overall food market. But its growth is fueled by news reports about mad cow disease, cancer-promoting pollutants in farm-raised salmon, and concerns about chemical pesticides in fresh fruits and vegetables.

Produce is the most popular organic food, and may contain more natural antioxidants linked to reduced risk for cancer, stroke, heart disease, and other illnesses, according to research at the University of California. A 2001 study in the *Journal of Alternative and Complementary Medicine* found that organic crops had higher average levels of twenty-one nutrients studied, including vitamin C and iron. At the 2004 First World Congress on Organic Food, keynote speaker Kathleen Merrigan, director of Tufts University's Agriculture Food and Environment Program, reviewed studies that found organic food had fewer pesticide residues and higher levels of omega-3 fatty acids. They also had higher levels of some secondary plant metabolites that may help prevent cancer. She called the research "not conclusive, but tantalizing."

Some call the trend the Mainstreaming of Organics. Kroger, Safeway, Publix, Albertsons, and Wal-Mart number among traditional supermarkets that now set aside space for organic foods. When Super Target grocery stores began selling organic chicken and beef in 2004, it drew praise from the New York–based Global Resource Action Center for the Environment, which promotes sustainable food.

The natural foods industry could be described as a victim of its own success. Some foods now are marketed by mainstream giants that want a share of the trend, including General Mills, Kellogg's, Mars, ConAgra, and Archer

Daniels Midland. Boca Burgers come from Kraft. So do Back to Nature cereals, a line that originated in 1960 in the back of a health food store in Madison, Wisconsin. Kellogg's makes Natural Touch organic soy burgers. Mars owns Seeds of Change, known for its organic seeds and bottled organic tomato sauces.

ConAgra offers organic bread flour. Heinz Company owns a stake in Hain Celestial Group, which makes Garden of Eatin' snacks, Earth's Best Baby Food and, among other things, Celestial Seasonings teas. General Mills' Small Planet Foods makes organic products under the Muir Glen and Cascadian Farms labels. Procter & Gamble's Millstone specialty coffee line sells some organic beans. Archer Daniels Midland in 2003 opened its first organic processing plant to make an organic soybean powder, and when a company official spoke at the Soyfoods Summit 2004, his talk included a discussion on "Organic whole soybean products: the face of the future?"

All of this makes it easier for consumers to buy organic foods, but causes some observers to lament that the movement has strayed from its original vision that went beyond healthy, environmentally friendly food to also favor small local farms and thus serve as a counterpoint to agribusiness. Corporate organic firms now are squeezing out small producers in Britain. "Industrial Organic" is how Michael Pollan terms today's multibillion-dollar industry.

"When I think of organic farming, I think family farm, I think small scale, I think hedgerows and compost piles and battered pickup trucks. I don't think migrant laborers, combines, thousands of acres of broccoli reaching clear to the horizon. To the eye, these farms look exactly like any other industrial farm in California . . . ," Pollan wrote in 2001. During a California trip, he discovered that five conventional megafarms control half of the state's organic produce market. So, "the same farmer who is applying toxic fumigants to sterilize the soil in one field is in the next field applying compost to nurture the soil's natural fertility. Is there something wrong with this picture? It all depends on where you stand."

Competing forces—including large food chains and organic purists—are trying to control the industry, resulting in a tug-of-war over federal organic standards, which define what can or cannot wear the official "organic" label. The federal Environmental Protection Agency (EPA) has leaned toward the loosest possible interpretation of the rules; as of 2004, it favored a proposal to allow sewage sludge as a fertilizer on "organic" crops, among many other outrages to organic advocates.

Meanwhile, a furious battle is being waged over a major competitor of organic foods: products containing genetically modified organisms (GMOs), which are found in six out of ten processed foods at the supermarket yet currently aren't labeled as such for American consumers. Since genetically engineered crops became available to farmers in 1996, the planted acreage has mushroomed—from 4.3 million acres that year (an area smaller than Vermont) to 2003's worldwide tally of 167.2 million acres (nearly the size of Texas). Seventy percent grow in the United States. Most soybeans and cotton grown in the United States are genetically engineered (81 percent and 71 percent, respectively). So is about 40 percent of all corn.

Eating GE

You definitely eat genetically engineered soy, corn, canola, and cotton, whether you realize it or not, according to Cornell University. Corn, soy, canola, and some cottonseed turn up in processed foods as oils. Biotech soy binds hot dogs and turns up in some nutritional supplements such as protein extracts and vitamin E. Ground corn ends up in taco shells and chips. Other corn-based ingredients include cornstarch, flour, dextrose, maltrose, baking powder, and the nation's leading sweetener—high-fructose corn syrup (the average American consumes 62.6 pounds a year).

Most corn and soybeans end up in animal feed, so consumers likely eat meat and poultry from animals raised on biotech feed. Flax, canola, Hawaiian-grown papayas, and some squashes are other U.S. crops authorized to be genetically engineered. Wheat and rice are potentially next. Down the road could come lettuce, as well as crops engineered to produce drugs, vaccines, and plastic.

Many European countries refuse to accept U.S.-grown produce for fear it contains biotech ingredients. While the industry and government officials assert that biotech foods are perfectly safe, a broad range of scientists, academics, and ethicists are concerned about the use of never-before-seen techniques such as adding jellyfish genes to wheat to make plants glow whenever they need water. Or inserting a bacteria gene into corn to ward off pests. Biotech foods have sparked a campaign among farmers calling for a moratorium on genetically engineered wheat, and prompted some parents to campaign against genetically engineered foods in school cafeterias.

It's particularly troubling that no one knows how to keep these newfangled genes from contaminating nearby organic or conventional crops. Eleven percent of organic farmers surveyed say they're already experiencing genetic pollution of their crops, according to a nationwide survey conducted by the Organic Farming Research Foundation. In a newsmaking 2004 pilot study by the Union of Concerned Scientists, researchers bought seeds at retailers used by U.S. farmers and found that the seeds of three major crops—corn, canola, and soybeans—are "pervasively contaminated with low levels" of genetically engineered material. Study authors estimate that 0.5 percent to 1 percent of seeds on the market are contaminated. At the 1 percent rate, that potentially translates to enough errant transgenic corn seeds, the study says, to "fill 240 large tractor-trailer trucks."

"You cannot build a wall high enough to keep GMOs out of the environment, as pollen often drifts for miles on the wind. And in the case of GMO pollen, it potentially contaminates everything in its path," argues Arran Stephens, president and founder of Nature's Path Foods, maker of organic food products.

This drift is particularly devastating for the organic farmer, and takes money right out of his or her pocket. Eight percent of organic farmers surveyed say they've borne costs or damages related to the advent of genetic engineering in agriculture, including costs to test their seeds or crops and the loss of sales or markets due to contamination or perceived contamination risk, according to the Organic Farming Research Foundation. Once contaminated, the harvested crops can't be sold at the premium paid by the organic market—or even conventional market. Gail and Tom Wiley, soy-

From Farmers to You

Farmers' markets are mushrooming around the country and have become a fun, green, inexpensive way to shop for people passionate about flavorful food, especially produce grown from rich black organic soil. The richer the organic matter in soil, the higher the sugar content and tastier the peach or turnip grown in it, says Jon Rowley, a Seattle food consultant.

Laura Miller of Wisconsin takes the farmers' market concept a step further: She buys a share of a farmer's harvest. A fun option increasingly chosen by green consumers, the concept is called Community Supported Agriculture (CSA). Miller gets a basket of farm-fresh, seasonal produce each week during summer and fall—about twenty weeks, in all. She gets it in return for paying in full in advance. Produce for a family of four through CSA programs typically costs $300 to $600, averaging up to $30 weekly for freshly picked, bagged, all-set-to-go, often organic produce. Some people split shares with a friend to lower the tab. Either way, the cost is generally comparable to a supermarket's. More than 1,000 U.S. farms participate in "teikei" ("putting the farmer's face on food"), as it's called in Japan, where the movement began about three decades ago in response to the nation's dwindling farms and increasing reliance on imported food.

Find the farmers' market closest to you by inquiring at your local chamber of commerce or City Hall, or by going online (www.ams.usda.gov/farmersmarkets). To find a Community Supported Agriculture program near you, inquire at your favorite vendors at farmers' markets or go online (www.localharvest.org or www.foodroutes.org).

bean growers in North Dakota, were ready to ship their high-protein conventionally grown food-grade soybeans to Japan in the summer of 2000 when tests found that 1.37 percent of the beans were contaminated with genetically engineered beans. The Wileys don't know the cause, whether drift from neighboring farms, pollen, the work of bees, or contamination of the original seed, but "we lost that contract," says Gail Wiley. "We sold the soybeans just on the open market, and the difference . . . was about $10,000 for our farm."

Seed contamination, if left unchecked, could unfairly burden the organic industry and allow potentially hazardous materials into the food supply, the authors of the Union of Concerned Scientists study contend. As demand for organic foods rises at supermarkets, it becomes that much more important for organic farmers to avoid transgenic contamination.

"It's important for people to know that if we don't stop genetic engineering, we're not going to have a thriving system of organic agriculture," says Simon Harris, national campaign director for the Organic Consumers Association.

Despite industry lobbying against labeling genetically engineered foods, most Americans polled overwhelmingly say they want labels. Without such labels on beverage cans and food packages, the only way to be certain to avoid biotech ingredients is by buying foods that are certified organic.

Yet, consumers often vote against organics and—often unwittingly—in favor of GE foods at the checkout line. It is that disconnect that is helping fuel the growth of the biotech food industry.

All of these issues have led to great confusion in the marketplace. Should I buy the "natural" eggs, the "free range," or the "organic"? When I can't afford organic food, is there any other way to definitely avoid products containing genetically engineered ingredients?

More and more, "ordinary people are becoming more demanding about everything they buy," *American Demographics* reported in a 2004 article headlined, "Food Safety: Why People Are Turning to Organics." "They want to know precisely what's in what they buy. What are the ingredients? What was the manufacturing process? Who made it? How was it made? Where? Were the conditions safe? Humane? What impact did the manufacture of the item have on the environment, and the people in the environment? People are asking these questions and demanding 'transparency' and forthrightness in answers to them."

GREEN PRODUCTS

It's easy to find healthy, green foods if you rethink the way you shop and employ the smart strategies outlined below. Arm yourself with shopping guides like those found in the accompanying charts. Beyond that, it's time to learn to look at food shopping in a different way.

Shop the perimeter of your typical supermarket and ignore the middle, advises Jane Rissler, a former biotechnology regulator with the EPA who now works for the Union of Concerned Scientists.

That way, your cart fills with fresh vegetables, fruits, fish, and (possibly) meats. You'll avoid thousands of mass-produced junk foods, frozen pizzas, muffins, taco shells, frozen foods, and other items likely to contain GE corn, canola, or soy. Plus, you'll stay clear of ample additives including sodium. This also is a good strategy for saving money; fresh foods cost less than processed edibles. Pat Hendricks of Zephyrhills, Florida, learned this perimeter-shopping strategy the hard way. Hospitalized with congestive heart failure at age forty-four and told she had seven years to live, the single mom of two children outlasted that prediction by kicking her reliance on fast-food cheeseburgers and processed foods, as well as by getting a pacemaker and following a firm piece of advice.

"You have to eat what comes off a tree or off the ground," Hendricks recalls being told. She now avoids the interior of the supermarket. She feels healthier than she has in years.

Strategy No. 2: Buy organic foods—and when that's not possible (or affordable), know which organic fruits and vegetables are essential. You can slash your exposure to pesticides by 90 percent by avoiding the "dirty dozen." Here are the most contaminated conventionally grown fruits and vegetables, according to Environmental Working Group, so buy these organic: apples, bell peppers, celery, cherries, imported grapes, nectarines, peaches, pears, potatoes, red raspberries, spinach, and strawberries.

Perhaps you don't eat any of those things often, but regularly consume other foods. The Organic Trade Association suggests buying organic versions of whatever foods you eat most. Another strategy for prioritizing your organic-food dollars is to avoid the ten conventionally produced foods most likely to be contaminated with long-banned chemicals that persist in the environment and are linked to developmental disorders and serious disease, including cancer. Merely by eating food, Americans can experience up to seventy daily exposures to residues from "persistent organic pollutants" such as dieldrin, a pesticide banned in the 1970s, according to research conducted by the Pesticide Action Network North America and published in the *Journal of Epidemiology and Community Health* in 2002. The Organic Trade Association suggests avoiding the nonorganic versions of the top ten contaminated foods uncovered by that research, which are (in alphabetical order): butter, cantaloupe, cucumbers/pickles, meatloaf, peanuts, popcorn, radishes, spinach, summer squash, and winter squash.

Hawaiian-grown papayas so far are the likeliest to be genetically engineered. More than half of papayas grown in that state are genetically modified. The chances of finding them at the supermarket are highest in Hawaii or the West Coast, according to Cornell University's Genetically Engineered Organisms Public Education Project. If your papaya comes from somewhere else—Brazil, Mexico, or the Caribbean—it isn't genetically engineered (at this point, at least).

What about other produce? It's possible but unlikely that you'll find green zucchini and yellow squash grown from the GE seeds marketed by

Asgrow Vegetable Seed, according to Cornell, since very few farmers use them. Genetically engineered strawberries have been field-tested since 2000, but hadn't hit the market by 2004. Your fresh potatoes are "probably not" genetically engineered, according to Cornell, since all GE potatoes were discontinued (due to poor sales) and since 2001 haven't been sold to farmers for planting. Biotech sweet corn—sold as fresh ears—represent 3 to 5 percent of the sweet-corn crop.

If convenience or preference dictate that you shop at a traditional super-market, then a good strategy is to head to the sections devoted to organic produce and natural products. Depending on the store, some prices for teas, natural sodas, and other items may be lower than at health-food stores, particularly at sale time. Mary Lee Treter of Toledo, Ohio, is impressed by the organic produce section at her local Kroger. "It's not very big, but it's a start," Treter says. "Being from Toledo, we don't have a lot of organic food markets in this area." The trend at traditional stores is hopeful, though not a panacea. At some giant chains, organic produce may sit in a "tiny little ghettoized section," complains Charles Margulis, a chef by training who sits on the steering committee of Californians for a GE-Free Agriculture. Some fruit comes packed on Styrofoam boards and, he says, "looks weeks old."

"I go to a traditional chain store to buy diapers and toilet paper, and that's about it," says Margulis, whose toddler outgrew organic cotton diapers. He finds it easier to be a socially conscious consumer at a natural food store, especially when the object is buying organic produce and the destination is a national chain with ample, well-lighted displays such as Whole Foods Market or Wild Oats. The number of organic produce varieties to choose from easily can top one hundred at Whole Foods in summer.

A longtime expert critic of genetic engineering, Margulis—like other shoppers—also can avoid biotech ingredients in processed foods by willy nilly grabbing any of the hundreds of store-brand items sold at Whole Foods, Wild Oats, or Trader Joe's. All three refuse genetically modified ingredients in their private-label products, which are the low-cost competitors to name-brand soups, spaghetti sauces, peanut butter, and so on. Whole Foods reformulated its sodas, ice cream, and frozen-fruit bars to remove corn syrup—an ingredient that is difficult to ensure to be GE-free. Trader Joe's became the latest to require its private-label suppliers to be GMO-free, explaining in a 2003 company statement: "We determined that, given a choice, our customers would prefer to eat foods and beverages made without the use of genetically engineered ingredients."

Raw and Uncooked

Will the oven ever become a passé appliance as health-conscious Americans decide to eat most of their food uncooked? Raw foods are being touted as one of the newest ways to eat healthfully and have a low impact on the environment, but can a person get all the nutrients they need without cooking their food?

Advocates say yes, and swear that eating raw cleanses your body, mind, and spirit. If you think eating raw means consuming nothing but salads and smoothies until you sprout wheatgrass from your ears, you would be surprised to hear what is on some of these new menus, from many-layered lasagna to veggie burgers to ice cream, as well as gourmet offerings such as chocolate mousse that are worthy of being served at upscale restaurants.

For most people who follow a raw food diet, going vegan is integral, meaning no animal products are consumed. But a minority of raw foodists consume unpasteurized, unhomogenized dairy products, and an even smaller minority eat raw animal flesh. And few are complete purists; though most raw food enthusiasts avoid meals that have been heated above temperatures of 110 to 120 degrees Fahrenheit, many practitioners supplement their diet with small amounts of cooked food from time to time.

The anecdotal, and widely touted, benefits of eating raw include increased energy, clear skin, weight loss, better digestion, and even reversal of chronic disease. Certified nutritionist Monica Dewart says, "When heat is applied, food enzymes are quickly destroyed, followed by many vitamins and other nutrients. In the case of extreme heat, such as when something is deep fried, the actual chemical structure of the food changes."

But Claudia Gonzalez, a registered dietitian and spokesperson for the American Dietetic Association, says that eating all raw, all the time would be an "extreme" diet. She says the enzymes needed to digest foods don't come from the food we eat, but are made by our bodies. Gonzalez adds, "If you eat more raw foods without adding calories that's always a good thing. Replacing refined, processed foods with raw foods is a healthy move. Eating a few raw meals a week can be great, but it's important not to go to the extreme."

Gonzalez says it's hard to eat more than 1,200 calories a day in uncooked foods. While this might be great for weight loss, once the weight comes off, that might not be enough to sustain a typical person's energy. Gonzalez also points out, "Cooking food below 160 degrees can lead to food-borne illness."

Don't automatically assume that everything sold at natural markets is sustainable or organic, and that's especially true at the seafood counter (as at restaurants and regular fish markets). Signs seen hanging behind the fish counter at a Whole Foods Market in 2004 touted sustainable seafood and the Marine Stewardship Council, which could lead consumers to believe that all fish in the display case adhere to sustainable principles. Yet, the ample offerings included fresh swordfish and several selections of shrimp, which the Audubon Society Pocket Seafood Selector deems among the worst ecological seafood choices. It's true that fish certified as sustainable by the independent Marine Stewardship Council were also on sale in the store, but as of 2004 only one North American fishery—Alaska salmon— earned the right to bear the distinctive blue MSC label.

The best strategy for buying seafood is to arm yourself with a wallet-sized guide to the best and worst seafood choices, which you can print at Audubon.org, among other websites (see "What You Can Do"). Another way to go: Consider seafood marketed by EcoFish, a small New Hampshire-based company that asserts its seafood is only from ecologically sound, well-managed fisheries, whether wild or farmed. Some stores carry only a few EcoFish products. But the full frozen line-bay scallops, albacore tuna, calamari rings, coho salmon fillets, mahi mahi, halibut, and shrimp—is ordered by some natural food stores such as Nutrition World in West Palm Beach, Florida. "I've had a lot of customers who have been like, 'Oh, I've been looking for this,'" says Michelle Cummings, Nutrition World manager. "The more educated the consumer becomes, the more they start asking for it."

Food cooperatives—another destination for savvy shoppers—are customer-owned or worker-owned, so they give customers greater control over product range and quality. The stores also are strongly committed to buying from regional farms and producers, meaning your dollars spent there impact your community further. Willy Street Co-op in Madison, Wisconsin, sells local organic dairy products and seasonal produce from more than twenty local growers (eighteen certified organic). The goals of Rainbow Grocery in San Francisco's Mission District include selling affordable vegetarian foods that have minimal negative environmental or social impact.

Typical of co-ops, Fort Collins Co-op in Colorado encourages customers to reuse bags and containers when buying bulk items because it's cheaper for the store and better for the environment. At the seven PCC Natural Markets in Greater Seattle, the contrast with mainstream supermarkets is clear: Ready-to-eat prepared chickens are free range. Not only are organic products sold, but some actual departments themselves are certified or-

Urban Oases

In the heart of downtown Manhattan, peeking out from between towering brick high-rises, is a little green oasis called the Liz Christy Garden. Inside, urban sojourners can watch fish and turtles glide beneath the surface of a pond. The Soho neighborhood created and tends this leafy niche, which grows a huge variety of natural produce, and the residents have defended its right to exist. Not everyone in the city appreciates this "frivolous" use of valuable real estate, which could support office and apartment complexes.

Urban community gardens aren't simply window dressing. Hong Kong, the most densely populated city in the world, produces two-thirds of its own poultry and about half of its vegetables from urban gardens. In Moscow, nearly 65 percent of families engage in some kind of food production.

In fact, the United Nations Development Program reports that urban gardens provide 15 percent of the world's food supply. In the United States, they are creating sorely needed jobs in neglected neighborhoods and introducing concrete-raised children to the wonders of nature.

South Central Los Angeles' "Food from the 'Hood" program has brought attention to the potential of its embattled Crenshaw district, while providing college funds for the high school students who maintain organic gardens. San Francisco's Fresh Start Farms employs homeless families to grow produce for the city's many restaurants. And U.S. prisons have taken to gardening projects in a big way, like San Francisco County Jail's Garden Project, which has prisoners growing food for local soup kitchens.

ganic. For instance, the organic produce section is "certified organic" because separate sinks are used for washing organic produce versus traditionally grown varieties.

Buy Locally

The consensus is that the single best thing a food lover can do to live lighter on the land is this: Buy locally produced foods and fresh local produce in season, whether they're organic or not. Avoid the transcontinental strawberry. The downside is you'll enjoy berries and sweet corn and tomatoes only in summer, if you follow this credo strictly. But did you ever notice how much better locally grown versions taste anyway? This strategy is better for the local economy, the Earth, your health and, let's be frank, the tastebuds.

"Really, for flavor, you can't beat anything that's local. Ideally it would've been picked more recently that anything from far-flung places," says Jennifer Hall, a board member of the Chefs Collaborative, a national network that promotes sustainable seasonal cuisine. "So for anyone who wants to please the palate, seasonal and local is a big, big driver." Hall is also general manager for Bon Appétit Management in Seattle, which serves produce from area farms and sustainable seafood at the café it manages at the Seattle Art Museum.

Most consumers don't understand today's highly complex global food system, in which most food production and processing occurs far from where they live, according to a report by the Iowa-based Leopold Center for Sustainable Agriculture. Food must now travel farther to reach consumers. One study found that importing fresh peas required nearly three times more energy than locally grown peas. To reach the Chicago terminal market from elsewhere in the continental United States, produce traveled 1,518 miles by truck in 1998, up 22 percent from 1,245 miles in 1981, according to a Leopold Center report.

A Swedish study considered the ingredients of a typical Swedish breakfast—apple, bread, butter, cheese, coffee, cream, orange juice, and sugar—and determined that to reach a breakfast table, these foods travel a mighty long way. "The mileage estimated for the meal," according to the Leopold Center report, "was equivalent to the circumference of the Earth."

The Leopold Center has floated the idea that grapes and other foods should bear an "ecolabel" stating the number of miles and days required to transport them from farm to store and the amount of carbon dioxide (CO_2) emitted en route. After all, the more miles traveled, the more greenhouse gases emitted.

Don't look for this label anytime soon. An Internet survey of a prototype label found a cool reception to the CO_2 reminder, though consumers partial to fresh foods did like pithy labels that stated the time it took (in days) for the product to travel from farm to store. More and more, consumers are showing interest in regionally produced foods, whether for environmental reasons or not. When researchers at Oregon State University surveyed working class and more affluent Portland-area residents, 44 percent of both groups, according to the Leopold Center report, "expressed moderate to strong support for buying local products."

In sum, it's clear that eating is voting. Every purchase at the supermarket, drive-through window, vending machine, food co-op, restaurant, and natural foods market amounts to a vote for or against genetic engineering, for or against organic agriculture, for or against regional farms.

How will you vote?

WHAT YOU CAN DO

Shoppers need to be armed with knowledge, especially about the terminology used on labels and ingredients. One of the best activist organizations to provide such information is the **Environmental Working Group**, which supplements its database research and analysis with carefully targeted monitoring of chemical contaminants in food, air and water. The group shocked many with its analysis of pesticide contamination in baby food. 1436 U Street NW, Suite 100, Washington, DC 20009, (202)667-6982, www .ewg.org.

Food First. Also known as the Institute for Food and Development Policy, Food First "works to reform the global food system from the bottom up, offering an antidote to the myths and obfuscations that make change seem difficult to achieve." It was founded in 1975 by Frances Moore Lappé and Joseph Collins, following the international success of the book *Diet for a Small Planet*. The Food First Information and Action Network (FIAN) is the action and campaigning partner of the institute. Contact: Food First, 398 60th Street, Oakland, CA 94618, (510)654-4400, www.foodfirst.org.

International Natural Hygiene Society. This is a longtime raw foods advocacy group, formerly the American Natural Hygiene Society. Subscribes to the "natural ways of life," including fasting, based on the teachings of Dr. Herbert Shelton. http://naturalhygienesociety.org.

Organic Consumers Association. Campaigns for food safety, organic agriculture, fair trade, and sustainability, and provides information on many issues including genetic engineering, irradiation, toxic sludge fertilizer, and mad cow disease. 6101 Cliff Estate Road, Little Marais, MN 55614; (218)226-4164, 1(888)403-1007; www.organicconsumers.org.

The Campaign to Label Genetically Engineered Foods. The campaign does an excellent job staying on top of the genetic engineering issue and sends out frequent free e-mail alerts containing key news articles about biotech foods. Its stated mission is to "create a national grassroots consumer campaign for the purpose of lobbying Congress and the President to pass legislation that will require the labeling of genetically engineered foods in the United States." As executive director Craig Winters sees it, "We're coming to a point in human history where we really need to get more involved in the political process than ever before. The only way we're going to combat [corporate influence in politics] is through grassroots political activism." His organization is among the many affiliates of the umbrella organization Genetic Engineering Action Network (www.geaction.org). P.O. Box 55699, Seattle, WA 98155, (425)771-4049, www.thecampaign.org.

To download a Shopper's Guide listing non-genetically engineered foods to substitute for your mainstream-produced favorites, go to www.TrueFood Now.org.

To print a wallet-sized card listing sustainable seafood choices, go online to download a free Seafood Watch card from Monterey Bay Aquarium (www.mbayaq.org), the Pocket Seafood Selector from Environmental Defense (www.edf.org), or the Audubon Seafood Wallet Card (www.audubon .org/campaign/lo/seafood). Some people might believe that fishing is as good as ever, but scientists and filmmakers graphically depict the decline of the oceans in a free online slide show you can view at www .shiftingbaselines.org.

Resources

Food from the 'Hood. The nation's first student-managed natural food products company, started at Crenshaw High School in 1992 as a response to the Los Angeles riots. P.O. Box 8268, Los Angeles, CA 90008, (888)601-FOOD, www.foodfromthehood.com.

Green Guerillas. Works to turn rubble-strewn lots in New York City into vibrant, food-producing community gardens. 151 West 30th Street, New York, NY 10001, (212)594-2155, www.greenguerillas.org.

San Francisco League of Urban Gardeners. 2088 Oakdale Avenue, San Francisco, CA 94124, (415)285-SLUG, www.grass-roots.org/usa/slug.shtml.

An Ounce of Prevention
Natural Health Care

Photo by Creatas/Punchstock

*H*ave you ever had a doctor offer treatment as if you were little more than a collection of isolated spare parts, and that your broken arm, swollen knee or sore throat had nothing to do with the rest of your body? Or perhaps you're tired of using conventional drugs with side effects that make you feel worse than the disease itself. Natural health care appeals to patients who want someone to care for their body, mind, and spirit. Holistic health practitioners give all of these factors equal weight as they help restore balance. Instead of focusing on sickness, natural health emphasizes wellness. While practitioners in India and China have been treating the whole person for more than 5,000 years, Westerners have only begun to embrace the concept.

A variety of caregivers practice natural health: massage therapists, acupuncturists, nutritionists, and aromatherapy experts, to name a few. Many patients use holistic health care to supplement their family physician's advice. And more primary-care doctors are seeking additional training in this area because so many patients want natural alternatives.

Obviously, it wouldn't be wise to treat a heart condition with herbs if your doctor recommends bypass surgery, but alternative medicine does offer considerable benefits for other, less severe conditions. A massage therapist or chiropractor, for example, is often able to do wonders for sciatica. An acupuncturist helps smokers and dieters control the cravings that drive their addictions. And a good herbalist can help menopausal women survive their hot flashes without relying on synthetic hormones.

Environmental exposures and diet are the root cause of many of the most serious diseases, such as cancer, asthma, and heart disease. A wide body of research, for instance, shows the negative health consequences of dioxin, a chemical by-product of pesticide, paper and plastic manufacturing. Garbage incinerators also produce dioxin. In 1993, University of Wisconsin researcher Sherry Rier came out with one of the first studies to link dioxin with endometriosis, a women's disease that causes painful cramps and infertility.

Vietnam veterans who were exposed to the dioxin-laced herbicide Agent Orange also developed long-term health problems. One of the most well-documented effects is an increased incidence of diabetes. Dioxin is an endocrine disrupter, a chemical that interferes with the body's natural hormones.

In this relatively new field of research, scientists have published many examples of animals being harmed by endocrine disrupters—from Florida alligators born with deformed genitals to Great Lakes seagulls with crumbling eggs. Now, researchers are linking these compounds to human health effects as well. Possible consequences of exposure include low sperm counts, early puberty, and reproductive system defects. One recent study showed women who eat a lot of Great Lakes fish contaminated with polychlorinated biphenyls (PCBs) take longer to become pregnant.

Scientists also are taking a closer look at all kinds of harmful substances in our diet. For example, dozens of studies have shown milk containing genetically engineered (GE) growth hormones appears to cause an increased risk of colon, breast, and prostate cancer. GE food, irradiated meat, and pesticide-laden produce pose other potential health threats consumers must consider.

A POUND OF PREVENTION

The good news is taking simple steps to safeguard health can have a definite impact. According to the U.S. Centers for Disease Control and Prevention, 19 percent of health problems are caused by environmental factors, but 53 percent are caused by poor lifestyle choices. Groups such as the American Holistic Health Association offer these commonsense tips for preventing harmful environmental exposures and promoting wellness:

- **Eat Healthy Food.** Reduce sugar, alcohol, and processed foods; add more fresh produce. Try to eat lower on the food chain. Simple changes in the diet can protect against serious diseases. One study, at the University of Illinois, showed eating more lycopene (found in tomatoes) prevents prostate cancer. Switching to low-fat, organic dairy products cuts dioxin exposure.

- **Drink Pure Water.** The federal Environmental Protection Agency estimates 8.6 percent of U.S. communities do not comply with clean drinking water standards. To be safe, install a filter or drink spring water. Consume at least eight glasses of water per day—more if you drink a lot of caffeine.

- **Exercise.** Aim for twenty minutes of aerobic activity three times per week. Exercise staves off everything from arthritis to clogged arteries. Physical activity increases oxygen levels and reduces cancer-causing free radicals. It also helps people maintain a healthy weight and build stronger bones.

- **Dump the Chemicals.** Green cleaning products, from a growing list of manufacturers, are safer than conventional cleansers, especially for children who spend a lot of time on the floor. Since dioxin traces have been found on everything from bleached paper towels and diapers to tampons, look for alternatives made with unbleached paper or organic cotton.

Meanwhile, other health advocates are highlighting the special needs of women and children, who react to environmental health threats differently than does a typical adult male. Until recently, most medical studies failed to take those differences into account.

For example, women show different—and more subtle—signs of a heart attack than men. Instead of the classic chest pain moving up the arm, a woman may have middle back pain and nausea. To add to the confusion, doctors thought hormone replacement therapy offered extra protection for menopausal women at risk for heart disease. But new research shows certain types of hormone therapy may actually increase the risk of heart attacks and strokes. Frustrated by the lack of conclusive information, more women are turning to natural alternatives.

Breast cancer is another deadly disease that affects thousands, and the government is funding research into the cause. One study, by the National Institute of Environmental Health Sciences (NIEHS), is looking into chemical exposures during early childhood that can cause breast cancer later in life. Lung cancer is the leading cause of death for women in the United States, however. That's because women are more sensitive to the harmful effects of smoking (and secondhand smoke) than men. As a result, they are more likely to develop a fatal form of lung cancer than men.

Children also face tougher odds. Babies and toddlers have a higher percentage of body fat, so toxic chemicals affect them more than adults. If they eat fish contaminated with polychlorinated biphenyls (PCBs), for example, their exposure will be higher because PCBs are stored in fatty tissue. Also, children consume a lot of fruit and juice, so they ingest more pesticide residue. Most pesticide safety tests, however, only provide data for adult exposures, so little is known about their effect on smaller bodies.

CURRENT EVENTS/LEGISLATIVE/POLITICAL

Natural health care offers obvious benefits. Alternative therapies are especially helpful for chronic pain caused by migraine headaches or lower back problems. But they also can be dangerous. Certain herbal diet pills can aggravate heart conditions, for example. And there is evidence that St. John's Wort, an herb that helps depression, can make birth control pills less effective.

With the popularity of alternative medicine gurus like Dr. Andrew Weil, holistic health is taking off in the national marketplace. One survey, published in the *New England Journal of Medicine* in 1993, estimated that one-third of all Americans have tried complementary therapies such as massage or echinacea. Most of the people who responded to the survey said they hid this fact from their family doctor. The study estimated Americans spend $13.7 billion per year on natural health care services and products. For this reason, organizations like the American Medical Association are paying more attention—and stepping up efforts to regulate alternative medicine practitioners.

In a recent report, the AMA urged the National Institutes of Health to provide more objective, scientific data that shows whether therapies such as acupuncture and homeopathy are helpful to patients. The organization takes a skeptical position about most alternative treatments, arguing many are no more effective than a placebo. But the AMA does urge its members to educate themselves about potential adverse reactions caused by herbs and other treatments, and to ask their patients whether they use natural health care.

Supervision for natural health providers varies in different regions of the country. At the federal level, the Food and Drug Administration regulates the use of herbs and vitamins as food supplements. But the products are not as carefully tested as traditional prescription drugs and manufacturers are not required to publish warnings about side effects.

Some states, such as Arizona, Connecticut, and Nevada, have more stringent rules for alternative practitioners. They have special medical boards that regulate homeopathic practitioners, chiropractors, and acupuncturists. Many other states require licenses for massage therapists and naturopathic doctors.

In recent years, more health insurance companies offer coverage for clients who prefer alternative therapies. In the late 1990s, several big health plans, such as Blue Cross in Washington State and Oregon, added alternative medicine to their coverage. Most HMOs in California also cover chiropractic care and acupuncture. Some companies will only pay for alternative therapies if the patient gets a referral from their primary care physician.

GREEN PRODUCTS

Once consumers make the decision to try natural health care, they often feel overwhelmed by the vast marketplace. With so many different therapies, how do we know which one is best for our needs? And how do we know it will work? Objective scientific evidence is not always available because it's hard to design effective clinical studies with certain alternative therapies. But some helpful data does exist. Agencies like the National Center for Complementary and Alternative Medicine are good resources. In addition, we offer the following guide to different natural health approaches:

Naturopathic Medicine

Naturopathic physicians use nutritional counseling, exercise, herbal medicine, hydrotherapy, stress reduction, and other noninvasive techniques to help their patients. They believe in the intrinsic healing power of nature. Naturopaths also strongly believe in their role as teachers.

Naturopathic medical students study traditional medical school topics such as anatomy and biochemistry, but they also learn holistic therapies like acupuncture and homeopathy. At the end of the four-year program, they earn a Doctor of Naturopathic Medicine (ND) degree. Many naturopaths also are educated in other approaches, such as Chinese medicine or Ayurvedic medicine. One of the most respected naturopathic training programs is Bastyr University in Seattle.

While seeing patients, naturopaths may use traditional methods of diagnosis, such as a physical exam or laboratory tests. Instead of handing the patient a prescription, however, they might offer an herbal tincture or suggest acupuncture treatments. Naturopathic physicians do not perform major surgery or use X-ray or radiation treatments.

Some states license naturopathic physicians and require them to take rigorous board exams just like conventional physicians with an MD degree. In states that do not have licensing, the best choice is a naturopath who is a member of the American Association of Naturopathic Physicians.

Herbs

From Native American medicine men to Chinese healers, ancient cultures have used plants to treat disease for thousands of years. Many of our most effective modern pharmaceuticals are plant-based drugs. Physicians rely on the flower digitalis (foxglove), for example, to help heart patients.

In the past decade or so, herbal therapies have become more popular, creating a $3.5 billion industry. Surveys show nearly half of all U.S. consumers have tried herbal products for everything from a cold to arthritis pain. Herbal therapy is particularly attractive to people who have diseases with no known cure and few treatments. In the early days of AIDS, before AZT was developed, many patients turned to traditional Chinese medicinal herbs for relief.

The American Botanical Council offers the following list of the most effective plant-based remedies: cayenne pepper for arthritis pain, cranberry for urinary infections, aloe vera for burns, echinacea for colds, evening primrose oil for premenstrual syndrome (PMS), and ginger for nausea.

In other cases, conclusive data does not exist. Scientists have been debating the merits of St. John's Wort, an herb for depression, in recent years. At first, researchers believed St. John's Wort was just as effective as an antidepressant. Later, in a study published in the *Journal of the American Medical Association*, Duke University scientists concluded the herb was not appropriate for people with severe depression.

Groups like the American Medical Association warn consumers to always

Picking "Good" Vitamins

Nutrition and medical experts agree eating a balanced diet with plenty of fruits and vegetables provides enough vitamins and antioxidants for the average healthy person. But studies also have shown vitamins and supplements can offer tremendous benefits, preventing everything from birth defects to heart disease and osteoporosis. So it can't hurt to add them to your daily routine. Choosing vitamins and supplements can be overwhelming, however. Here are a few helpful guidelines:

- Pass up anything that offers more than 100 percent of the recommended daily allowance (unless your doctor prescribes it). Fat-soluble vitamins, like A, D, and E, can build up to toxic levels over time.

- Look for vitamins with "USP" on the label, which means they have passed absorption and purity tests by the U.S. Pharmacopeia, a trade group for the supplement industry. Vitamins without this symbol could pass right through your system without doing any good. Studies have also shown many vitamins and supplements have too little or too much of the active ingredient. Do some research and find a reputable manufacturer.

- Be wary of miracle cure health claims. Avoid buying vitamins on the Internet. Stick with established companies with a long-term track record.

- Check the expiration date. Store vitamins in a cool, dry place out of reach of children (iron overdose is a leading cause of death for infants and toddlers). Store fish oil capsules and other oil-based supplements in the refrigerator so they don't become rancid.

- Take vitamins and supplements with meals to increase absorption. Also, combining them with certain foods can make them more effective. For example, the body processes iron better with vitamin C. So take iron pills with a glass of orange juice.

- Avoid supplements with herbs if you are pregnant or trying to conceive.

- In general, it's a good idea to check with a doctor before adding large doses of vitamins, herbs, and supplements to your diet. *Consumer Reports'* "dirty dozen" list of dietary supplements (available on the magazine's website at www.ConsumerReports.org) that can cause serious harm includes chaparral, ephedra, comfrey, lobelia, and yohimbe.

check with their physician before trying an herbal remedy because it could interact with other drugs. People with disorders like lupus should not take echinachea because it could make their immune system too active. Pregnant women should also avoid herbal remedies.

Essential Oils

Aromatherapy uses the sense of smell as a pathway to stimulate the brain. The chemical components of essential oils have different effects on the mind and body. For example, practitioners use lavender to relax their clients, jasmine to lift their moods, and lemon to sharpen their concentration and boost their energy.

Clinical studies show aromatherapy is most helpful for reducing stress and anxiety. People with PMS, panic attacks, chronic pain, insomnia, and menopausal mood swings are among those who benefit most from this type of treatment. Researchers reported in the British journal *Lancet* that a group of elderly patients were able to reduce their sleeping pill use after scientists piped a soothing lavender scent into their rooms at night. Another study, at Memorial Sloan-Kettering in New York, found patients felt 63 percent less claustrophobic when exposed to the scent of vanilla before entering a magnetic resonance imaging (MRI) machine.

Stress-busting lavender is one of the most useful and basic essential oils. Peppermint oil combats fatigue and eases stomach discomfort. Tea tree oil erases athlete's foot. Products range from special spray bottles to candles and bath salts.

Aromatherapy is not for everyone, however. Scented products can aggravate allergies and should be used with caution—or not at all—if pregnant. Essential oil fumes also can bother the eyes and irritate sensitive skin.

Massage

Of all the treatments available in the vast world of alternative medicine, massage therapy is the most popular and universally accepted by consumers, physicians and insurance companies alike. The Evanston-based American Massage Therapy Association estimated 18 percent of the U.S. population got a massage in 2002. That figure had doubled since 1997. Another survey, published in the *Journal of the American Medical Association* in

1998, showed 27 percent of the money Americans spent on natural health care went to massage therapists.

Massage enjoys broad acceptance because so many studies prove it works. The benefits of touch therapy have helped premature infants gain weight more quickly, hospital patients heal wounds faster and gave solace to AIDS patients at the end of life.

Physicians from Beth Israel Hospital in Seattle published a report that showed massage to be extremely effective for chronic lower back pain. Several other studies have shown massage helps breast cancer patients reduce pain and swelling in their arms caused by a build up of lymphatic fluid. At Cedars-Sinai Medical Center in Los Angeles, researchers found massage reduced muscle spasms in patients who had just undergone heart bypass surgery.

There are as many different types of massage as people who need it. Choosing the right one can be confusing. Some therapists will be trained in only one method, while others may use a combination as needed. Swedish massage is a common type, which emphasizes lighter, soothing strokes. Other styles include sports medicine massage for athletes and deep tissue massage, which releases tension from deep within the muscles.

Most massage therapy sessions last an hour, or a half hour at minimum. It's a good idea to bring along any medical history information the therapist might need to know about beforehand. Women who are pregnant should be sure to notify their massage therapist, since some types of bodywork can be too rough for a growing baby.

Body Work: Reiki and Reflexology

People looking for hands-on care may find these two therapies appealing. Reiki is based on ancient Tibetan beliefs that the body is surrounded by an invisible electromagnetic energy field. Practitioners believe they can heal patients by pressing on certain points to bring the energy flow back into balance and remove blockages.

Body work experts say people carry tension and past emotional hurts inside their muscle tissue. By doing deep massage, these experts say, patients can release stress and old psychic wounds, giving them more energy and a new feeling of well being.

Reflexology—first developed thousands of years ago in China, Greece, and Egypt—divides the body into sections, running in vertical bundles from head to toe. By pressing mainly on the feet and hands, practitioners believe they can improve the function of different organs, glands, nerves, and the brain. Proponents say it can help with everything from chronic back pain to headaches and PMS.

While mainstream medical scientists have not been able to prove reiki and reflexology actually work, they also appear to be relatively harmless and perhaps worth a try for those who are open to their potential benefits. Since most health insurance companies do not cover these procedures, however, they can be expensive to pay for out of pocket.

Different Approaches

Ayurveda, developed in India, and traditional Chinese medicine (TCM) are ancient medical systems formed by Hindu and Buddhist scholars thousands of years ago. They are both enjoying renewed popularity because they emphasize prevention and the mind-body connection. Both ayurveda and TCM use a combination of diet, herbs, and exercise to bring a patient's physical, emotional, and spiritual elements into balance.

Ayurvedic practitioners classify people according to their dominant nature—wind, fire, or earth (known in sanskrit as *vata*, *pitta*, and *kapha*). People who are predominately *vata* are slender perpetual-motion machines, which can make them very productive and charismatic. But when they are out of balance, with too much wind, they may become irritable and flighty, according to ayurvedic teachings. If *pitta*, or fire, predominates, a person (likely to be of medium build) can be intense and driven—or judgmental and temperamental if out of balance. *Kapha* people, like the Earth, tend to have round bodies and a calm, nurturing personality. If unbalanced, however, they have a tendency to become depressed and sluggish.

When *vata*, *pitta*, and *kapha* get out of sync, ayurvedic physicians believe diseases and illnesses appear. To diagnose their patients, they may feel the person's pulse or examine their tongue, eyes, face, fingernails, and lips for telltale signs of imbalance in certain organs. Typical treatments include special diets that correspond to the patient's predominant nature (such as cooling foods for a person with "excess fire"), sweating therapies, yoga, massage, and herbal remedies. Ayurvedic healers also use a system known as *pancha karma* to clear toxins from the body. *Pancha karma* treatments can

Chiropractors

Chiropractic therapists have benefited from the surge of interest in natural health care. A survey published in the *Journal of the American Medical Association* showed nearly half of all visits to alternative practitioners were for chiropractic care. At the same time, the conventional medical establishment has been highly critical. The American Medical Association has dismissed chiropractic care as quackery. Despite this opposition from mainstream physicians, many consumers prefer their chiropractors—not just for spinal adjustments, but also for advice on nutrition, stress reduction, and other healthy lifestyle changes.

Chiropractors are mainly known for treating back pain. But by realigning the spine and taking pressure off it, chiropractors believe they can improve nervous system function. This, in turn, has a positive impact on the entire body's ability to heal itself, they say.

Like physicians, chiropractors will take a medical history and do a physical exam during a patient's first visit. They may also order X rays or lab tests to make a diagnosis. To correct back and spine problems, chiropractors will do a series of physical manipulations, similar to a deep massage.

Most insurance companies will pay for chiropractic care. It's a common type of therapy for workers who have been injured on the job. Chiropractors are most helpful for people with back and neck pain, muscle strains and sprains. To find a reputable chiropractor, look for someone who attended an accredited training program, has several years of experience, and is a member of a professional organization such as the International Chiropractors Association.

include everything from swallowing oil and undergoing a colonic enema to emotional counseling and bloodletting.

Most of the positive clinical studies have shown ayurvedic herbs, such as Gynema Sylvestre, to be helpful in controlling the high blood sugar levels caused by diabetes. While those studies were small in size, officials at the National Center for Complementary and Alternative Medicine agreed they warranted further study. Ayurvedic herbs also may help Parkinson's disease patients.

Drawbacks include reports of some ayurvedic herbal supplements containing dangerous levels of impurities, such as lead. Also, many people find some aspects of this approach, such as *pancha karma* enemas and bloodletting, to be distasteful and risky.

Traditional Chinese medicine draws on similar concepts. Instead of *vata*, *pitta*, and *kapha*, this system emphasizes *yin* and *yang*. Each person has both of these opposing elements in their mind and body. *Yang* is the fiery, hot, light energy while *yin* represents water, cold, and darkness. If one predominates over the other, it can cause a series of physical problems.

Like their ayurvedic counterparts, TCM practitioners examine their patient's pulse, skin, and tongue as they make a diagnosis. They believe an electrical life force, called *qi* (pronounced "chee") flows through the body along energy channels, or meridians, that correspond roughly with veins and nerves. By placing their fingers on certain spots that correspond with certain organs, they can determine the cause of a person's illness. Chinese medicine experts may manually stimulate or insert a needle into these energy channels to treat an imbalance with acupressure or acupuncture. Other TCM treatments include special diets, herbs, and exercises such as tai chi.

Endometriosis is one of the most promising areas for TCM treatment, according to the National Center for Complementary and Alternative Medicine. Several studies have shown Chinese herbs and acupuncture effectively ease endometriosis symptoms. A new, larger and more comprehensive clinical trial sponsored by the NIH will compare herbs and acupuncture to conventional medical treatment with hormones. TCM also is known to be helpful for anxiety, insomnia, and minor flu and colds.

As with ayurveda, TCM patients need to be cautious about herbal impurities. Improper acupuncture treatments also can lead to blood clots. Experts say it's best to choose a TCM practitioner who has several years of experience and was trained in China.

Modern Illnesses

Many of the illnesses that cause people to seek treatment from a natural health specialist are relatively new syndromes. Diseases like multiple chemical sensitivity (MCS) and chronic fatigue did not exist a hundred years ago (or at least were not diagnosed). One explanation is that there were then fewer toxics circulating in the environment. Today, patients who suffer from these conditions often go through years of frustration before they are properly diagnosed. More physicians are becoming aware of them, but few treatments are available.

The medical community is still debating whether MCS is actually a valid syndrome. The American Medical Association argues it does not exist. Similarly, the federal Centers for Disease Control and Prevention do not have an official diagnosis on the books for MCS.

But doctors across the country say they are seeing more patients with this debilitating disease, which causes them to be allergic to everything from household cleaners to carpet and perfume. MCS can be caused by a short-term exposure, such as a chemical spill, or a long-term, low-level exposure, such as an office building with poor ventilation. Symptoms vary, but may include headaches, rashes, memory loss, insomnia, irritability, and joint pain. Scientists currently have no cure for MCS, other than avoiding as many chemicals as possible.

Awareness of MCS increased when hundreds of Persian Gulf War veterans came down with these same symptoms. After doing brain scans on a group of Gulf War veterans, researchers from the University of Texas reported evidence of brain damage caused by low-level exposure to nerve gas, pesticides, and insect repellants containing DEET. The veterans had impaired decision-making ability, memory loss, and depression, according to the study.

If chemicals can, in fact, affect our brains and cause central nervous system disorders, natural health advocates say it makes sense to avoid them as much as possible. Some tips for nontoxic living include installing air purifiers and water filters, and selecting organic cotton fabrics for the home.

Cancer Prevention

While diseases like multiple chemical sensitivity are relatively rare, approximately 500,000 people will die of cancer in 2004, according to the American Cancer Society. From secondhand smoke to dry-cleaning solvents and asbestos, cancer-causing chemicals are all around us. To some extent, there is no way to avoid all of the carcinogens in our environment, but experts say it's wise to minimize exposure. They also recommend some basic steps to boost your body's ability to prevent cancer before it takes root.

Diet is the biggest risk factor for cancer, and it's also the easiest one to control. Scientists at the University of Illinois' Functional Foods for Health program have flagged the following foods for their cancer-prevention potential: blueberries, red grapes, tomatoes, garlic and onions, oats, broccoli, and green tea. Other good choices include orange and yellow vegetables (full of the antioxidant beta keratine) and cruciferous vegetables: cabbage, cauliflower, and brussels sprouts. Certain herbs have also been shown to be helpful tools, such as saw palmetto for prostate cancer prevention.

Being overweight is a key risk factor for colon, uterine, and breast cancer. By contrast, studies show exercising thirty minutes per day can significantly reduce your risk for colon and breast cancer. For smokers, it's time to quit. Smoking causes toxins to crowd out the cells so they can't get enough oxygen, which leads to cancer mutations.

Government regulators keep track of hundreds of carcinogenic chemicals in the workplace. If you are exposed to carcinogens on the job, take precautions to protect yourself. Asbestos is one common threat construction workers experience while demolishing buildings. Dry-cleaning workers also face a cancer risk due to solvent use. Agricultural workers have a higher rate of certain cancers, including leukemia, non-Hodgkin's lymphoma and myeloma. Researchers from the National Cancer Institute, the National Institute for Environmental Health Sciences and the U.S. Environmental Protection Agency are studying whether pesticides may be linked to those statistics.

Cancer-causing chemicals can sneak into our lives in other, smaller ways. Nitrates contaminate some rural water supplies. Radon seeps through the foundations of our homes. Microwaving leftovers in the wrong kind of plastic container can be a mistake. Even barbecue lovers may be ingesting carcinogens that form when meat is cooked at high temperatures.

While the statistics and sheer numbers of cancer-causing substances can be overwhelming, the good news is it's easy to protect yourself with a few practical changes. Just reaching for a carrot stick, wearing sunscreen, and taking an extra walk can go a long way toward reducing the risk of cancer.

WHAT YOU CAN DO

How to Evaluate a Natural Health Care Provider

Complementary and alternative medicine is a riskier place for consumers than the conventional marketplace. That's because objective scientific research reports are just beginning to emerge. Without good data, it's hard to know if certain treatments actually are effective and worth the money.

Meanwhile, there are safety concerns. The U.S. Food and Drug Administration recently took the herbal weight-loss supplement ephedra off the market because it was linked to strokes, seizures, and heart attacks. Local regulations have holes in them too. Most states license chiropractors, naturopathic doctors, and massage therapists but in many areas, providers can start up a business with little or no proof of their training and abilities.

That said, it pays to do some homework before choosing a natural health practitioner. Here are some recommendations:

- When possible, verify the therapy's effectiveness by searching for scientific information on clinical research trials. The National Cancer Institute and the NIH's National Center for Complementary and Alternative Medicine (NCCAM) both have excellent searchable databases online (see resource section).

- Before trying a new therapy, check with your primary care doctor to make sure it will be compatible with the conventional drugs and treatments you currently receive.

- Find a reputable practitioner by seeking referrals from professional organizations such as the American Massage Therapy Association (AMTA) or the American Academy of Medical Acupuncture (AAMA). Other good resources include the American Holistic Health Association and the Coalition for Natural Health.

- Check to see if the provider has a current license to practice in your state.

- If possible, get a personal referral from a friend who has used this person before and was happy with the care. If a personal referral is not available, go with a provider affiliated with a major hospital or university.

- Ask about the provider's training. A therapist with a degree from an accredited program, such as Bastyr University in Seattle, is better than someone who completed a correspondence course.

- Similarly, look for a practitioner with several years of experience instead of someone fresh out of school.

- Don't be afraid to ask a lot of questions: find out the risks and benefits of the treatment, potential side effects, drug interactions and whether it will be covered by health insurance.

Following these guidelines should help consumers find a competent alternative medicine provider. But since health care is such a personal and subjective endeavor, it may take some time. Don't be afraid to try several people. Good health is so essential to our well being, it's important to find the right fit.

Natural Health Resources

Information Sources

American Environmental Health Foundation. Promotes the study and treatment of adverse environmental effects on health. The foundation funds research projects to help physicians diagnose and treat environmentally related illness and publishes semiannual and quarterly newsletters. 8345 Walnut Hill Lane, Suite 225, Dallas, TX 75231, (214)361-9515, www.aehf.com.

American Holistic Health Association. A neutral clearinghouse for natural health resources. P.O. Box 17400, Anaheim, CA 92817-7400, (714)779-6152, www.ahha.org.

Functional Foods for Health. A joint program of the University of Illinois at Chicago and the University of Illinois at Urbana-Champaign, Functional Foods for Health identifies safe and effective natural products that can reduce chronic disease risk and promote optimal health. 103 ABL, 1302 W. Pennsylvania Avenue, Urbana, IL 61801, (217)333-6364, www.ag.uiuc.edu /~ffh/ffh.html.

National Center for Complementary and Alternative Medicine. Offers a searchable database of natural health research studies. National Institutes of Health, Bethesda, MD, www.nccam.nih.gov.

Trade Organizations

American Association of Naturopathic Physicians. 3201 New Mexico Avenue, NW, Suite 350, Washington, DC 20016, (866)538-2267, (202)895-1392, www.naturopathic.org.

American Botanical Council. 6200 Manor Road, Austin, TX 78723, (512)926-4900, www.herbalgram.org.

American Massage Therapy Association. 820 Davis St. Evanston, IL 60201, (847)864-0123, www.amtamassage.org (online referrals by state).

National Ayurvedic Medical Association. 620 Cabrillo Avenue, Santa Cruz, CA 95065, info@ayurveda-nama.org, www.ayruveda-nama.org.

American Academy of Medical Acupuncture. 4929 Wilshire Boulevard, Suite 428, Los Angeles, CA 90010, (323)937-5514, www.medicalacupuncture.org (online referral service for MDs trained in acupuncture).

International Chiropractors Association. 1100 North Glebe Road, Suite 1000, Arlington, VA 22201, (703)528-5000, www.chiropractic.org.

Suppliers

Nature's Plus. Major supplier of vitamins and nutritional supplements. 548 Broadhollow Road, Melville, NY 11747, (631)293-0030, (631)293-2934, www.naturesplus.com.

Nature's Way. Sells herbal products, vitamins and specialty supplements. 1375 North Mountain Spring Parkway, Sandy, UT 84663, (801)489-1408, www.naturesway.com (leading brand of herbal, vitamin, probiotic and specialty supplements).

chapter three

Personal Care

Pampering Your Body and the Planet, Too

Photo by Kevin Jordan/Getty Images

*F*or most of us, putting our best face forward means delving into our stash of cosmetics and personal-care products. After all, we've *got* to look good, right? But those pricey moisturizers, foundations, lipsticks, shampoos, antibacterial soaps, and deodorants come with a hidden cost—to your health and to the environment.

According to a report by the National Institutes of Occupational Safety and Health, 884 of the ingredients routinely used to make cosmetics and personal-care products are toxic and another 500 are skin sensitizers. Although most of us don't give a second thought to these common products, using them can put you at increased risk for cancer or reproductive damage. Short-term exposure can cause neurotoxic effects or bring on an allergic reaction, ranging from itchy skin to anaphylactic shock.

But there is a way to look and feel your best without applying a toxic soup of chemicals to your body every day. From herbal shampoos to organic toothpaste, a host of more natural alternatives are now becoming available to help anyone feel more beautiful without risking their health or fouling the environment. Here's how to tell the good stuff from the bad.

COUNTER INTELLIGENCE

Wandering the cosmetic aisle in your local supermarket or department store can be like walking through a minefield of toxic chemicals.

Two of the biggest hazards to look out for:

- **Carcinogens.** Topping the list of these cancer-causing substances are coal tar colors, listed on labels as FD&C and D&C colors. Made from bituminous coal, these synthetic tints are a common ingredient in hair dyes, dandruff shampoos, and cosmetics. Nearly all coal tar colors have been found to cause cancer in animals and most have never been tested for safety in people, despite the potential risks for long-term use. Lead, found in some hair dyes and easily absorbed through the skin, is also a carcinogen, as well as a hormone disruptor (see below).

  Another potential threat lurking within those pretty bottles is formaldehyde. This suspected carcinogen, released by preservatives as they degrade, is found in shampoos, nail polish, nail hardeners, and hair-growth products.

  And then there's the toxic trio of DEA, TEA, and MEA—diethanolamine, triethanolamine, and monoethanolamine. Combined with nitrites, these three chemicals, found in many shampoos, body washes, and soaps, produce highly carcinogenic compounds that are readily absorbed into the skin.

- **Endocrine Disruptors.** These chemicals interfere with the normal functioning of hormones and may cause infertility, miscarriage, birth defects, reproductive and breast cancer, as well as thyroid, heart, lung, liver, and kidney damage. Some of the most common types of endocrine disruptors include:

  - **Phthalates.** These chemicals (not generally listed by that name on product labels) accumulate in the body's fatty tissue and can remain there for years. In a 2002 test of seventy-two popular beauty products, researchers found phthalates in nearly three-quarters of them, including perfume, hair-care products, nail polish, and hand lotions.

  - **Surfactants.** A group of chemicals known as nonylphenols also can disrupt hormones, yet they are widely used in shampoos, hair dyes,

Making Better Scents

Increasingly, perfumes and fragranced products are being blamed for contributing to health problems such as asthma, migraines, neurotoxic effects, and upper respiratory irritation. That's because although perfumes were once distilled simply from flower essences, today's fragrances are complex mixtures of more than 4,000 chemicals, 84 percent of which have never been tested for safety.

While many popular fragrances evoke natural scents, 95 percent of all perfume ingredients are derived from petroleum, which the National Academy of Sciences has identified as capable of causing cancer, birth defects, central nervous system disorders, and allergic reactions. When EPA researchers tested thirty-one fragrance products, they found that more than half the products contained ingredients listed under the EPA's Toxic Substances Control Act.

Since perfume can enter the body through either the skin or by inhalation, many of these chemicals are readily absorbed. Some, particularly synthetic musks, have been shown to accumulate in the body's fatty tissues and have been detected in human blood and breast milk. But because the chemical formulas of fragrances are considered trade secrets, manufacturers aren't required to list their ingredients—so consumers are none the wiser when they buy scented products.

If you're hooked on fragrance, but would rather avoid the risks posed by these chemical cocktails, look for products that contain only pure, preferably organic, essential oils. Good quality essential oils are extracted from a plant's flowers, leaves, stems, and bark through steam distillation. But, be aware that some manufacturers use chemical solvents to coerce the oils from plants. Since these products contain a chemical residue, they cannot be considered true essential oils.

and shaving creams as wetting agents. According to a 1998 report by the environmental group Friends of the Earth (www.foe.org), nonylphenols interfere with normal reproductive function in wildlife and can confuse sexual development.

- **Parabens**. Pick up just about any cosmetic or personal-care product and you're likely to find one or more of them listed on the label. Although the FDA considers parabens safe, new research published in *Food Chemistry and Toxicology* shows that these substances mimic estrogen and can adversely affect testosterone levels and reproductive functioning in men. Thankfully, some forward-thinking companies have begun using antioxidants such as vitamin C or grapefruit seed extract to preserve their cosmetics. Not only are these natural alternatives effective, they are nontoxic.

BAD HAIR DAZE

Love to lather up? While you might think that shampoo is fairly benign, the FDA reports that this hair-care essential is the product most often reported for causing adverse reactions like contact dermatitis.

According to Dr. Samuel Epstein, professor emeritus of environmental and occupational medicine at the University of Illinois School of Public Health, using shampoo day in and day out may also increase your risk of cancer. At least 90 percent of all mass-produced shampoos contain detergents (listed on ingredient labels as DEA, TEA, or MEA) that have a tendency to react with other common shampoo ingredients to form the potent cancer-causing nitrosamine NDELA.

Fortunately, many natural cosmetic manufacturers are beginning to reformulate their shampoos, dumping chemicals in favor of plant-based ingredients.

Even greater danger lurks in hair-coloring formulas. Short-term consequences can include allergic reactions, eczema, asthma, and sun sensitivity. Over the long term, phenylenediamine, a tongue-twisting chemical often preceded by an m-, o-, or p- on the label, has been found to cause cancer in both animals and humans. Although the chemical is protected by a 1938 law and the FDA is unable to ban its use, the agency attempted to require manufacturers to place warning labels on products containing the chemical. But as often happens, powerful cosmetic industry lobbyists successfully defeated the proposal, and no warning was ever made.

And women aren't the only ones at risk. A study by Xavier University of Louisiana found that many of the gradual hair dyes popular with men contained so much lead acetate that the researchers couldn't wash it off their hands.

The good news is that synthetic chemicals aren't the only way to wash away the gray. Natural hair dyes that use color-rich plants or henna to alter hair color are widely available.

WHO'S FOOLING FATHER TIME?

Most of us stock up on cleansers, toners, and moisturizers in the hope of achieving and maintaining glowing, youthful skin. But conventional skin-care products are packed with petroleum-based chemicals, synthetic detergents, and alcohols that strip the skin of its natural oils and degrade its protective function.

Cleansers come in two flavors—foaming liquids or creamy lotions. Foaming cleansers often contain antibacterials and harsh detergents like DEA and SLS, along with alcohol that can sap moisture from skin.

Cleansing lotions, on the other hand, are based on mineral oil (made from refined liquid hydrocarbons) to create a water-repellent film that coats the skin and plasticizers to give skin a soft feeling. To whisk away dirt and grime, cosmetic manufacturers also rely on chemical solvents made by combining fatty hydrocarbons with ammonia. Both foaming liquids and cleansing lotions are also chock full of preservatives and parabens.

Removing the last traces of dirt and dead skin cells left after cleaning your face requires a splash of skin-freshening astringent or toner. Yet astringents contain mostly denatured alcohol, plus chemicals that can remain in the body for months after use. Moisturizers can also harbor petroleum-based emollients such as mineral oil and petrolatum that, studies show, inhibit the ability of skin to heal itself. And lanolin, while natural, is a common allergen that may be contaminated with pesticides.

Another product that has become a hands-down best-seller is the anti-aging treatment. The most popular creams available today employ alpha hydroxyl acids (AHAs) to slough off old skin cells and stimulate the generation of new healthy cells. But while natural AHAs are derived from sugarcane or fruits, conventional products often add an alphabet soup of harsh chemical "peelers" that remove the top layer of skin. The FDA reports that use of these caustic chemical compounds has led to more than a hundred reports of severe redness, swelling, burning, blistering, bleeding, rash, itching, and skin discoloration.

Fortunately, a range of nonabrasive creams are now on the market, offering age-defying results without harming your skin.

CLEAN AND MEAN

Let's face it: Americans are obsessed with cleanliness. In our zeal to kill bacteria, we've switched from good old soap and water to a host of high-tech antibacterial products. But a number of researchers have speculated that the overuse of antibacterials may cause genetic mutations, essentially creating new strains of drug-resistant bacteria, or "super bugs" for which the human immune system has no defense.

Another problem is that most antibacterial soaps, body washes and toothpastes are based on triclosan—a kissing cousin to a common pesticide that is toxic to the blood, liver, and kidneys. And, like most pesticides, triclosan accumulates in the body's fatty tissue. During a study by Stockholm University, Swedish researchers noted that high levels of this commonly used bactericide were found in three out of five randomly selected samples of human breast milk.

To keep us fresh throughout the day, most of us automatically reach for the deodorant or antiperspirant. But deodorants rely on chemical biocides to inhibit the growth of microorganisms (those little critters that feed off perspiration) and often contain common allergens like lanolin and fragrance, which can cause breakouts and irritation under your arms. Antiperspirants, on the other hand, contain aluminum compounds to stop sweat. Not only are these compounds irritating and capable of causing an allergic reaction, some researchers believe that, since aluminum exposure may be linked to Alzheimer's disease, these products pose an unnecessary risk.

But there are less-risky alternatives. Companies with safety and the environment in mind, like Tom's of Maine, have found that tea tree oils, sage, lemongrass, and other natural ingredients work wonders in keeping the skin and teeth clean and odors in check.

NAILING DOWN THE PROBLEM

When you paint your nails, you can pick your poison. Nail polish can contain up to 50 percent toluene, a petroleum-derived chemical regulated under California's Proposition 65. Manicurists exposed to this solvent experience five times more spontaneous abortions than women who aren't exposed. The EPA's Office of Pollution Prevention and Toxics warns that breathing large amounts of toluene for short periods of time can adversely affect the kidneys, liver, and heart.

Along with toluene, nail polish can harbor formaldehyde. Research has linked exposure to severe asthma attacks, skin rashes, and hives. Studies also show that this highly reactive chemical, banned for use in cosmetics in Japan and Sweden, can cause DNA damage and may combine with other chemicals to produce mutagenic effects. Fortunately, many manufacturers, including Earthly Delights, Honeybee Gardens, Sante Kosmetics, and Firoze Nail Care, have begun removing formaldehyde and toluene from their nail products. These products are well worth seeking out.

There are other hidden hazards. A number of manufacturers add phthalates to help the polish form an even film as it dries. Since this hormone-disrupting plasticizer is water soluble, it leaches out of the polish every time your nails come in contact with water, making it a source of repeated exposure.

Acrylics come with their own set of problems. The chemicals used in making and applying false nails have been linked to asthma, birth defects, neurological damage, and cancer in animals. Even brief exposure—the kind you would get visiting a nail salon—can cause throat and eye irritation, headache, and nausea, say researchers with the Canadian Centre for Occupational Health and Safety.

Bottom line: The healthiest nails are those in the nude. To keep nails and cuticles clean and well-groomed the natural way, try one of the nontoxic lotions and creams now on the market.

CURRENT EVENTS/LEGISLATIVE/POLITICAL

The Body Politic

Most consumers believe that the FDA ensures the safety of the cosmetic and personal-care products we use every day. But the sad truth is that the agency doesn't have the authority to require safety testing before a product appears on store shelves. What's more, manufacturers aren't required to report cosmetic-related injuries or submit safety data on the ingredients used in their products.

The FDA's authority comes directly from the U.S. Congress, a body that has never put much importance on cosmetics or their safety. As a result, the agency is chronically underfunded and understaffed. Thanks to this weak, ineffective regulatory climate, the cosmetic industry is in the

The Bunny in Your Bathroom

Even though many cosmetics claim to be "Cruelty-Free" or "Not Tested on Animals," there's still a lot of confusion over what these terms really mean. Like the words "natural" and "organic," they don't have any legal meaning, and cosmetics companies have used them liberally, leaving consumers wondering if these claims just refer to the finished product or if any of the ingredients have been tested on animals. To cut down on the confusion, eight animal rights groups banded together to form the Coalition for Consumer Information on Cosmetics (CCIC). The result of this partnership was the international Leaping Bunny logo—the only independently certified "cruelty-free" mark that indicates that a cosmetic is free from any animal testing on the ingredients, formulations, or the finished product.

Also, many ingredients are derived from animals and can be hard to spot. For instance, hydrolyzed animal protein might be replaced by the term "hydrolyzed collagen," a gelatin derived by boiling animal bones and tendons. Here are a few other ingredients you'll want to watch for:

- **Benzoic acid.** While found in some plants, benzoic acid is derived primarily from vertebrates. It is used as a preservative in mouthwashes, deodorants, skin creams, and fragrances.

- **Carmine, cochineal, or carminic acid.** Red pigment from the crushed female cochineal beetle. Reportedly 70,000 beetles must be killed to produce one pound of this red dye.

- **Cetyl alcohol.** This wax can be derived from sperm whales, dolphins, or plants. Look for products that specify "vegetable" or "coconut" sources.

- **Glycerin.** A by-product of soap manufacturing using animal fat. Look for products that specify "vegetable glycerin."

- **Keratin.** Protein from the ground-up horns, hooves, feathers, quills, and hair of various animals. This ingredient is often used in hair-care products.

- **Lanolin.** Extracted from the wool of sheep and used as an emollient in many skin and body-care products.

- **Royal jelly.** Secretion from the throats of worker bees that is fed to larvae in the colony.

- **Silk powder.** Obtained from the secretion of the silkworm and used in some powdered cosmetics.

- **Stearic acid.** Fat from cows, pigs, and sheep, and from pets euthanized in animal shelters.

- **Urea.** Excreted from animal urine and other bodily fluids.

enviable position of policing itself—and the Cosmetic, Toiletry and Fragrance Association (CTFA) is working to keep it that way.

But not everyone in Congress is convinced by the CTFA's tactics. Senator Edward Kennedy (D-MA), noting that "the cosmetic industry has borrowed a page from the playbook of the tobacco industry by putting profits ahead of public health," attempted to strengthen cosmetic regulations in 1997. And former representative Ron Wyden (D-OR) introduced a bill that would have required manufacturers to list the ingredients on the products used by professional cosmetologists, especially hair dyes. When the legislation failed, one congressional staff member reportedly said, "Until further action is taken, [consumers] are worse off than guinea pigs. At least with guinea pigs, someone is watching."

GREEN PRODUCTS

Even though shopping for cosmetics may seem daunting, an ever-broadening spectrum of good-for-you products can be found in health and natural food stores.

Here are a few ingredients to look for as you browse the cosmetic aisle in your local health food store:

- **Hair products**. A good alternative to the detergents in shampoos is tea tree oil, which cleanses without harsh chemicals. Coconut oil, corn oil, olive oil, castile, wheat, and soya protein moisturize and strengthen. Natural preservatives include antioxidant vitamins A, C, E, and citrus seed extract—all of which also help fight premature skin aging. Natural fragrances such as geranium, lavender, orange blossom, and jasmine oils add a touch of nontoxic scent.

- **Hair colors.** Plant dyes made from beets, walnuts, tea, or marigolds provide effective alternatives for enhancing hair color, bringing out highlights, and toning down gray. Another healthy option is henna, which is made from the powdered leaves of a desert shrub called Lawsonia and has been used for centuries. Oat, soy, corn, and wheat extracts enrich natural dyes, and rosemary extract is an effective conditioning agent.

- **Skin- and body-care products.** Several natural anti-aging creams are now on the market, and a wide spectrum of healthy skin-pampering lotions are available, too. Antioxidant vitamins, including A and E, help protect skin from the elements and minimize the signs of aging. Super-rich macadamia nut oil and cocoa butter keep skin supple and smooth; extracts of green tea and algae make excellent facial moisturizers. To reduce stretch marks, sesame oil and shea butter are a good bet.

- **And don't forget to cover up.** Wearing protective clothing and sunglasses can go a long way in preventing skin cancer as well as the aging of the skin.

- **When it comes to smelling good**, deodorants using the natural antibacterials found in plant extracts do a wonderful job of preventing odors.

- **Oral care.** To keep teeth clean without caustic cleansers, try toothpastes with zinc citrate, which helps control tartar buildup, and plant extracts like peppermint and fennel—natural breath fresheners.

- **Nail care.** Natural cosmetic company Jason offers nail treatments that strengthen nails, soften cuticles, and soothe hangnails. Ingredients include green tea extracts and shea butter.

Generally speaking, look for personal-care products based on plant oils instead of petrochemicals, colors derived from natural minerals such as titanium dioxide, fragrance from essential oils, and natural preservatives such as vitamins C and E or grapefruit seed extract. Herbal extracts also provide a range of healthy benefits, from promoting strong, shiny hair to repairing aging skin. But if you are chemically sensitive, please be aware that even these safe choices may cause an adverse reaction.

Some care must be taken when looking for alternative products, however. Some people may have allergic reactions. There are no federal standards for organic labeling of cosmetics, and words like "natural" and "botanical" have no legal meaning.

Separating truly nontoxic cosmetic and personal-care products from natural wannabes requires reading the ingredient label. Here are a few tips:

Cosmetic ingredients are listed in descending order, with the largest amount of a particular ingredient listed first. If the first few ingredients are obvious synthetic chemicals, put the product back on the shelf. Artificial colors, fragrances, and preservatives usually appear near the end of the ingredient label. Colors are the easiest to spot because of the FD&C or D&C designation. Synthetic fragrance is also easy to decipher since it is listed simply as "fragrance." Finding the preservatives in a product can be trickier, although the parabens are preceded by the prefixes butyl-, ethyl-, methyl-, or propyl-.

Natural cosmetic and personal-care companies, like those listed below, offer a wide array of effective but nontoxic alternatives:

Abaka Republic. California-based company known for its hand soaps, which are made using extracts of the abaca plant. The soaps can help soothe skin conditions like psoriasis and eczema, and also contain anti-aging properties. 208 East Carson Street, Suite 101, Carson, CA 90745, (888)95-ABAKA, www.abakarepublic.com.

Aubrey Organics. Full line of chemical-free skin, hair, and body-care products, many of which include organic ingredients. Although the products have not been tested on animals, some do contain animal by-products. 4419 N. Manhattan Avenue, Tampa, FL 33614, (800)282-7394, www.aubrey-organics.com.

Avalon Natural Products. Makers of the popular Alba Organics line of skin care products, which are made of ocean-derived ingredients such as sea kelp (toner) and sea moss (moisturizer), Avalon offers everything from tinted lip balms with SPF 18 protection to herbal shampoos. 1105 Industrial Avenue, Petaluma, CA 94952, (707)347-1200, www.avalonnaturalproducts.com.

Aveda. A socially conscious company that applies eco-friendly principles not only to its entire product line, but also its manufacturing and packaging. Aveda offers a wide array of cosmetics, perfumes, shampoos, and conditioners, and other personal-care products, many made from pure flower and plant essences. Also operates several stores, hair salons, and spas. 4000 Pheasant Ridge Drive Northeast, Minneapolis, MN 55449, (866)823-1425, www.aveda.com.

Red Alert!

Our mothers may have had few options when it came to feminine protection, but today's woman has a mind-boggling array of products to choose from. But while mainstream feminine hygiene manufacturers promise "confident protection," those chaste pads and tampons stashed under your bathroom sink have a more sinister side.

Twenty-five years after tampons were linked to toxic shock syndrome, which causes high fever, vomiting, diarrhea, and even death, women are still falling prey to TSS. The malady was blamed on a type of superabsorbent tampon that increased the production of toxins in women who carried the *Staphylococcus aureus* bacteria. While tampon manufacturers finally pulled these products off the market, there's a new offender: rayon. Although manufacturers insist that rayon is just as safe as cotton, it doesn't absorb toxins the way cotton does, says Philip Tierno, adjunct associate professor of microbiology at New York University Medical Center. Instead, the toxins roam freely in the vagina, where they can be absorbed into the delicate tissue.

To make sanitary pads and tampons "whiter than white," feminine hygiene companies historically bleached them with chlorine. But as consumers became aware of the dangers chlorinated bleaching posed to their health and the environment, mainstream manufacturers switched to elemental chlorine-free (ECF) bleaching. Yet, even though both the industry and the FDA maintain that ECF bleaching produces no dioxin, at least two independent studies have found detectable levels of the chemical in popular brands of tampons.

Women can reduce their risk by using organic all-cotton tampons and pads like Organic Essentials and Natracare. Not only are these products free of synthetics, natural brands use organic cotton and a harmless oxygen process for bleaching. To cut down on the waste from sanitary products, try reusable flannel pads, such as GladRags or Lunapads. For internal protection, some companies offer highly absorbent washable sea sponges as an alternative to tampons. Another reusable product, The Keeper, is a natural rubber cup, which is worn internally during your period.

Aztec Secret. This deep-cleansing, 100 percent bentonite clay from Death Valley is made without additives, animal products, or animal testing. P.O. Box 841, Parhump, NV 89041, (775)727-8351.

Bare Escentuals. Full line of color cosmetics created from 100 percent pure minerals. 1290 59th Street, Emeryville, CA 94608, (510)844-0707, www.bareescentuals.com.

Beeswork. Face, hair, and body-care products based on beeswax, plant oils, and organic herbal extracts. Most products are packaged in reusable glass bottles. 122 Hamilton Drive, Suite D, Novato, CA 94949, (415)883-5660, www.beeswork.com.

Better Botanicals. Herbal products that work with the skin's "natural intelligence" to address root causes of skin conditions. 335 Victory Drive, Herndon, VA 20170, (703)481-3300, www.betterbotanicals.com.

Botanical Earth. Herbal skin and body-care products. Ingredients are sustainably grown and organic whenever possible. None of the products are animal tested. P.O. Box 86, Winfield, MO 63389, (636)528-7789, www.botanicalearth.com.

Burt's Bees. All-natural skin, hair, and body care, as well as color cosmetics. Some items do contain animal by-products. P.O. Box 13489, Durham, NC 27709, (800)849-7112, www.burtsbees.com.

Crystal. Fragrance and additive-free deodorant stones, sticks, and sprays. Products do not contain aluminum chlorohydrate, commonly found in conventional antiperspirants. Cruelty-free and environmentally safe. French Transit, Ltd., 398 Beach Road, Burlingame, CA 94010, (800)829-7625, www.thecrystal.com.

derma e. Founded in the 1960s, making organic body-care products that are never tested on animals. 9751 Independence Avenue, Chatsworth, CA 91311, (800)521-3342, www.dermae.net.

Dr. Bronner's Magic Soaps. The 1960s counterculture icon still offers the same castile-based liquid and bar soaps, plus a few newer items. Many of these cruelty–free products are now certified organic under the USDA's organic food regulations and come in recycled plastic bottles. P.O. Box 28, Escondido, CA 92033, (760)743-2211, www.drbronner.com.

Dr. Hauschka. Holistic skin, hair, and body care, as well as color cosmetics. Synthetic chemical–free; however, some items do contain animal products. All products list an expiration date. 59C North Street, Hatfield, MA 01038, (800)247-9907, www.drhauschka.com.

Earthly Delights. A nontoxic, water-based nail polish that peels right off for quick, convenient color changes. No solvents like toluene or hardeners like formaldehyde are in these tiny bottles. 767 Union Chapel Road, Cedar Creek, TX 78612, (512)303-3448, www.earthlydelightsusa.com.

Earth's Beauty. A division of Cosmetics Without Synthetics. P.O. Box 701, Dewey, AZ 86327, (888)586-9719, www.earthsbeauty.com.

Ecco Bella. Natural and holistic cosmetics and skin care. 1123 Route 23, Wayne, NJ 07470, (973)696-7766, www.eccobella.com.

Giovanni Organic Hair Care. All products are cruelty-free and many contain organic ingredients. 21580 South Wilmington Avenue, Long Beach, CA 90810, (310)952-9960, www.giovannicosmetics.com.

Glad Rags. Reusable menstrual pads made from organic cotton. The company also offers The Keeper, a soft, reusable natural gum rubber cup that collects menstrual flow rather than absorbing it like tampons do. P.O. Box 12648, Portland, OR 97212, (800)799-4523, www.gladrags.com.

Grateful Body. All-natural skin and body-care products based on organic herbal formulas. 1342 Virginia Street, Berkeley, CA 94702, (800)600-6806, www.gratefulbody.com.

Hemp Organics. Lipsticks and lipliners made from a blend of organic plant oils and herbs, beeswax, and minerals. P.O. Box 170507, San Francisco, CA 94117, (415)861-4070.

Honeybee Gardens. Petrochemical- and fragrance-free skin, hair, and body care, along with color cosmetics. Ingredients are sustainably harvested, and none of the products are tested on animals. 311 South Street, Morgantown, PA 19543, (888)478-9090, www.honeybeegardens.com.

Jade & Pearl. Offers bath and body products, along with a DEET-free insect spray and natural sea sponge tampons. Products are synthetic chemical–free. P.O. Box 1106, Hawthorne, FL 32640, (800)219-9765, www.jadeandpearl.com.

Shining the Light on Sunscreens

You've heard it before: Wear sunscreen. According to the American Cancer Society, an estimated 60,000 people will be diagnosed with some form of skin cancer this year alone. But just when people have become convinced that sunscreen can protect them from premature wrinkles and skin cancer, new evidence is casting a shadow of doubt about the safety and effectiveness of these products.

The controversy stems from a parallel rise in skin cancer and sunscreen use. Epidemiologist Dr. Merianne Berwick of New York's Memorial Sloan-Kettering Cancer Center has found that there is no scientific evidence that the use of sunscreen prevents skin cancer. Five of the studies Berwick cited found that sunscreen users actually had an increased risk of melanoma.

Some experts suspect that certain sunscreen ingredients may be the culprit. In the late 1990s, John Knowland of Oxford University reported that sunscreens containing Padimate-O can damage DNA when exposed to sunlight.

More recently, scientists have found that sunscreen ingredients also promote cancer by generating free radical damage. Free radicals are unstable molecules that cause cellular damage by stealing electrons from healthy cells, a process called oxidation. Scientists at the University of Zurich, Switzerland, have also found that many widely used sunscreen chemicals mimic the effects of estrogen and trigger developmental abnormalities in rats.

Fortunately, Mother Nature has supplied her own UV screening agents. Zinc oxide and titanium dioxide are natural minerals that, unlike chemical sunscreens which absorb UV light, scatter UV rays away from the skin's surface. Often paired in natural sun protection products with mild botanical sunscreens like shea butter, wild pansy, green tea, and coffee extracts, these minerals safely protect against both UV-A (which promotes melanoma, the deadliest form of skin cancer) and UV-B rays.

And, of course, staying out of the sun offers the surest bet for protecting yourself from skin cancer.

Jakaré. Chemical-free skin care that includes organic or wildcrafted herbs and plant oils. Products are made fresh weekly and packaged in reusable glass bottles. P.O. Box 10124, Bozeman, MT 59719, (877)525-2731, www.jakare.com.

Jason Natural Cosmetics. The company has reformulated its product line to remove artificial surfactants and preservatives. Many of the products include organic ingredients and all are cruelty-free. 8468 Warner Drive, Culver City, CA 90232, (800)527-6605, www.jason-natural.com.

From Botox to Breast Implants

Extreme makeovers. Botox parties. For people who aren't happy with their looks, these modern "miracles" can give them what nature—or time—has deprived them of. One of the most radical makeovers is breast implantation. Since breast implants first became an option for women in the 1960s, these medical devices have been fraught with problems. More than 190,000 adverse reports have been collected by the FDA, including 123 deaths directly resulting from breast implants.

A 2000 FDA study of women with silicone breast implants found that out of 344 women who underwent Magnetic Resonance Imaging, 69 percent had at least one ruptured implant. Another study, published in the *Journal of Rheumatology*, found that women with leaking silicone gel were 2.8 times more likely to suffer from fibromyalgia. Other serious problems include pain, a tightening of the capsule surrounding the implant, a dislodged implant, serum collecting below the skin, blood clots, infection, toxic shock syndrome, or extrusion (an implant pushing through the skin).

Because of these safety concerns, the FDA issued a moratorium limiting the use of silicone gel implants in 1992. But the new saline breast implants may not be any safer. New research shows that 60 percent of women with saline breast implants have complications within the first four years.

Women who want to turn back the effects of Father Time are increasingly turning to Botox, collagen, or other so-called lunchtime procedures. But, whether you're looking to erase a few wrinkles, plump up your lips, or get a whole new complexion, these treatments carry risky side effects.

Botox is the brand name for botulinum toxin A, the poisonous bacteria that causes botulism. Although dermatologists use a highly diluted amount of the toxin to smooth out wrinkles (which it does by paralyzing the muscles), it can cause bruising, headaches, nausea, flu-like symptoms, respiratory infection, double vision, or a temporary drooping of the eyebrow or lid. Dermal fillers use animal fat or collagen to plump up lines and wrinkles and to make features like lips appear fuller. But allergic reactions aren't uncommon and the procedure can also cause joint and muscle pain, headaches, blistering, soreness, and respiratory problems.

Chemical peels can soften skin, remove blemishes, and improve pigmentation. But since these treatments rely on harsh chemicals, stinging, redness, blistering, and an increased sensitivity to the sun are common. Of more concern, this treatment can cause infection, burns, and scarring.

While these treatments may offer a quick fix, none are permanent or a cure-all for aging skin. So buyer beware: When it comes to cosmetic surgery, you may just get more than you pay for.

John Masters Organics. Organic skin and hair-care products, made from (among other things) sage, lemongrass, and evening primrose. 77 Sullivan Street, New York, NY 10012, (212)343-9590, www.johnmasters.com.

Kiss My Face. All-natural body-care company operating out of a 200-acre organic farm in New York's Hudson Valley. P.O. Box 224, 144 Main Street, Gardiner, NY 12525, (845)255-0884, www.kissmyface.com.

Lily of Colorado. Botanically based skin and body-care products free from chemicals. Many ingredients come from the company's own certified organic farm. All products are cruelty-free. P.O. Box 437, Henderson, CO 80640, (800)333-5459, www.lilyofcolorado.com.

Living Nature. New Zealand company offering chemical-free skin, hair, and body-care products packaged in glass bottles and labeled with an expiration date. Products are cruelty-free and don't contain animal by-products. Box 193, Kerikeri, New Zealand, (011)+64-9-4077895, www.livingnature.com.

Lotus Brands/Light Mountain. Pure henna powder in various shades. Cruelty-free and packaged as a complete application kit. P.O. Box 325, Twin Lakes, WI 53181, (800)824-6396, www.internatural.com.

Lunapads International. Reusable menstrual pads made from organic cotton. The company also offers The Keeper, sea sponges, and organic cotton tampons. 207 West 6th Avenue, Vancouver BC, Canada V5Y 1K7, (604)681-9953, www.lunapads.com.

Mad Gab's. All-natural lip glosses and skin salves. The company produces and packages their products with minimal waste. P.O. Box 426, Westbrook, ME 04098, (800)547-5823, www.madgabs.com.

Mera Naturals. Alcohol-free botanical hair-care products. Products do not contain any synthetic dyes, fragrances, or animal by-products, and are not animal tested. P.O. Box 218, Circle Pine, MN 55014, (800)752-7261.

Moom. Chemical-free skin and body-care products. Moom offers a unique all-natural hair removal product containing only sugar, water, lemon juice, chamomile, and tea tree oil. All products are cruelty-free and the company strives to eliminate unnecessary packaging. 1574 Gulf Road, #1115A, Point Roberts, WA 98281, (800)492-9464, www.imoom.com.

Morganics Essential Botanicals. Natural skin-care products. Morganics offers products from gentle scrubs and moisturizers to shampoos and bath salts. 7302 E. Helm Drive, Scottsdale, AZ 85260, (800)820-9235.

Natracare. Certified organic cotton tampons, pads, and panty shields. (303)617-3476, www.natracare.com.

Natural Dentist. Offers mouthwash and toothpaste based on medicinal herbs and essential oils. Woodstock Natural Products, 140 Sylvan Avenue, Englewood Cliffs, NJ 07632, (201)944-0123, www.thenaturaldentist.com.

Nature's Gate. Personal-care products based on botanical remedies. 9200 Mason Avenue, Chatsworth, CA 91311, (819)882-2951, www.levlad.com.

Nonie of Beverly Hills. Anti-aging skin care for men and women. Based on plant oils, organic juices, and plant proteins, all of the products are hand mixed and packaged in glass bottles. 812 Seward Street, Los Angeles, CA 90038, (888)666-4324, www.nonieofbeverlyhills.com.

Organic Essentials. Along with tampons and sanitary pads, this company offers nursing pads, cotton balls, cotton swabs, and cosmetic rounds. All the products are 100-percent certified organic by the Texas Department of Agriculture and are bleached using hydrogen peroxide. 822 Baldridge Street, O'Donnell, TX 79351, (806)428-3486, www.organicessentials.com.

Pandora Pads. Offers organic, reusable, and non-chlorine bleached disposable sanitary and nursing pads. The company also offers Natracare products and sea sponges. 955 Frances Harriet Drive, Baton Rouge, LA 70815, (888)558-7237, www.pandorapads.com.

Paul Penders. Chemical-free skin, hair, and color cosmetic products. All of the products are cruelty-free and contain no animal by-products. 3002 Giant Road, #215 Center Court, San Pablo, CA 94806, www.paulpenders.com.

Peelu. Natural toothpaste, tooth powder, dental floss, and peelu gum. P.O. Box 2803, Fargo, ND 58108, (800)457-3358.

Real Purity. Chemical-free skin, hair, and body products, along with a growing line of color cosmetics. The products are cruelty-free and contain no animal products. P.O. Box 307, Grass Lake, MI 49240, (800)253-1694, www.realpuritytm.com.

Recycline. Toothbrushes, tongue cleaners, and razors made of 100 percent recycled plastic. The reusable toothbrush packaging is made from renewable wood resources. 236 Holland Street, Somerville, MA 02144, (617)776-8401, www.recycline.com.

Sappo Hills Soapworks. Natural bar soaps made traditionally with saponified plant oils and herbs. Cruelty-free and contains no external packaging. 654 Tolman Creek Road, Ashland, OR 97520, (541)482-4485.

Sun Dog. Hair and body products based on plant oils, botanical extracts, and essential oils. Although some products may contain animal by-products, none are tested on animals. Ten percent of all profits go to Native American cultural preservation. P.O. Box 64, Westby, WI 54667, (608)634-2988, www.sundoghemp.com.

TerrEssentials. Hand-crafted line of natural skin, hair, and body-care products. Many of their products contain organic ingredients and all are cruelty-free. 2650 Old National Pike, Middletown, MD 21769, (301)371-7333, www.terressentials.com.

Tisserand. Aromatherapeutic essential oils and natural hair and body care. 1129 Industrial Avenue, Petaluma, CA 94952, (707)769-5120, www.tisserand.com.

Tom's of Maine. Natural toiletries including toothpastes, mouthwashes, deodorants and soaps made from plant extracts, essential oils, and other nontoxic ingredients. Also offers cough and cold remedies. P.O. Box 710, Kennebunk, ME 04043, (800)FOR-TOMS, www.tomsofmaine.com.

Trillium Herbal Company. Based on ayurvedic healing principles, these body polishes, oils, and lotions contain certified organic plants and essential oils. They're cruelty-free. 185 East Walnut Street, Sturgeon Bay, WI 54235, (920)746-5207, www.aromafusion.com.

Cosmetics in the Kitchen

If you really want to know what's in your cosmetics, make them yourself! Not only are homemade cosmetics and personal-care products just as effective as store-bought varieties, they are always fresh and they cost a fraction of what you'd pay at the cosmetic counter.

While creating your own cosmetics is a simple art to master, you'll need to follow a few general guidelines:

- Always use fresh, high-quality ingredients, preferably organic.

- If you are using dried herbs, look for non-irradiated ones with a vibrant color and strong aroma.

- Buy only pure essential oils. Never use synthetic fragrance oils.

- Except for olive oil, all plant oils should be stored in the refrigerator to prevent them from becoming rancid.

- Make sure all of your equipment is scrupulously clean, since microscopic bits of dirt and bacteria can quickly spoil a whole batch.

- To avoid homemade cosmetics going bad, make small batches and preserve them naturally with a few drops of vitamin E or grapefruit seed extract.

Making your own skin and hair treatments is fun. Once you've nailed down the basics, get creative! Experiment with different fruits, vegetables, herbs, grains, nuts, and essential oils to create your very own custom cosmetics. To get you started, here are a few recipes:

Stress-Less Bath Salts
Adding these fragrant salts to your bath will relax tight muscles and wash away tension.

> 1 cup epsom salt
> ¼ cup baking soda
> ¼ cup sea salt
> 15 drops lavender essential oil

Measure the dry ingredients into a bowl and blend them together thoroughly. Add the essential oil and mix well. Package in an airtight glass jar and label. To use, add ¼–½ cup to bath water.

Yield: 12 ounces.

Simple Sugar Scrub
This scrub brightens a dull complexion and leaves skin incredibly soft and smooth.

> ¼ cup white cane sugar
> ⅛ cup sesame oil
> ½ teaspoon vitamin C crystals
> 2 drops chamomile essential oil

Combine the ingredients in a wide-mouth jar and cap with an airtight lid. To use, massage a small amount into your face using circular motions. Rinse well with warm water.

Yield: 4 ounces.

Tea Rose Toning Mist

The antioxidants in white tea help protect skin from environmental pollution and free radical damage. As an extra bonus, the tea and rose water help soften the appearance of fine lines.

½ cup strong white tea
½ cup rose water
5 drops carrot seed oil

Pour all the ingredients into a spray bottle. Cap and shake to mix well. To use, spritz on face after cleansing. Allow to dry before applying moisturizer.

Yield: 8 ounces.

Avocado Hair Mask

This nutrient-rich recipe gives dry, damaged hair the deep conditioning it craves.

½ ripe avocado, mashed
1 teaspoon avocado oil
5 drops rosemary essential oil

Combine all ingredients in a small bowl. Massage into clean, wet hair, making sure you coat each strand. Cover with a plastic shower cap and relax for 30 minutes. Rinse the mixture out of your hair with warm water, then shampoo as usual.

Yield: 1 application.

Cocoa Butter Cuticle Oil

Keep cuticles soft and healthy with this chocolate-scented oil.

2 tablespoons jojoba oil
1 tablespoon wheat germ oil
1 tablespoon cocoa butter

Place all ingredients in a small saucepan. Heat gently until the cocoa butter has completely melted. Stir well and cool. Pour into a glass jar with a tight-fitting lid. To use, massage a small amount into the base of each nail, gently pushing back the cuticles.

Yield: 2 ounces.

Vermont Soapworks. Offers organic bar soaps and bath products. All of the products are biodegradable and the company is working with consumer groups to strengthen regulations for organic cosmetics. 616 Exchange Street, Middlebury, VT 05753, (866)762-7482, www.vtsoap.com.

Vita-Myr. Natural toothpaste and mouthwash made without sodium lauryl sulfate, fluoride, alcohol, or artificial sweeteners. P.O. Box 230576, Las Vegas, NV 89123, (888)558-8482, www.vitamyr.com.

V'tae. Essential oils (organic when possible) are the basis for this line of natural perfumes, bath, and body products. More than 10 percent of the company's profits go to environmental groups. All products are cruelty-free and encased in recyclable or reusable packaging. 569 Searls Avenue, Nevada City, CA 95959, (800)643-3011, www.vtae.com.

Weleda. All-natural skin, hair, and body-care products from Germany. 175 North Route 9W, Congers, NY 10920, (845)268-8572, www.weleda.com.

Wild Earth. The company's Inara line of 100 percent organic bath and body-care products are made by women or indigenous cultures throughout the Americas. Some products may contain animal by-products. 918 Sherwood Drive, Lake Bluff, IL 60044, (888)688-7565, www.inaraorganic.com.

WHAT YOU CAN DO

Now that you know the truth about cosmetic and personal-care products, you can make informed decisions when it's time to go shopping. Use your purchasing power—and your pen—to let irresponsible cosmetic companies know that you won't buy their products until they clean up their act.

Instead, put your money where your values are. Hundreds of natural personal-care products that are just as effective as their toxic counterparts are available at your local health food store or online. You can also whip up your own healthy, beauty-enhancing concoctions at home, usually with just a few easy-to-find ingredients (see p. 58).

One of the best ways to get involved in changing how conventional cosmetics are made and marketed is to educate your congressional representatives about the dangers they pose and urge them to draft legislation supporting healthier beauty products. (Check your local telephone book for the address and phone number of your congressional representatives or check online at www.congress.org for contact information.)

You can also learn more about what's being done to change how mass-marketed cosmetics are created by checking out the following organizations:

The Cancer Prevention Coalition. A nationwide alliance of health experts, activists, and representatives from organized labor, environmental, and women's groups. Their primary goal is to reduce the preventable causes of cancer, including the carcinogens found in cosmetics. CPC, Samuel S. Epstein, M.D., c/o University of Illinois at Chicago School of Public Health, MC 922, 2121 West Taylor Street, Chicago, IL 60612, (312)996-2297, www.preventcancer.com.

The Coalition for Consumer Information on Cosmetics. A partnership of eight animal rights organizations that promotes a single comprehensive standard for "cruelty-free." The group has also introduced the Leaping Bunny logo as the international symbol denoting that a product is free of animal testing. CCIC, P.O. Box 75307, Washington, DC 20013, (888)546-2242, www.leapingbunny.org.

The Environmental Health Network. A nonprofit advocacy group for chemically injured people. Its website is full of information on the chemicals found in fragrance and scented products. EHN, P.O. Box 1155, Larkspur, CA 94977, (415)541-5075, www.ehnca.org.

The Environmental Working Group. Investigates environmental threats to the planet and to personal health and safety. Their 2002 "Not Too Pretty" report contains a wealth of information on the phthalates found in cosmetics and personal-care products. EWG, 1436 U Street N.W., Suite 100, Washington, DC 20009, (202)667-6982, www.ewg.org.

Green Products Alliance. A consortium of natural cosmetic manufacturers who believe that socially responsible business practices can help create a sustainable economy and ecosystem. Members pledge to avoid petrochemicals or other harmful chemicals, animal testing, and animal by-products, and to use organic ingredients and recycled or reusable packaging whenever possible. GPA, 616 Exchange Street, Middlebury, VT 05753, (802)388-4302, www.greenproductsalliance.com.

The Organic Consumers Association. Fights to keep strong standards for organic cosmetics. OCA, 6101 Cliff Estate Road, Little Marais, MN 55614, (218)226-4164, www.organicconsumers.org.

The Organic Trade Association. The membership-based business association for the organic industry in North America. Its website is packed with fact sheets and useful information about organic products of all kinds. OTA, P.O. Box 547, Greenfield, MA 01302, (413)774-7511, www.ota.com.

chapter four

Wear Your Love Like Heaven
Natural-Fiber Clothing

Photo by coolnotcruel

Despite its association with things "new agey," there's nothing new about natural-fiber clothing. Until the twentieth century, all clothing was "natural," made simply from cotton, wool, and other fibers.

But the American love of all things modern (along with the urge for convenience) produced a chemical revolution. Starting with the first polyamides—long-chain synthetics that could be spun into cloth—in the 1930s, man-made fibers became highly desirable because they delivered a plethora of apparent benefits for clothing manufacturers and the buying public.

Clothing made from synthetics is strong; resists stretching, wrinkling, and shrinking; and is easy to wash—all of which contributed to synthetics' rise in popularity and a ready marketplace for any new "wonder fabric" that came along. Synthetics also take dyes easily and cling to the body, qualities that proved irresistible as the disco era hit its peak in the 1970s. We were treated to such "classic disco" looks as formfitting Lycra stretch pants in strident colors and bright, patterned shirts worn open to expose astrologically inspired medallions on many a manly chest.

However, as consumers become more discerning and fashion trends shift toward a more organic look, people have started seeking out clothing that is more comfortable—and less harmful to the wearer's health and to the environment. Now consumers are saying no to conventional dyes, "wrinkle-free" treatments, and pesticide-doused fabrics. Many are making the switch to natural, breathable, chemical-free alternatives. Hemp, organic cotton, flax, and tencel fabrics, in a growing variety of styles and colors, are some of the options now found in mail-order catalogs and retail stores.

Why the switch? Making clothes is a seriously polluting business. According to natural yogurt maker Stonyfield, "The clothing industry is energy intensive, requiring the transportation of raw materials and finished products around the world. It's natural-resource intensive, with the production of synthetic fibers from petroleum products, and environmentally impactful, with releases of toxic bleaches, dyes and finishes."

Even such seemingly innocent products as the common all-cotton T-shirt trip alarms. Did you know that cotton exhausts the soil, and uses 25 percent of the world's pesticides, making it the most pesticide-intensive crop?

The production of man-made fibers is even more harmful to the environment. According to a report by the Environmental Protection Agency (EPA), in 1995 alone man-made fiber manufacturing released 399 million pounds of toxic chemicals into the air and water (the statistic includes toxics that were "transferred," either shipped off site or discharged into sewers). Large amounts of wastewater are also generated. Rayon is usually made by the viscose process, which the EPA says "is typically associated with a large volume of air emissions."

There is also growing concern about the link between the use of such cleaning chemicals as formaldehyde and the spread of multiple chemical sensitivity (MCS), in which people experience severe reactions to even very low levels of chemicals. Those concerns are driving changes in the dry-cleaning industry, where the use of more environmentally friendly processes is becoming widespread.

The Sustainable Cotton Project (SCP) reports, "Once the raw materials are transformed into garments, they may be subjected to other chemical onslaughts, including treatment with formaldehyde—also used in embalming. Applied to prevent wrinkles in permanent press clothes, formaldehyde can cause such symptoms as dizziness, light-headedness, memory impairment, attention disorders, and allergies.

"Repeated exposure to this toxin may weaken the immune system, and may lead to Multiple Chemical Sensitivity Syndrome (MCSS) or Environmental Illness (EI), a medical condition that affects the neurological, immune, respiratory, skin, gastrointestinal, and musculoskeletal systems. With time it takes less and less exposure to the toxins to cause symptoms and, as the body systems break down, an ever-increasing number of chemicals, including some unrelated to the initial exposure, are found to trigger a reaction."

As American consumers become more aware of conditions in sweatshops around the world, many are avoiding garments sold by companies that exploit workers in developing countries such as Bangladesh, China, and Morocco.

However, while there is clearly a market for natural-fiber clothing, it remains something of a specialty item. This is true, in part, because of the relatively higher cost of clothing made from natural fibers. Simply put, many mainstream stores don't carry natural-fiber clothing because they aren't convinced that the public will pony up the additional bucks.

In addition, according to Sara Cross, owner of the website coolnotcruel .com (which specializes in natural-fiber clothing that works as a business wardrobe), the spread of her industry remains somewhat stymied by a "Catch-22" dilemma. "While there is a market for this kind of clothing," says Cross, "it's not widely available because distribution is a problem."

Having made the decision to dress according to her values while still looking good, Cross made a startling discovery. "I found that a conscious consumer has to do several hours of research in order to find a few websites or catalogues, most of which are small businesses directly marketing their limited product lines," she says. But things are getting better. Although finding the right clothes is still a challenge, new Internet-based companies give the buying public unprecedented access, making it easier than ever to "go natural."

Some of the new entrepreneurs are motivated by social concerns, such as legalizing industrial hemp or doing away with sweatshops. Others are spurred on by an appreciation of such fabrics as organic cotton or natural merino wool from New Zealand. And others simply see a marketing opportunity.

CURRENT EVENTS/LEGISLATIVE/POLITICAL

A Renewed Interest in Hemp

Despite the fact that versatile industrial hemp is a highly renewable resource, it is currently illegal to grow in the United States because it has been classified as a "drug" under the Controlled Substances Act.

Activists are mobilizing to legalize U.S. cultivation of this natural fiber, which has many environmental benefits. Hemp has been used in textiles since at least 8000 B.C., making it perhaps the longest-used fiber. Both George Washington (who wrote in a letter to his farm manager, "make the most you can of the Indian hemp seed. Sow it everywhere") and Thomas Jefferson were hemp boosters. Hundreds of thousands of acres of hemp grew in America's heartland until the 1930s, when the industrial crop was caught up in the anti-marijuana crusade (though it has only 1 percent THC, the drug's active ingredient). Hemp's fortunes were briefly revived during World War II, when the federal government launched an aggressive "Hemp for Victory" campaign that convinced farmers to devote more than 400,000 acres to its cultivation. The fiber was used in manufacturing badly needed canvas, rope, and even uniforms for the military. Between 1942 and 1945, the War Hemp Industries Corporation built forty-two hemp mills in the Midwest to handle the demand.

Despite the U.S. ban, the hemp industry around the world is as large as $100 million annually. According to Candi Penn, executive director of the Hemp Industries Association (HIA), fourteen states have passed legislation to petition for the right to study or cultivate industrial hemp. Both the Association of State Departments of Agriculture and the Association of State Legislatures have adopted pro-hemp resolutions. These urge the Department of Agriculture, the DEA and the Office of National Drug Control Policy (aka the "Drug Czar's office") to develop an official definition of industrial hemp. Supporters have urged Congress to adopt policies allowing U.S. farmers to grow industrial hemp, legally making a division between that crop and marijuana.

Hemp produces 250 percent more fiber than cotton, using virtually no pesticides. At the same time, the crop suppresses weeds and leaves the soil rich in nitrogen deposits, increasing yields on rotational crops such as soybeans and corn.

Hemp clothing is relatively costly in the United States because producers import fabric from major suppliers like Canada and Spain—which raises the price on the end product. Given the wide-ranging market for hemp products, including clothing, there are clear economic advantages to legalizing hemp cultivation.

The Organic Fabric of Your Life

Another natural fiber with a growing popularity is organic cotton, though it remains relatively scarce. In 1998, organic cotton harvests from U.S. growers were as low as 20,000 bales (10 million pounds). Consequently, organic cotton clothing is also more expensive than "regular" cotton. However, there are hidden costs associated with the "fabric of our lives."

Farmers worldwide spend $2.6 billion on cotton pesticides annually, including such hazardous chemicals as parathion, which has effects that reach beyond farm workers to affect wildlife and ecosystems. Some 20,000 deaths per year and a million poisoning cases can be attributed to cotton-related pesticides. According to James Liebman, staff scientist for the Pesticide Action Network (PAN) in San Francisco, the United States grows 13 million acres of cotton each year, and most of it is doused with pesticides.

The Sustainable Cotton Project says the average acre of California cotton is blasted with an estimated 300 pounds of synthetic fertilizers (nitrogen, phosphorous, and potash) along with about thirteen pounds of pesticides, herbicides, insecticides, and defoliants. Run-off from cotton fields has been found to contaminate drinking water in farm communities and pose other long-term threats to the environment. And the workers who are exposed to these toxins are at increased risk for cancer and many other diseases.

The goal of SCP's Cleaner Cotton Campaign is to substantially increase organic cotton acreage in California in hopes of achieving "the critical mass necessary to redirect the future of the world's favorite natural fiber."

"Organic cotton is grown without any of the 200 agricultural chemicals used in the standard process," says Christine Nielson, founder of Coyuchi, a California-based company that was a U.S. pioneer in developing full-width organic cotton sheets. Certified organic cotton is frequently rotated in compost-rich soil, and uses beneficial insects, rather than spraying, to control bugs, Nielson explains.

Other groups have also taken up the cause of organic cotton. A group of fifty-five companies—including Nike, Cutter & Buck, Mountain Equipment Cooperative, Norm Thompson, Patagonia, and Timberland—formed the Organic Exchange, a nonprofit business organization focused on expanding the global organic cotton industry. The group wants to see 10 percent of the world's cotton supply certified as organic by 2012.

One issue of concern is that while there are regulations about how organic products are grown, those regulations don't extend to sectors other than food and beverages. "There aren't any regulations that talk about how that cotton boll or wool off the sheep are turned into organic fiber goods," says Holly Givens, communications director for the Organic Trade Association (OTA).

"It's not like food," adds Bena Burda, cofounder of Ann Arbor, Michigan's Maggie's Organics. "T-shirts don't come off T-shirt trees."

The first step was developing agricultural guidelines for organic cotton and wool. The next step was harder. According to *Earth Times*, "The steps between commodity and cloth—ginning, spinning, knitting, wet finishing, and then on to the cut-and-sew house—make codifying a process difficult." But the OTA has developed standards for natural fibers that speak to the issues of production. "It took us five years and it was a consensus-driven process," Givens explains. "We sought comments from people in the industry and from the public."

OTA's standards are available for license by certified manufacturers of organic fiber products.

The Hidden Costs of "Mainstream" Clothing

Beyond strictly environmental concerns, conscious consumers might want to consider that sweatshop labor often comes along with the "bargain" of less-expensive clothes.

According to Co-op America, a national nonprofit organization, "A sweatshop is any workplace where workers are subject to extreme exploitation. This includes hazardous working conditions, arbitrary discipline, and a lack of a living wage, self-determination, benefits, dignity and basic human rights."

In a few cases, especially when the sweatshop connections of prominent celebrity clothes lines have been exposed (Kathy Lee Gifford provides one celebrated example), guilt-motivated checks have been written and promises made. But the exploitation of workers so that we can buy "reasonably priced" clothing continues throughout the world.

A 2002 *New York Times* op-ed story discussed sweatshop conditions for young, mostly female workers in Bangladesh. "[They] are paid an average of 1.6 cents for each baseball cap with a Harvard logo that they sew," the op-ed asserted. "The caps retail at the Harvard bookstore for $17, which means the garment workers, who often are younger than the Harvard students, are being paid a tenth of 1 percent of the cap's price in the market. Also in Bangladesh, women receive five cents for each $17.99 Disney shirt they sew." Similar conditions exist in China, Morocco, and Central America.

According to Juliet Schor and Betsy Taylor's book *Sustainable Planet: Solutions for the Twenty-first Century* (Beacon Press, 2003), there is an emerging "global sweatshop" cranking out the T-shirts, jeans, and other clothing U.S. consumers demand. In these factories, women—as much as 70 percent of the labor force—are often locked inside overcrowded buildings without fire exits while working for starvation wages. The women are reportedly sexually and physically harassed by their supervisors, subjected to beatings, forbidden to speak, and denied such basic rights as permission to go to the bathroom.

A number of manufacturers are making an effort to develop equitable partnerships in Third World countries. For instance, Maggie's Organics has pledged its company's sewing contracts to Maquilador Mujeres, a cooperative in Nueva Vida, Nicaragua.

GREEN PRODUCTS

Suellen Fisher Henney's interest in natural clothing stems from her sensitivity to formaldehyde. To escape the chemical assault, Henney introduced her Fisher Henney Naturals organic and chemical-free clothing line for women in 1995. Henney's clothes use naturally colored cotton in mocha, tan, gray, and reddish brown. These pastel shades were first cultivated around 2700 B.C., and were common in Ancient Indo-Pakistan, Egypt, and Peru. The natural cotton is certified organic, free of all dyes, pesticides, herbicides, and chemical fertilizers.

Henney says her clothing line is "for people who want style and don't want to look frumpish." She says that about 30 percent of her customers are chemically sensitive, while others are just environmentally conscious people who know the harm caused by conventional cotton production and cloth dyeing. Available by mail-order, Henney's line includes formal business attire, shorts, sweaters, lingerie, and jeans.

Cheryl Hahn, proprietor of Tomorrow's World, says that her mail-order company offers a full line of natural clothing, shoes, and bedding items made from organic cotton and hemp fabrics. Hahn says that best-sellers include hemp jeans and organic cotton undergarments. Tomorrow's World also sells bulk hemp and "transitional" cotton fabric (grown with the same process as organic, but in soil that's in the three-year transition period to becoming certified). "These are products that feel good because they are good—in more ways than one," she says.

Other companies are creating eco-fabric blends. In 2000, natural products leader Gaiam took over the EcoSport company, which became known for blending organic cotton with tencel, a biodegradable fiber made from wood pulp (and the first natural fiber introduced by the industry in over thirty years). Taken from managed tree farms, tencel appeared on the market in the early 1990s. EcoSport's cofounder, Marylou Marsh-Sanders, says that tencel drapes like rayon and is extremely durable. However, it is not chemical-free, since it relies on low-toxic chemicals during production. Sanders' current company is Spiritex, which makes organic cotton clothing, including sweatshirts, loungewear, and T-shirts.

Northern California–based Coyuchi specializes in organic cotton bedding. According to founder Christine Nielson, "All our organic cotton is grown in three developing countries—India, Turkey, and Uganda—on family farms that range in size from two to 250 acres. We pay premium prices to these small-scale growers because it encourages organic practices that protect not only the environment, but also these farmers, their families, and their communities from exposure to toxic agricultural chemicals. Also, by purchasing our cotton at a better price per pound, we help support local and economically sustainable production."

Planet Hemp makes homespun, handwoven, and crocheted "fiber arts" from 100 percent hemp fiber, using mostly organic dyes. The line includes oxford shirts, drawstring and fishermen's pants, hats, belts, jean jackets and robes, scarves, backpacks, hammocks, and even hacky sacks.

California-based Organic Threads makes naturally colored FoxFibre organic cotton socks. Sally Fox of Athena Mills spent decades developing FoxFibre from naturally colored long-staple cotton, which is far stronger than the natural cotton used in ancient times. Owner Gail Richards says, "FoxFibre uniquely deepens with each washing." She adds that her socks are "a totally U.S.-made product, from farmer to knitter."

Natural Clothing Resources

American Apparel. Sweatshop-free T-shirts, made in downtown Los Angeles. 747 Warehouse Street, Los Angeles, CA 90021, (213)488-0226, www.americanapparel.net.

Blue Canoe. Features a wide range of clothing designed by a yoga practitioner. While much of the line is active wear, including bras, tops, and pants, there is also a cotton cashmere line, and baby gear. The Sheer Organics collection is made "for hot yoga or just looking hot." P.O. Box 543, Garberville, CA 95542, (707)923-4111, www.bluecanoe.com.

coolnotcruel. Specializes in men's and women's clothing for business and casual wear. You can buy coolnotcruel products—including organic tees emblazoned with your choice of six different phrases—at the website or at Swirlspace, 593 Guerrero Street (at 18th Street), San Francisco, CA 94110, www.coolnotcruel.com.

Decent Exposures. Specializes in bras, but also features a full line of products "designed by women for women," including hard-to-find Latex-free swimsuits. All of the products—many of which are made with recycled materials—are made in Seattle and, in keeping with the company's dedication to being a socially responsible business, employees are paid good wages, receive benefits, and have flexible work schedules. Decent Exposures, (206)364-4540, www.decentexposures.com.

Earth Speaks, Organic Fashion. Classic women's clothing made from hemp and hemp blends. 33 Flatbush Avenue, Brooklyn, NY 11217, (866)ESPEAKS, www.earthspeaks.com.

Genopalette. This collection of scarves, wraps and throws are handwoven on a small family farm in Missouri. The all-virgin wool from the family's flock of Romney and Merino sheep—raised with sustainable agriculture methods—comes in a variety of natural, undyed colors. 1110 County Road 319, Franklin, MO 65250, (888)374-5371, www.genopalette.com.

Heartland Products. Non-leather footwear, from dress pumps to hiking boots. The snappy men's dress shoes look and feel like supple leather but actually have uppers made from Vegetan, a cruelty-free synthetic that is water-resistant, scuff resistant, lightweight and breathable like leather. P.O. Box 218, Dakota City, IA 50529, (515)332-3087, www.trvnet.nets/~hrtlndp.

Indigenous Designs. Specializing in knitwear and casual clothing made by artisans, 50 percent of whom come to the work through knitting cooperatives or nonprofit groups. 975 Corporate Center Parkway #110, Santa Rosa, CA 95407, (707)571-7811, www.indigenousdesigns.com.

Kasper Organics. Features clothing, socks and underwear made from organic cotton and hemp. 6500 Hazeltine Avenue, Van Nuys, CA 91401, (818)988-3924, www.kasperorganics.com.

Maggie's Functional Organics. Dedicated to making affordable clothing from environmentally sustaining materials and methods, the company began with socks and T-shirts but has expanded to a full line of undergarments, sleepwear, dress oxfords, and more. Supports the work of Maquilador Mujeres, a worker-owned cooperative in Nueva Vida, Nicaragua. "We believe our company should scorn the planned obsolescence of the fashion industry, and instead produce solidly constructed basics." 306 West Cross Street, Ypsilanti, MI 48197, (800)609-8593, www.maggiesorganics.com.

Making It Big. Proving that style is not defined by size, this natural-fiber clothing manufacturer specializes in quality clothing for plus-sized women (traditional sizes 32 to 70). Clothes are available on the company's website and at one retail location in Rohnert Park, California. The company's products include underwear, activewear, business attire, special occasion attire, and casual fashions. (877)644-1995, www.makingitbigonline.com.

Of the Earth. The casual clothing and active wear are made of such natural fibers as hemp, tencel, ramie, soy, and organic cotton. P.O. Box 1124, Bend, OR 97709, (541)317-9266, www.oftheearth.com.

Planet Hemp. Makers of 100 percent hemp clothing and lifestyle accessories. "The Garden of the Goddess," 114 Xenia Avenue, Yellow Springs, OH 45387, (937)767-9001, www.planethemp.net.

Rawganique. From sandals to a truly classic Oxford shirt, Rawganique offers high-quality, affordable hemp clothing in classic styles. The company is committed to the environment and fair trade workplaces. 9000

Rayelyn Lane, Denman Island, BC V0R1T0, Canada, (250)335-0050, www.rawganique.com.

S.O.S. From Texas. "We're growing organic T-shirts, from seed to sewing," say these Texas entrepreneurs. Having made the transition to organic practices, the family-run farm—in the Oldham family for more than 100 years—produces a wide range of tees and a limited number of other garments, including men's underwear, socks, sweatpants, and polo shirts. P.O. Box 767, Samnorwood, TX 79077, (800)245-2339, www.sosfromtexas.com.

Under the Canopy. Sold online, in catalogs, and in some retail stores, this product line includes men's, women's and children's clothes made of a wide variety of natural fibers, including organic cotton stretch denim, hemp-silk, organic cotton-tencel, organic linen, and organic cotton blended with angora. Plans are underway to introduce organic cashmere, yak, soy, and even bamboo clothing. Hemp shoes and boots are also available. 1141 South Rogers Circle, Suite 7, Boca Raton, FL 33487, (888)226-6799, www.underthecanopy.com.

Utopian Living. Home of Ecolution's complete line of hemp clothing, including shirts, pants, dresses, shoes, and bags. Utopian Living is an Earth-friendly hemp store, also selling hemp bags and accessories. If you like making your own clothes, you can buy hemp fabric by the yard. P.O. Box 300646, Austin, TX 78703, (512)255-4065, www.utopianliving.com.

Vegetarian Shoes. If you just have to have a pair of eco-friendly purple Para boots, here's your source. Featuring a full line of footwear—from sneakers and sandals to an adorable pair of women's boots—British-based Vegetarian Shoes sells footwear made-to-order by such European factories as Birkenstock and the oldest co-op in England. Yes, they ship internationally. 12 Gardner Street, Brighton, East Sussex UK BN1 1UP, (011)44(0)-1273-691913, www.vegetarian-shoes.co.uk.

Wildlife Works. These T-shirts, yoga pants, and clothes for people of all ages are available online and in high-end retail stores, supporting the mission of saving endangered and threatened wildlife. The entire line is made from organic cotton, hemp, and other environmentally friendly fabrics. 475 Gate Five Road, Suite 120, Sausalito, CA 94965, (415)332-8081, www.wildlifeworks.com.

Zappos. We found a pair of incredibly flirty, red strappy dress sandals that may just stamp out the stereotype of "crunchy granola frump" in Zappos' "Vegetarian Shoes" section. While this site doesn't specialize in eco-friendly footwear, what it does offer is a wide range of options in that category— from sneakers to work boots to everyday shoes for the real world. 271 Omega Parkway, Suite 104, Shepherdsville, KY 40165, (888)492-7767, www.zappos.com.

Clothing Lines to Look For

Two Star Dog. Founded by brothers Steven and Allen Boutros in 1992, Two Star Dog manufactures hemp clothing for women and men. The company has only one retail outlet (at 1370 Tenth Street, Berkeley, CA 94710) and does not sell directly to the public. (510)525-1100, www.twostardog.com.

Nike Organics. Features clothes made of certified organic cotton. "While this initial offering is modest in size, we hope that it will signal to our retailers and consumers that we are sincere in our commitment to organic cotton," said Heidi McCloskey, Nike's global director of sustainability, talking about the company's first product line in 2002 to BeautyBuzz.com. "We're not sourcing organic because it's easier, faster, or cheaper—in fact, in many ways it's harder, slower, and more costly. We're doing it because we believe that it's the right thing to do." One Bowerman Drive, Beaverton, OR 97005-6453, (800)344-6453, www.nike.com.

Patagonia. The company converted its entire sportswear line to 100 percent organic cotton in 1996, vowing never to go back to conventionally grown cotton, which it criticized for "extensive and intensive use of synthetic fertilizers, soil additives, defoliants, and other substances [that] wreak terrible havoc on soil, water, air and many, many living things." 8550 White Fir Street, P.O. Box 32050, Reno, NV 89523-2050, (800)638-6464, www.patagonia.com.

WHAT YOU CAN DO

Naturally, the easiest course of action is to vote with your pocketbook—choose clothing made from natural fibers. However, there is more you can do to support the cause. You can, for instance, join with groups working to change the way fibers are grown.

The Hemp Industries Association (HIA) describes itself as "at the forefront of the drive for fair and equal treatment of industrial hemp." It lobbies to change government policies that prohibit growing the plant.

"In addition to the HIA website, we've set up the Vote Hemp website to help educate about the use of industrial hemp," explains Candi Penn, HIA executive director. The Vote Hemp website offers a state-by-state guide to the status of hemp legislation, straight facts about industrial hemp, and alerts about the latest hemp news.

In keeping with its educational mission, the Vote Hemp site also provides voter guides so you can track the position of any federal candidate or incumbent (including Presidential candidates) on industrial hemp. The site also provides links to hemp product sites and information on a range of other environmental issues. The Vote Hemp website is at www.votehemp.com.

The Sustainable Cotton Project (SCP) builds bridges between farmers, manufacturers, and consumers to pioneer markets for certified organically grown cotton. Visit SCP's website, www.sustainablecotton.org, to learn more about sustainable farming, the dangers of pesticides, and links to more information.

Ask around. Consumers will probably create awareness of organic fabrics simply by inquiring if they're available. According to Holly Givens of the Organic Trade Association, "If you walk into a store and ask if they have any clothing made from organic fibers, [the retailers] will begin to understand that this is something that their customers want." She points out that choosing products like organic cotton can manifest other changes, as well. "A lot of these products are all connected—for instance, once organic cotton has been processed for textiles, the remaining fibers can be made into organic cotton feed meal, which is fed to organically raised livestock, which produce dairy products and meat." Choosing an organic cotton T-shirt, then, can have a greater effect than you realize.

Sustaining the Momentum

Once you've bought your natural-fiber wardrobe, you'll have to care for it.

CLEANING CLOTHES

A range of environmentally friendly laundry products are now readily available in even the most mainstream supermarkets, as well as in the more specialized national chains such as Trader Joe's and Whole Foods. The real trick is to approach doing laundry with an eye toward conservation.

- Always use cold water for the rinse cycle. Choose the cold or warm water wash cycle.

- Make sure you use the right water level for the load you're washing—and try to hold off on doing laundry until you have a full load.

- Use the shortest setting possible. If you're doing a load of heavily soiled clothes, take advantage of the soak cycle—then wash for ten minutes.

- Don't underload or overload your dryer—and bear in mind that it's most efficient to dry clothes that have the same bulk, i.e., T-shirts with other relatively lightweight clothing, jeans with other jeans, towels with towels. And use the warm to cool settings.

- If you're in the market for a new washing machine and/or dryer, make sure you find the one that puts the least burden on the environment.

- If you're very particular about your delicates, consider hand-washing with shampoo. Any shampoo that leaves your hair clean and shiny will probably deliver good results—and no pesky residue—on your clothes (see page 42).

Green Dry Cleaning

Look inside your closet or dresser and you're certain to find some items of clothing that you simply can't care for on your own. Dry cleaning is, at some point in nearly everyone's life, the only option. The bad news is that traditional dry cleaning uses perchloroethylene or perc, which not only makes your clothing smell bad, it's also bad for the environment. The good news is that there are some environmentally friendly dry-cleaning alternatives that are becoming more widely available.

- **Silicone-based.** The GreenEarth method uses a silicone-based solvent and reportedly delivers good results. It is odorless, nontoxic and—as an added incentive to dry-cleaning professionals—affordable. You can search for dry cleaners that use this process at GreenEarth.com.

- **Carbon-dioxide based.** Using patented technology and liquid carbon dioxide, the process relies on Earth-friendly detergents to dissolve dirt and doesn't use high heat. So the process is energy efficient as well as being less damaging to your clothes. You can find cleaners who use this technology at hangersdrycleaners.com.

- **"Wet" cleaning.** Not considered as effective as silicone or carbon-dioxide, wet cleaning uses water and special detergents in computer-controlled machines.

OFF-SEASON STORAGE

Part of "treading softly on the Earth" is cutting down on our consumption. It's important, then, to try and ensure that our clothing lasts through many seasons. Barring either a truly minimalist wardrobe or expansive closet space, most of us need to put seasonal clothing away somewhere when it's not in use. Some simple precautions will ensure a long "shelf life" for most clothing.

- Because light—incandescent, fluorescent, and natural—contains ultraviolet rays, any clothing that contains dyes of any kind needs to be protected from exposure during storage.

- Store only clean clothes. Stains from food and drink can attract insects and turn yellow with age. Avoid using chlorine bleach, starch, sizing, and fabric softeners, however.

- Store clothing in breathable materials—in other words, *not in plastic*. Plastic prevents air circulation, allows moisture to collect on the clothes and can lead to mildew. Canvas garment bags with cedar tops and bottoms, or an infusion of dried lavender, are great for hanging garments. If you need to lay clothing flat, use a suitcase and place your folded items inside pillowcases or sheets. That way it's easy to remove the stored items if the travel bug hits suddenly. When it's time to switch wardrobes again, let the clothes you remove from storage air out completely before you put them in the closet or drawers.

Don't Buy Sweatshop Clothes

Another way to take action is to boycott products from corporations that exploit workers in sweatshops. One of the best resources for learning about this issue is Sweatshop Watch. Founded in 1995, this coalition of more than thirty groups serves low-income workers globally, with a special emphasis on garment workers in California.

The coalition believes that "workers should earn a living wage in a safe, decent work environment, and that those responsible for the exploitation of sweatshop workers must be held accountable." The group offers information on supporting boycotts of companies that employ sweatshops, organizes students to make their campuses "sweatshop free" (no more $20 baseball caps made in near slave-labor conditions by workers receiving eight cents apiece), and provides responsible shopping guides.

Co-op America, a national nonprofit organization founded in 1982, educates and empowers people through economic strategies, organizing power and practical tools for businesses and consumers. And that includes providing resources on sweatshop labor and how to stop it.

The Center for a New American Dream, which began with a mandate to foster the "new simplicity" movement, helps "Americans consume responsibly to protect the environment, enhance quality of life, and promote social justice." Check out the group's "Conscious Consumer" project for sources for sweatshop-free clothing and information about the anti-sweatshop movement.

Get more information about how the buying choices you make can make a difference at the I Buy Different website. Part of "Be, Live, Buy Different—Make a Difference," a national campaign from World Wildlife Fund (WWF) and the Center for a New American Dream, this site's goal is to help young people learn how they can make a difference by buying differently. While the information and buying tips are aimed at teens, they're useful for people of all ages.

Sweatshop Resources

Center for a New American Dream. 6930 Carroll Avenue, Suite 900, Takoma Park, MD 20912, (877)68-DREAM, www.newdream.org.

I Buy Different. www.ibuydifferent.org.

Sweatshop Watch. 310 Eighth Street, Suite 303, Oakland, CA 94607, www.sweatshopwatch.org.

chapter five

Perfect Pets

Healthy Food, Chemical-Free Collars, and Organic Bedding

Photo by Petstages

*E*xplore the farthest reaches of recorded history, and you'll discover that humans were keeping animals as pets. Sometimes the animals have been revered—such as the dogs in Chinese royal courts that were assigned their own servants, or the cats that were declared demigods in ancient Egypt and even dragged from house fires before their human family members.

But we humans have also gone to the other extreme. First-century Romans went to great lengths to import domestic dogs, only to throw them into gladiator rings and pit them against each other in bloody battles. A century later, European churches decided cats were a direct link to the devil and sent out their death squads. (It was a move that was as bad for people as it was for cats: With felines nearly wiped out of human communities, rats flourished and bubonic plague boomed.)

Today, many pets enjoy a status that their forbearers would envy: Neither god nor demon nor object of sport, they are simply part of the family—and, quite often, they are doted upon. Americans share their homes with more than 112 million cats and dogs, not to mention an assortment of reptiles, birds, horses, and exotic animals. And, as pet owners become more health- and environment-conscious, their new awareness is beginning to include their companion animals.

Even if you've been on the fringes of the modern environmental movement, you probably know about the simple, three-step program of reducing, reusing, and recycling. If you're going green, or already went there years ago, it's important to remember to take your pets on the journey.

CURRENT EVENTS/LEGISLATIVE/POLITICAL

You may think that choosing a pet is a simple act, affecting none other than you and the creature you decide to share your life with. Think again. How you acquire your pet and how you care for it throughout its life can affect many other animals, too.

Every year, legions of animal advocates work to make life better for the animals sold or kept as pets in the United States. Law enforcement officers routinely enforce, and try to strengthen, animal cruelty laws in their towns, cities, and states. Animal protection groups lobby local, regional, and national legislative bodies to consider laws that would afford cats better care and protection through licensing, force owners to spay and neuter their pets, outlaw dangerous or neglectful practices, clamp down on unsavory pet dealers, and a whole host of other concerns.

But animal advocates know that compassion begins at home. They also know that most pet owners want to do the right thing, but they often don't know how. That widespread lack of understanding explains why pet-owner education has become the leading goal among companion-animal divisions of humane societies nationwide. Ideally, that education starts before you choose your pet, not after.

Choosing a Companion Animal

You may already have a dog, cat, hamster, or even an exotic animal that you share your life and times with. But if you don't, then your first order of business is to choose wisely. At no other point in your pet-owning life will the three Rs—reduce, reuse, and recycle—come more into play.

Rule number one: Get thee to an animal shelter. It is so easy to be wooed by a wondrous creature you see in a pet store, to be lured by a "puppies for sale" sign posted in someone's yard, or to decide that a particular character trait you want in a dog or cat can only be assured through "perfect" breeding.

But, all these impulses feed the most dramatic problem of modern pet-hood: massive overpopulation.

No one knows exactly how many dogs and cats are brought into animal shelters every year, but the Humane Society of the United States (HSUS) puts the number between eight and twelve million. Of these, a small percentage is lost pets that are eventually reunited with their owners. Others, between 25 to 35 percent, find new homes. But at least half are euthanized—a sad reminder that there are still many more animals than there are people willing to adopt them.

You can reduce this suffering by adopting a homeless animal from your local shelter rather than buying one at a pet store, through a dealer's classified ad, or through a breeder. This act alone can reduce waste at its most basic level: There is no reason to create consumer demand for more animals when millions die needlessly each year.

Moreover, if you do purchase a dog rather than adopt one from a shelter, you are likely supporting the particularly noxious businesses known as puppy mills. These breeding facilities mass-produce puppies and sell them to animal dealers and pet shops. They also sell directly to the public, mainly through the Internet or newspaper ads. The puppies born in these mills often suffer medical problems from overbreeding and inbreeding—problems that surface later in the dog's life. Worse yet, the animals that are forced to live at the mill and continually produce puppies have minimal veterinary care, substandard food and shelter, overcrowded cages, little interaction with humans, and a sure death once they can no longer breed. Still, according to the Pet Industry Joint Advisory Council (PIJAC), about 3,700 of the nation's 12,000 pet stores choose to sell puppies—and consumers buy up to 400,000 puppies from stores each year.

If this doesn't make a shelter sound grand, I don't know what does. But just in case you need convincing, here are some shelter facts:

- Most shelters have a great selection of animals for adoption— everything from kittens and puppies to mature adults. They also have small mammals like rabbits, gerbils, hamsters, and rats, and of-ten have parakeets and other common birds as well.

- Mixed-breed animals are often healthier and more moderately tem-pered than purebreds, but even if you're convinced you want a specific breed, a shelter may still work: On average, a quarter of a shelter's dog population is purebred, and new animals arrive daily. If you have a specific breed in mind, you can often put your name on a waiting list and the shelter will call you when animals that meet your description arrive. There are also breed-specific rescue groups, which can be found online.

- Responsible shelters screen animals for health and behavior issues, and pass that information along to you before you adopt.

- Shelters charge minimal adoption fees—unlike a pet store or breeder—and also often vaccinate, deworm, and spay or neuter animals before they go home with you.

To find your local shelter or humane society, just go to your Yellow Pages, or search the Internet for listings. Many shelters profile animals available for adoption on their websites. There are also a few general websites—such as Pets 911, Petfinder, and 1-800-Save-A-Pet.com—that list pets available from shelters. Your shelter can also refer you to rescue groups who specialize in placing homeless animals of certain breeds.

Rule number two: Don't buy exotics. If you are considering an exotic pet, the best advice is Reaganesque: Just say no. Exotic animals may be the fastest-growing craze in pet ownership, but it is also a most dangerous one—for animals, ecosystems, and sometimes for people, too. There are many reasons to avoid exotic pets, but here are the main ones.

- By purchasing an exotic pet you are supporting the commercialization of wild creatures.

- You are also likely supporting animal dealers who go to many legal and illegal lengths to remove "saleable" animals from their wild homes. Every year, millions of birds, reptiles, primates, and other creatures are snatched from the wild and transported to various countries to be sold as pets. For every animal that makes it to a customer, many more die en route or are killed so that their young may be captured. Ecosystems, too, are compromised.

- The booming business in exotics has also fueled a bevy of backyard breeders, with varying levels of skill and compassion for treating animals in their care.

- Exotic animals do not adjust well to a captive environment and do not make good companions.

- The average person cannot provide the special care, housing, diet, and maintenance these animals require. As a result, most end up suffering significantly and often die of neglect.

If you aren't swayed by these factors, then consider human safety. Exotic animals pose undeniable risks. Monkeys may look cute as babies but their tolerance for captivity wanes and they can inflict serious bites as they mature. Of the 7.3 million reptiles kept as pets in American homes, some are deadly. Snakes routinely escape—and reports of bites and strangulations are not rare. Children and adults have been mauled by escaped tigers. (Some 7,000 large wild cats are thought to be kept as pets in the United States.) Finally, there is disease to consider. Depending on the species, exotic animals can and do transmit herpes B, monkey pox, and salmonellosis to humans, among other diseases.

Bear in mind, too, that wildlife experts estimate that the illegal trade in exotic animals is a $10 billion-a-year business: As contraband, it is second only to the illegal trade in drugs. Many animals, ounce for ounce, are worth more to smugglers than cocaine.

What can you do to reverse this astonishing trend? Resist buying exotic animals from dealers or pet shops. Support or introduce legislation that would make owning exotic animals illegal in your community. And fight efforts by breeders and pet store owners to dismantle existing laws.

Rule number three: Choose a pet for life. Being environmentally responsible is often about resisting the urges of a throw-away society. This applies to pets, too. Many people acquire pets impulsively, and are later surprised by the amount of time it takes to train, exercise, groom, and otherwise care for them. Often, this leads to the disposable-pet syndrome: easy come, easy go.

You and your pet will fare better if you do your homework. Find out what your pet will need from *you* in order to have a good life. Also, check into how much money you should plan on spending each year for routine veterinary care—which differs from animal to animal—and make sure you are comfortable with that. And consider how long your pet might live: Adopting a kitten is a potential twenty-year commitment; a large dog will be with you for perhaps twelve years; some birds live for more than sixty years.

GREEN PRODUCTS

Once you've chosen your pet, you will see that there is no shortage of ways to pamper him or her. Enter an average pet store and a world of products awaits you. Aisles are lined with everything from chew toys to pet sofas. Again, put the three Rs into play. As tempting as it might be to buy your lapdog that polka-dot rain slicker and matching booties, think twice. Don't overconsume. Instead, evaluate what your pet really needs—for food, comfort, protection, and play. Then, look for the best, least-harmful products and avoid excessive packaging.

Selecting Healthy Pet Food. The vast majority of us only barely understand the specifics of what it takes to keep our own bodies properly fueled. When it comes to our pets, we understand even less. And if you have a household filled with many types of animals, you already know their needs are all radically different.

Where to start? According to Rebecca Remillard, pet nutritionist at Angell Memorial Animal Hospital in Boston, dogs and cats should be fed diets specifically designed for their breed, age, and activity level. What to feed your pet depends on what balance of nutrients she needs, and how much energy she burns each day. To find out what that balance must be for your dog or cat, visit Remillard's website, www.petdiets.com, and use the online calculators to measure energy requirements and nutritional needs.

Once you know your pet's general requirements, the next step is to choose a food. Many resources on natural pet care urge homemade diets, and if you decide to take that route, read the sidebar on homemade pet food (see page 85). Otherwise, get ready to explore the world of pet food, and begin your journey by reading labels.

For starters, look for a label statement guaranteeing that a pet food meets the American Association of Feed Control Officials (AAFCO) standards for a nutritionally complete and balanced diet. But don't stop there. Food carrying this label still may not meet your criteria for an environmentally sound diet.

Are Homemade Diets Right for Your Pet?

Go online, flip through pet magazines, or check out the pet section at a local bookstore and you'll find slews of homemade recipes for dogs and cats. Choosing which to try can be baffling, and feeding the wrong one to your pet over time can even be harmful. If you want a safer way to create a homemade buffet, ask your veterinarian—but still beware. One recent survey found that even 90 percent of veterinarian-prescribed homemade diets were not nutritionally adequate for adult dogs or cats. If you want to be as confident as possible, consult a pet nutritionist.

According to Rebecca Remillard of Angell Memorial Animal Hospital in Boston, "Making homemade foods requires knowledge, motivation, additional financial resources, and careful and consistent attention to recipes."

If you do decide to play chef, here are some of Remillard's words of wisdom:

- **Follow supplement instructions to the letter.** Pet owners often seek one veterinary supplement that can make homemade recipes for dogs or cats meet all the micro mineral and vitamin requirements adequately—but it doesn't exist. Carefully crafted recipes usually call for various supplements, but often pet owners eliminate them because they are hard to find, expensive, or because they don't understand their importance. To keep your pet's diet as balanced as possible, follow instructions precisely.

- **Stick to the recipe.** Variety may be the spice of our own dinner plates, but mixing and matching dinner fare doesn't work quite the same way for pets. Remillard warns that pet owners unwittingly unbalance their pet concoctions by substituting ingredients from the same tier on the human food pyramid, or leaving them out altogether.

- **Ignore human diet fads.** Just because you're avoiding fat, cholesterol, and sodium doesn't mean your pet should.

The American Veterinary Medical Association reports that Americans spend approximately $11 billion per year on pet food. But it may be time to examine how those shiny but foul-smelling cans and cute-shaped kibble measure up to what Mother Nature provides.

Food Pets Die For (New Sage, 1997) by Ann N. Martin, and Dr. Richard H. Pitcairn's *Natural Health for Dogs and Cats* (Rodale Press, 1995) spell out in great detail the reasons commercially processed pet food is dangerous to your animal's health. For example: Listing the protein source as "meat or poultry by-products" allows the manufacturer to include meat processing waste. This includes "4-D" animals: dead, diseased, dying, or disabled, whose meat often contains tumors and drugs used to try to treat the animals before they died. According to the Association of American Feed Control Officials, pet food can and does include spray-dried animal blood, hydrolyzed hair, dehydrated garbage, unborn carcasses, and many other things.

To add insult to injury, according to the National Animal Control Association, of the more than 13 million pets shelters kill annually, five million are shipped to rendering factories to be used in pet food. Drugs used for euthanasia, such as pentobarbital, survive the rendering process. Carbohydrate sources of commercial pet food may consist of such factory waste as dust, floor sweepings, and husks. Restaurant grease has also become a major component of pet food in recent years.

To avoid this noxious mixture, sleuth out food labeled "natural" or "organic." But be aware that the same labeling inconsistencies that apply to human foods apply to pet foods: What these terms mean is open to interpretation. In general, you'll want to look for a food that lacks artificial colors, flavors, and preservatives as well as synthetic nutrient additives (such as amino acids, vitamins, or minerals). You'll also want to make sure the meat and grains used in the food were produced without synthetic hormones, pesticides, or fertilizers.

Many of us have chosen a vegetarian route for ourselves—either out of concern for the environment, for animals, for our health, or all of the above. The urge to carry these principles to our pets' dinner bowls is often strong. But bear in mind that dogs are by nature omnivores, and cats are carnivores. Professional opinions vary widely on how healthy a dog can be on a vegetarian diet. But the word on vegetarian diets for cats is quite clear: they can be fatal.

Health Care: Necessities and Natural Options

If you have a dog or cat, the most important medical step you will take for it is to have it spayed or neutered (see the sidebar on page 87). Once you've done that, make sure you make annual visits to a veterinarian and keep rabies and other vaccines up to date. Veterinary care is also available for your other pets—from birds, gerbils, hamsters, rats, and horses to rabbits—but vaccinations and other such routine needs differ considerably. The best

The Kindest Cut: Spaying and Neutering

If you've read the rest of this chapter you know that, for cats and dogs, overpopulation is a massive problem. One step all pet owners should take to help solve it is to have their cats and dogs sterilized—commonly referred to as spaying or neutering.

Even if your dog is constantly under your watchful eye, or your cat never ventures outside, they should indeed meet the knife for this one concession to the greater good. Pets always stand the chance of escape, and a pet with all of its biological yearnings in full swing will undoubtedly work hard to seek an exit route and find a mate.

Besides preventing unwanted litters, spaying and neutering will help your pets live longer lives. In females, sterilization also eliminates the possibility of ovarian cancer and reduces the incidence of breast cancer. In males, it eliminates testicular cancer and decreases the incidence of prostate disease. Another plus: The commonly heard musings that spayed and neutered pets are more even tempered, less aggressive, and more affectionate are not just folklore. Many studies have shown these notions to be true.

advice is that once you get a pet, ask a veterinarian how often it should be seen.

Beyond that, you have many options for keeping your pet healthy, and if you are partial to alternative medicine for yourself, you'll be happy to know that it is becoming increasingly popular for pets, too. Holistic practices are now routinely used to treat arthritis, hip dysplasia, and degenerative joint diseases—as well as to ease metabolic stress and strengthen immune systems. Even so, the traditional veterinary community usually reserves alternative therapies for aging animals who are too tender to undergo surgery or tolerate more medication.

If you want to make holistic care a routine part of your pet's life, though, you can turn to specialists in veterinary acupuncture, chiropractic manipulation, and homeopathy. Veterinarians are also using Chinese herbs to promote healing and kinesiology to diagnose muscle ailments. And they're experimenting with naturopathy—cleansing pet bodies through fasting, drinking water, exercise, and massage.

Fleas, Ticks and Toxins

What to Avoid. According to a study done by the Natural Resources Defense Council (NRDC), the chemicals commonly used in flea and tick products can cause serious health problems—particularly for children and pets. To avoid these chemicals, learn what to look for in a label. The chief culprits are organophosphate insecticides (OPs) and carbamates—which can harm the nervous system. To screen out OPs, avoid products with chlorpyrifos, dichlorvos, phosmet, naled, tetrachlorvinphos, diazinon or malathion. To screen out carbamates, avoid products with carbaryl or propoxur.

If you have any over-the-counter flea and tick products—dips, sprays, powders, bombs, or collars—in your household that contain these chemicals, dispose of them according to your local hazardous-waste guidelines. Don't underestimate their dangers.

Healthier Alternatives. Most experts advise the cautious pet owner to start by avoiding over-the-counter products and consulting a veterinarian for both preventive care as well as products for fending off invasions. But not all veterinarians are equally attuned to the pitfalls of various chemicals, so it helps to do your homework, too.

If you do want to treat your pet, ask about products that contain non-pesticide insect-growth regulators, also called IGRs. These are not a panacea, but are safer for pets and people than their more toxic relations. They won't kill the fleas already on your pet, but they will stop them from reproducing. With any flea and tick product, follow the guidelines closely; never use products designed for dogs on your cat or vice versa; and never apply pesticides to young, old, pregnant, or sick animals unless guided by a veterinarian.

Some holistic vets recommend natural remedies such as garlic, brewers yeast, and eucalyptus leaves. Unfortunately, while some pet owners report positive results, there's little data based on traditional veterinary trials to show that these are effective. The same goes for ultrasonic insect repellents.

Prevention Is the Key. The safest option for your pet, your family, and the environment is prevention. Simple measures can make the use of pesticides unnecessary. Here are a few peaceful weapons to deploy during flea and tick season.

- Bathe your pet frequently with a pesticide-free shampoo, and wash pet bedding weekly.

- Comb your pet regularly with a flea comb—and have a bowl of hot, soapy water nearby in which to drown any interlopers.

Keeping Your Pet Safe

There are all sorts of perils a pet can encounter in your home. Cats or dogs might munch on mistletoe or chocolate (toxic to some), swallow string, or chew chicken bones that could lodge in their throats. If you've ever baby-proofed a home, recall some of your tactics and put them to use: think about electrical cords and outlets, store your medicines out of reach, and keep doors closed or set up gates so that your pets don't wander out without you.

But, to truly take precautions, check pet-care books or websites to find out what could harm your particular animals. You might be surprised at some of the seemingly mundane items that could cause havoc. For instance, your Lab might steal your avocado sandwich with no ill effects, but giving a slice of avocado to your pet bird or mouse for a treat is akin to giving it poison.

There are some common environmental hazards that you'll need to know about, and dangerous chemicals are one of them. If our pets confront toxic invasions in their lifetimes, they will most likely come from the many products we heap upon them to keep them safe from fleas and ticks. See the companion article for helpful guidance on this thorny problem.

But other dangers abound, too. Julie Dinnage, a veterinarian serving the Massachusetts Society for the Prevention of Cruelty to Animals' shelter animals, points out that many toxic encounters are highly preventable. Here are some common ones:

- **Antifreeze**, even in very small amounts, is fatal to pets. Worse yet, its sweet taste attracts them. To prevent pet deaths, Safe Brands introduced SIERRA antifreeze—safer, and well worth the minimal extra price, but still not trouble-free. Keep all antifreeze safely stored and watch out for any driveway spills.

- **Lead poisoning** is a serious concern for pets, whose low-to-the-ground profile often brings them into close contact with contaminated dust and paint chips. Lead poisoning is a serious human problem, too, so screening your environment for dangerous lead levels is always a wise idea.

- When it comes to **chemical lawn treatments**, says Dinnage, "Don't do it. Dogs become heavily exposed to this and also track the chemicals inside on their paws. Some people employ sprinkler systems in order to avoid chemical lawn applications, but that wastes water." Says Dinnage, "Plant natural grasses that have less need for fertilizers and pesticides."

- **Synthetic carpeting** can create the same problem for pets as it does for people—asthma and allergies.

- Avoid **de-icing salts.** They may melt snow and ice, but they also irritate paws—causing your pet to lick them and in the process ingest poison. If you've walked your pet in areas where you think these salts have been used, wash and dry his feet before he has a chance to lick away. Some city dwellers have resorted to doggie boots to quell the problem in heavily salted areas.

If you're a bird owner, be aware that some fumes—such as those from nonstick cooking surfaces, self-cleaning ovens, and aerosol or pump sprays—can kill them. When selecting bedding for your small mammal, bear in mind that shavings from even cedar and pine can emit fumes that can be dangerous to hamsters and gerbils. When scoping out the chew-toy aisle, remember that rawhide bones have at times been infected with salmonella.

Simple steps should keep your pets safe and sound and ecologically in tune. And when it comes to going green in petland, remember: What your pet wants second only to food and water is attention—something that consumes no resources and is good for both of you.

WHAT YOU CAN DO

There are countless ways to help companion animals. Animal shelters always need good volunteers to help care for their animals, and to spread the word about homeless animals to potential adopters. Shelters also need help cleaning, teaching visitors about pet care, and raising funds. If your interests run more to the political, then consider lobbying for humane legislation—locally, nationally, or even internationally. Contact the groups listed below—particularly the Humane Society of the United States and People for the Ethical Treatment of Animals on the national front, and the World Society for the Protection of Animals on the international front—and find out how they can use your help. There may also be regional issues that need your voice.

Perhaps your state is trying to protect cats and dogs from dangerous leghold traps, strengthen laws that prevent former pets from being sold or surrendered to medical research laboratories, or strengthen fines and penalties for animal cruelty or neglect. Every letter you write to your legislators or local newspaper, and every voter you talk to, could make a difference in efforts like these. Finally, don't forget how useful your donations can be to the nonprofits that spend their days making life better for animals.

Resources

Animal Advocacy

1-800-Save-A-Pet.com. Free service connects users to detailed listings of animals available for adoption at public and private shelters across the nation. Search by phone or web. P.O. Box 7, Redondo Beach, CA 90277, (800)728-3273, www.1-800-Save-A-Pet.com.

American Society for the Prevention of Cruelty to Animals. Humane education, public awareness, government advocacy, shelter support, and animal medical services and placement. 424 East 92nd Street, New York, NY 10128-6804, (212)876-7700, www.aspca.org.

Animal Protection Institute. National animal advocacy group combining legislative and grassroots initiatives. P.O. Box 22505, Sacramento, CA 95822, (916)447-3085, www.api4animals.org.

CatsIndoors! A campaign of the American Bird Conservancy, whose website offers tips on keeping your indoor cat happy. 1834 Jefferson Place, NW, Washington, DC 20036, (202)452-1535, www.abcbirds.org/cats.

The Humane Society of the United States. Promotes the protection of all animals, including companion animals. 2100 L Street, NW, Washington, DC 20037, (202)452-1100, www.hsus.org.

Massachusetts Society for the Prevention of Cruelty to Animals. National advocacy programs, regional animal law enforcement, medical centers and adoption centers. 350 South Huntington Avenue, Boston, MA 02130, (617)522-7400, www.mspca.org.

PAWS. The Progressive Animal Welfare Society is the northwestern leader in education, legislation, and direct animal care. 15305 44th Avenue, W, Lynnwood, WA 98037, (425)787-2500, www.paws.org.

People for the Ethical Treatment of Animals. A leading national group, offering public education, cruelty investigations, research, animal rescue, legislation, and direct action to promote an understanding of animals' rights. 501 Front Street, Norfolk, VA 23510, (757)622-PETA (7382), www.PETA.org.

Petfinder.com. Website lists adoptable pets across the nation, connects users to local shelters and rescue groups, offers pet-care advice, and posts notices about lost pets or pets needing homes. www.petfinder.com.

Pets 911. Operates a website and toll-free phone hotline offering a wealth of information on saving homeless animals and ending pet overpopulation. (888)PETS-911 or www.1888pets911.org.

World Animal Net—USA. Lists more than 15,000 animal organizations around the world, by category and region. 19 Chestnut Square, Boston, MA 02130, (617)524 3670, www.worldanimal.net.

World Society for the Protection of Animals. Works with more than 460 member organizations to raise standards of animal welfare throughout the world and conducts organized campaigns, animal-rescue operations for natural and manmade disasters and education. 34 Deloss Street, Framingham, MA 01702, (508)879-8350 or (800)883-WSPA, www.wspa-americas.org.

Dealing with Doo

At the heart of all environmental conundrums is the question of how to deal with waste, and the question is no less complicated when we are considering how to deal with waste from our pets.

Urbanites walk their dogs with plastic bags in hand, and the result is millions of plastic-wrapped dog feces making their way into American landfills each day. Most observers of modern pathology consider this preferable to dog-borne parasites, or diseases like parvovirus, making their way into waterways or other ecosystems, or being flushed into municipal water systems. But, the eco-conscious still seek other ways.

Look for biodegradable scooping bags. And, if you have a yard, look into installing a mini septic system designed specifically for pet waste. They're relatively inexpensive, and quite small—fitting into a hole just two feet deep. Also, some cities are now set up to handle animal waste in water treatment facilities, and a call to your municipal water agency will let you know whether yours is among them—in which case, you can scoop and flush.

For cats, eco concerns mostly revolve around the contents of litter. Most is made of clay—but treated with a plethora of chemicals that control dust and odors. Newer, natural varieties are made from wood waste, peanut shells, sand, and other innovative materials. To make the best choice, consider not just the material, but also the energy required to transport it to your litter box. Use what's locally available if at all possible. And again, check on your municipal requirements before indiscriminately flushing things like clay into your local sewer system. Many have to strain it and cart it off to a landfill. An estimated two million tons—or more—of nonbiodegradable cat litter end up in municipal solid waste landfills each year.

Animal Care

The American Holistic Veterinary Medical Association. Website provides a gateway for in-depth information on alternative care and has an online referral service that can lead you to practitioners in your area. www.ahvma.org.

American Veterinary Medical Association. Association for conventional veterinary medicine; website offers pet care information. 1931 North Meacham Road, Suite 100, Schaumburg, IL 60173, (847)925-8070, www.avma.org.

The Animal Poison Hotline. Fee-for-service center staffed twenty-four hours a day, seven days a week, with veterinary professionals and experts in toxicology. (888)232-8870.

National Animal Poison Control Center. A fee-for-service call center staffed with veterinary health professionals who are familiar with how different species respond to poisons and treatment protocols. (900)680-0000 or (800)548-2423.

Products to Pamper Your Pet

Ark Naturals Products for Pets. All-natural, holistic remedy and wellness products and snacks. 6166 Taylor Road, #105, Naples, FL 34109, (239)592-9366, www.arknaturals.com.

Best Bones. Natural beef dog bones and treats made from cows humanely raised on sustainable farms with no antibiotics or added hormones. 159 East Livingston Avenue, Columbus, OH 43215, (614)228-1400, www.naturesreward.com.

Country Pet Foods. Frozen dog and cat food made in New Zealand from range-fed animals; no growth hormones, preservatives, colorings, or flavorings. P.O. Box 3033, Santa Monica, CA 90403, (310)394-7793, www.countrypet.com.

Earth-Friendly Products. Natural stain and odor removers—from pet stain removers to de-skunking shampoos. 44 Green Bay Road, Winnetka, IL 60093, (847)446-4441, www.ecos.com.

Eight in One Pet Products. Products for dogs, cats, birds, and small mammals range from grooming, healthcare, training, food, and cleaning items. 2100 Pacific Street, Hauppauge, NY 11788, (631)232-1200, www.eightinonepet.com.

Feline Pine. Natural alternative to clay litter for cats. 2200 North Florida Mango Road, 2nd Floor, West Palm Beach, FL 33409, (561)688-8101, www.felinepine.com.

Goldenlab Enterprises. Offers a recycled cardboard scoop with its Oops Scoops biodegradable plastic bags. (608)271-8663.

Integrated Pet Foods. All-natural pet food, dog biscuits, and cat litter. 1120 Chateau Drive, Exton, PA 19382, (610)594-2581, www.integratedpet.com.

Natural Life Pet Products. Organic pet food produced using whole grains, meat, chelated minerals, and natural antioxidants. 412 West St. John, Girard, KA 66743, (800)367-2391, www.nlpp.com.

Natural Products for Pets. All-natural multivitamins, supplements, and treats for dogs and cats. 2832 Walnut Avenue, Suite B, Tustin, CA 92780, (714)505-8188, www.dancingpaws.com.

Oops . . . I Pooped. Offers biodegradable plastic poop bags. (888)811-8804, www.oopsipooped.net.

Planet Dog/Planet Cat. All manner of dog and cat products—from leashes and toys to beds and serving dishes. 424 Fore Street, #2A, Portland, ME 04101, (207)761-1515, www.planetdog.com.

Pet Sage Products. Holistic health products—from food to alternative therapies. 2391 South Dove Street, Alexandria, VA 22314, (703)299-5044, www.petsage.com.

Swheat Scoop. All-natural, biodegradable, flushable, and scoopable litter made from naturally processed wheat. 1421 Richwood Road, Detroit Lakes, MN 56502, (800)794-3287, www.swheatscoop.com.

Petguard. Cat and dog food, treats, supplements, and grooming products. 165 Industrial Loop South, #5, Orange Park, FL 32073, (904)264-8500, www.petguard.com.

Wow-Bow Distributors. Purveyors of natural pet foods, shampoos, and other products, as well as homeopathic remedies. 13B Lucon Drive, Deer Park, NY 11729, (631)254-6064, www.wow-bow.com.

chapter six

The Color of Money
Socially Responsible Investing and Other Green Ways to Build Your Nest Egg

Photo by Myron Jay Dorf/Corbis

*T*he basic premise of socially responsible investing is simple: If money makes the world go 'round, greener, more humane investments can improve the way it spins. Want sustainably managed forests? Provide loans or capital to eco-minded timber companies. Want Monsanto to get out of the genetically engineered (GE) food business? Put forward a shareholder resolution demanding the company cease and desist. This isn't just wishful thinking; social investors can point to many positive efforts like these. And their strength is building. Yet before hailing a new era of green capitalism, it's also important to recognize that this new form of ethically tinged money management, socially responsible investing (SRI), does have some limitations.

SRI is something of a curious hybrid. It's part capitalism, part activist tool, and works within constraints that are usually oblivious to anything non-financial. When done well, social investors can earn attractive financial returns while also making the world a greener place. But the gains—both for yourself and the planet—may be modest.

So before investing in stocks, bonds, or even bank certificates of deposit (CDs), look closer to home for what may be overlooked investment opportunities. As you'll see elsewhere in this book, energy-efficient lightbulbs offer returns that beat any utility stock; insulating your house (especially if you do the work yourself) should give you a bigger bang for the buck than buying shares of a natural gas company; and buying a gas-sipping economy car (or better yet walking, biking, and taking mass transit) will give you a better return than General Motors or Toyota can—all the while producing direct dividends for the Earth.

Once you've exhausted the low-hanging fruit of energy-savings in your own life, you enter a rainforest of investment choices. In the broadest sense, you can invest your money in fixed-income vehicles (money lent out, via an institution that gives you a fixed rate of return, such as for bonds or bank CDs), real estate, stocks, and speculative investments like options or commodities. Except for the most seasoned investors, buying pork belly futures rarely makes financial sense and certainly doesn't qualify as green investing, so we'll focus on CDs, bonds, stocks, and, to a very limited extent, real estate. Each of these offers the chance to make your dollars work for a better future, both financially and environmentally.

GREEN PRODUCTS

Fixed-Income Investments

Community Investing: Where to Put Your Safe Money

Before investing a penny in that vegetarian restaurant your cousin promises can't miss, or even before putting money into the stock market, you should put aside enough cash—liquid, safe, readily spendable money—to cover at least six months of living expenses, plus a few thousand extra for potential emergencies, like a medical mishap, a fried car transmission, or an expired furnace.

There is no shortage of options for parking your cash. You're probably familiar with the most common: checking, passbook savings, money market funds, and CDs. Unless you're in a high enough tax bracket to justify buying a tax-free short-term municipal bond fund, the best choice is to use a progressive bank or credit union.

For funds you need to keep safe, but are unlikely to need soon, you're best off buying a CD, which typically gives a better return than a checking or money market account (stick with the money market if it seems likely you'll need those funds within a year).

Green Credit Unions and Banks

Most people don't think of their bank as a catalyst for social change. Yet the loan decisions your bank makes influence which projects get funded. So while one neighborhood bank may finance a new strip mall, yours could be helping retrofit a school with solar panels or financing equipment for an organic farm.

Long before the concept of socially responsible banking took root, credit unions were practicing a brand of community banking. Credit unions are federally insured, nonprofit, tax-exempt financial cooperatives that essentially act like banks. They exist solely to serve their members—which can be organized by a variety of criteria from union members or location to sexual orientation. The bulk of a credit union's deposits are invested in loans to its members, strengthening the community the credit union serves. While most banks resell mortgage loans to larger institutions (meaning your funds enter the great global financial community in the sky), credit unions typically do not. As an example, a credit union likely to appeal to committed environmentalists everywhere is the Permaculture Credit Union in New Mexico, which is organized to combine sound financial practice with Earth-sensitive ethics.

Community-development credit unions are a socially proactive form of credit union, designed to help disadvantaged communities. Sometimes socially motivated depositors are willing to accept a lower-than-market interest rate so more of their funds can be channeled into productive developments.

For eco-minded investors also interested in helping people who are experiencing hard times, Self-Help Credit Union in Durham, North Carolina, offers an appealing program that focuses on financing minority and low-income applicants who have environmentally friendly businesses. For instance, Self-Help loaned money for buying equipment to R24 Lumber, a minority-owned business that remanufactures discarded lumber into useable wall studs.

Banks with a strong or exclusive focus on loaning money to environmentally oriented businesses or nonprofits include Chittenden Socially Responsible Banking division in Vermont, Wainright Bank in Massachusetts, and Shorebank Pacific in Washington.

Although there are many socially responsible banks, credit unions, and loan funds, ShoreBank Pacific is one of the greenest. It stands out for investors eager to put their savings and banking dollars to work directly supporting eco efforts. ShoreBank's website (www.eco-bank.com) is full of loan stories that will warm any green-hearted soul. ShoreBank, for example, financed equipment for Panel Tech, a company that makes nontoxic plywood in an economically depressed former timber town in southwest Washington State. Panel Tech now supports thirty-six living-wage employees. Shorebank also gave an expansion loan to Stormwater Management, Inc., which uses composted leaves and other natural materials to filter oil, heavy metals, and other contaminants out of road runoff.

Why didn't conventional banks loan these businesses money? "Sometimes businesses come to us because of our reputation, but most often it's because of our staff of scientists," said Laurie Landeros, Shorebank's eco-deposit manager. "Our expertise gives us insight into business situations which other banks consider too risky or are uncomfortable assessing."

Loan Funds and Trusts

While most community investing is done through banks and credit unions, community development loan funds and trusts fill a niche that goes beyond the regulation requirements and risk-comfort zone of most banks, even socially conscious ones. Loan funds and trusts put less emphasis on financial returns and more on mission. Note, however, that although loan funds and trusts are nonprofit organizations, they aren't charities: They thoroughly research the credit worthiness of those they lend money to and expect to be paid back. Banks are famous for loaning money to people who don't really need it (since they only give financing to those who have the collateral to pay a loan back). Loan funds and trusts will fund borrowers that don't necessarily have the means to pay back a loan if their business fails.

The thought of unsecured loans may lead you to think a loan fund or trust is only for philanthropic, deep-pocketed investors, but since the loans in a trust are pooled, the risk of any single project failing is spread among a larger portfolio, making these investments generally quite safe. A National Community Capital Association report done in the late 1990s cited a 99 percent repayment rate of loans. Still, while loan funds and trusts typically offer conservative fixed-income investment vehicles, since they do *not* carry federal insurance, you shouldn't invest in them with the safest of your safe money.

Examples of loan funds likely to interest eco-minded investors include the Institute for Community Economics, which helps fight poverty, racism, decaying inner cities, and suburban sprawl through its urban housing loans; Cascadia Revolving Fund, which helps minority, women, and environmentally focused small businesses in the Pacific Northwest (during its first ten years, Cascadia Revolving Fund helped generate 7,000 jobs—many of them employing ex–timber company workers); and EcoLogic Enterprise Ventures (EEV), a Cambridge-based nonprofit that provides small loans to Latin American businesses that engage in fair trade and conservation. EEV targets alternative agriculture, non-timber forest products, renewable energy, ecotourism, and handicrafts. In the humid forest of northern Guatemala, for instance, EEV made $215,000 in loans available to organic spice growers, who will farm without damaging the surrounding biologically diverse and sensitive forest. Many of Guatemalans benefiting from these loans had been displaced from the country's long civil war.

Can't choose which loan fund to invest in? You can participate in a whole basket of loan funds at once through the Calvert Social Investment Foundation (a nonprofit independent of Calvert Funds), which offers professionally managed and diversified notes.

Investing for the Future

Once you have your safe funds wisely tucked away, adding their dash of green to the world's money supply, you're ready to invest for the future. And that's exactly how you should think of any of the investments mentioned below: bonds, real estate, and stocks—particularly real estate and stocks. When investing in stock and real estate, you should have at least a five- and preferably a ten-year time horizon. If you're counting on *quick* results, you're speculating, not investing.

Decisions about how much of your money should go in stocks and real estate and how much should go in bonds should be based on your age, wealth, and comfort with risk. So while there isn't a one-size-fits-all answer for asset allocation, a reasonable mix for most thirty- to fifty-somethings is 35 percent in bonds/fixed income and 65 percent in stocks. History has shown that bond/stock combination brings slightly lower returns than an all stock portfolio, but with considerably less volatility.

Bonds

At most banks, a long-term certificate of deposit means five years (though a few banks offer seven-year CDs, we're not aware of any SRI banks that do). If you want to lock up a guaranteed rate of return for longer than that, you have lots of options, but, alas, they're unlikely to be as environmentally beneficial as supplying funds to a progressive bank, credit union, or loan fund or trust. The classic long-term bond option is a U.S. treasury bond or, if you're in a higher tax bracket, tax-free municipal bonds.

The trouble with investing in U.S. government bonds is that you could be helping finance a nuclear bomb, aiding clandestine operations overseas, or subsidizing any number of causes related to the military-industrial complex. For that reason, try to keep as much of your fixed-income money as possible with one or more of the progressive institutions mentioned above.

If your financial situation or advisor demands you invest in something with a longer-term outlook, you can avoid the most unseemly side of the U.S. government by buying bonds or bond funds (money pooled with other investors and managed by a professional) issued by government agencies you can feel better about, such as bonds issued by the Government National Mortgage Association (known as GNMA or Ginnie Mae).

There are also a healthy half-dozen SRI bond funds that buy bonds issued by the more appealing government agencies (including the Bank for Cooperatives, Federal Farm Credit System, the Small Business Administration, and Postal Service) and ethically screened corporations. Among these are Domini's Social Bond Fund, Acquinas Fixed Income, Calvert Social Bond, Citizens Income Fund, Parnassus Fixed Income, and CRA Qualified Investment Fund.

CRA Qualified Investment Fund takes its name from the Community Reinvestment Act, a 1977 congressional regulation created to make federally insured deposit institutions address community credit needs. Through the CRA Qualified Investment Fund investors have an opportunity to make a direct impact on communities, as their investment helps create jobs, improve health care, and build low-income housing—all while earning good, fixed-income returns (at this writing, the fund has averaged 7 percent annual returns since August of 1999). The catch? The minimum investment is $250,000.

Odds are, if you have that kind of money to invest or *need* long-term bonds to balance your portfolio, you probably are in a high tax bracket. (Here's a simple formula to compare taxable and tax-free yields: Municipal bond yield/1 – your tax rate = tax-equivalent yield.) If that's the case, you're likely to benefit from municipal bonds, whose interest is free from federal income taxes (and state and local taxes too, if you buy bonds issued by the state you live in).

Tax-Free Bonds

Most municipal bonds are kosher for socially conscious investors. Cities and states tend to use their money for civic-minded and civilian purposes. You needn't worry, for instance, about Rhode Island using bond proceeds to buy missiles or fund the CIA. There are exceptions to be aware of, however; such as bonds that generate revenue for building a pollution-spewing incinerator, a wetlands-trashing real estate development, creating more highways, or the infamous nuke-funding, bankrupt WPPSS bonds (popularly known as "whoops," but officially the Washington Public Power Supply System).

Some socially conscious investors like knowing exactly what their investments are funding and seek out bonds issued for funding projects they support—such as hospital or school construction, housing projects for the elderly, rehabilitating a decaying urban area, or funding a recycling program. Such bonds aren't readily available, though, especially if you want your money to go directly to funding the bond project. If you live in a small or less-populated state and want something that's triple tax-free, your odds of getting just what you want go down even further. So you may need to be patient or purchase out-of-state bonds (even then, don't expect a big menu to choose from). With such restrictions, you'll need to find a sympathetic and patient broker or money manager who's willing to work with you.

There are a limited number of SRI tax-free bond funds available; namely Parnassus' CA (as in California) Tax-Exempt Fund, and Calvert's six tax-free funds. Two of these are state-specific funds (California and Vermont) and the others are national tax-free bond funds with very short-(a money market), short-, medium-, and long-term maturities. While your conscience can rest a bit more comfortably when you invest in these funds, note that only a small portion of the bonds in these portfolios will *directly* support environmentally helpful projects. Of Calvert's National Municipal Intermediate's holdings, for example, only 6 percent were in the category "Resource Recovery"—the most eco-friendly category listed (the long-term Calvert municipal fund had only 2 percent in that category); 33 percent of the bonds funded "transportation" (which means the biggest single use of the funds are for repairing and building roads and bridges).

Stocks

Some "hard-core" environmentalists refuse to invest in stocks. Considering Wall Street the ultimate headquarters of corporate America, they simply don't want to participate in any way in the harm generated by big business. If you feel similarly, you should keep your savings with enlightened lending institutions or—if you're looking for better returns—own some rental properties. But before committing to such an investment path, there are a couple things to be aware of.

Historically, stocks have proven to be the best returning investment vehicle ever invented. Owning a piece of public companies is the best chance for your savings to race ahead of inflation and taxes. Over time, with just a little bit of effort and know-how (and, at times, a strong stomach for holding pat when stocks head south), a consistent investment program can make you financially secure. Second, as a shareholder you get a voice, a chance to influence how corporations behave. It's a limited voice, and shareholder influence *alone* won't keep businesses from heading in the dangerous direction they're now going, but it can bring a bit more sanity and sustainability to how corporations operate, perhaps creating an opening for fundamental, lasting changes.

Since enough books have been written on the stock investing process to level large tracts of forest, let's briefly look at two tools available to investors for making Wall Street a bit greener, and how using them may influence your investment choices.

The most commonly used tool for social investors is screening, which is summed up with the maxim: "Invest your principal with your principles."

As we've seen, that guideline can be applied to bonds as well as stocks, and take the form of positive or negative screens. If, for instance, you're angry with Procter & Gamble for testing its products on animals, you'd either avoid their stock or if you already owned P&G, sell it. For a positive screen, you might consider adding Ballard Power Systems to your portfolio if you look forward to the days when automobiles are powered by fuel cells. This approach intuitively appeals to investors with a conscience. Stock screening is by far the most popular form of SRI.

Almost all SRI mutual funds (a professionally managed investment fund of pooled money, which is most often used to buy stocks) do negative screening (avoiding corporate louses); less do positive screening—seeking out good-guy companies. For most socially conscious mutual funds, an environmental screen is just one of many filters. There are a handful of funds, however, that emphasize environmental issues. For example, Portfolio 21, run by Progressive Investment Management of Portland, Oregon, seeks out sustainable corporations worldwide, like Electrolux in Sweden, which has made environmental sustainability central to its business strategy. As cofounder Carsten Henningsen says, "The goal of Portfolio 21 is to identify those companies that recognize the deepening ecological crisis and are positioning themselves to benefit from a new approach to business."

These mutual funds make environmental concerns a priority:

- **Winslow Green Growth Fund** is an "aggressive" growth fund (that is, it buys mostly younger, growing companies that tend to be more volatile than more-established businesses) that, at this writing, has the hot hand. In 2003, the Winslow Green Growth Fund was up about 70 percent, more than doubling the returns of its small company benchmark index. As Winslow sees it, there's no need to compromise between financial glory and being green. Their website lists fourteen studies that indicate eco-savvy companies do better than other businesses. The reasoning makes sense: environmentally sensitive businesses are likely to be forward thinking, more efficient, less wasteful, and less susceptible to litigation. All characteristics that make for successful companies.

- **The Green Century Balanced Fund** buys both stocks and bonds (bonds can often help to stabilize returns in down markets). Not surprisingly, both Winslow Green Growth Fund and Green Century Balanced Fund hold many of the same stocks, such as the water purification company Ionics. As a result, the Green Century Balanced Fund also achieved eye-popping returns of 61 percent in 2003 (through September 30, 2003).

- **The New Alternatives Fund** seeks to be "the greenest fund in America." It invests in industries that are oriented to a clean environment with a special interest in alternative energy, such as fuel cells, wind, and solar energy. The problem, unfortunately, has been its performance. In 2000, New Alternatives produced market-trouncing 51.5 percent returns, but otherwise it has lagged the returns of other funds. But according to a prospectus, through 2002 the fund's ten-year annual return was 2.64 percent.

Surprisingly, only a minority of companies held in most "green" stock funds are in decisively eco-focused businesses. Most of their holdings are more traditional businesses, such as the medical company PolyMedica, which Winslow or other fund managers deem to have excellent operations. Winslow portfolio manager Jack Robinson believes "that every company has the potential to be a green company"—an outlook shared by other funds, including the recently launched Sierra Club Funds. Among the top five holdings of the Sierra Club stock fund is Best Buy, Dell, Estée Lauder, and Charles Schwab. The Sierra Club's goal is to make full use of their shares under management for shareholder activism (see below). The group, for instance, has bought shares in large building companies, looking to use shareholder activism to direct them away from farm land, forests, and other open spaces.

For eco-investors interested in owning global companies, Portfolio 21 (as in 21st century), applies shareholder activism and filters inspired by Natural Step (an international science-based consulting and training organization that works for sustainability with communities and organizations around the world).

"The quality of Portfolio 21's environmental screening is very high," says Jay Falk, president of SRI World Group. Since its inception in 1999, Portfolio 21 has consistently beat its benchmark performance comparison index, MSCI World Equity Index, by about 3 percent.

Getting Results with Shareholder Activism

The other tool available to socially concerned stock investors is shareholder activism: taking advantage of the opportunities a stock shareholder has to change a company's policies. Shareholder activism has been described as the muscle in SRI. Though it works best in conjunction with other activist efforts such as consumer boycotts and letter-writing campaigns, shareholder activism is an excellent complement to these efforts because the corporation is being "provoked" from within.

Since shareholders are part owners of the company, even if you own only one share of Microsoft (the equivalent ownership stake of Bill Gates' closet door knob), you're allowed to attend annual shareholder meetings, ask questions at that meeting, and vote on any issues before shareholders (which can be done via mail or the Internet). Up your ownership stake to $2,000 worth of stock and, if you follow the proper protocol, you can propose a *nonbinding* corporate resolution—a shareholder referendum for a policy change. Or, as a mutual fund investor, your fund can do this for you.

One of the best-known cases of effective shareholder activism is Rainforest Action Network and cohorts' drive to get Home Depot to end the sale of old-growth lumber (see sidebar on p. 108). But shareholder activists have had other notable successes for the environment. They've influenced General Electric to allot $150 to $250 million for cleaning up PCBs polluting the Housatonic River in western Massachusetts; they've motivated Universal Health Services of Pennsylvania, the country's third-largest hospital management company, to agree to formally request that its suppliers phase out the toxic polyvinyl chloride (PVC) in medical products; and they have persuaded Ford, DaimlerChrysler, General Motors, and Texaco to quit the Global Climate Coalition—an organization that undermines efforts to curb global warming.

Another handful of funds have been leaders in using shareholder activism. At the forefront has been the Domini Social Equity Fund, a socially screened index fund that holds 400 companies. The Fund has closely matched the performance of the S&P 500, its less sensitive, but standard, benchmark cousin. In 1999, the Domini Social Equity Fund became the first mutual fund to publish how it votes on shareholder resolutions, allowing investors to hold them accountable for the positions the fund takes. Green Century's Equity Fund holds exactly the same portfolio as the Domini Social Equity Fund and also practices shareholder activism. It is run by a nonprofit environmental advocacy group, which donates 100 percent

Shareholder Activism, SRI's Most Powerful Tool, at Its Finest

On the agenda at the 1999 stockholders meeting of Home Depot, the $62 billion, Atlanta-based home-improvement retailer, was a shareholder resolution urging the company to stop sales of old-growth wood products from ancient trees. The tension in the room was palpable.

The resolution coming to vote was the culminating point in a year of relentless protests by activists from Rainforest Action Network (RAN). RAN's vigorous efforts had slowed the opening of new stores and kept existing franchises on their toes with guerilla tactics such as popping up mischievously on store intercoms to announce, "Attention shoppers, there's a special in aisle twenty-three on products made from old-growth timber."

The pressure tactics ultimately worked. Although the old-growth resolution received just 11.8 percent of shares voted at that May meeting, by the end of August, Home Depot had relented. CEO Arthur Blank made a sudden about-face and announced that Home Depot would phase out three kinds of endangered wood.

It was an extraordinary victory. The ripple effects from Home Depot's decision are still transforming the timber industry. Home Depot is the largest home-improvement retailer in the world and, according to its CEO, it controls a significant portion of the global lumber market. And if that weren't enough, Lowe's—the number-two home-improvement retailer—followed Home Depot's lead by also committing to phasing out old-growth wood products. Following suit were the big chains Wickes Lumber and HomeBase, who committed to nearly identical terms. "It's truly remarkable," says Michael Brune, who is now executive director of RAN. "Every large wood supplier acknowledges the impact Home Depot's action has had and is having. The whole industry is changing."

This unprecedented victory offers an inspiring example of the power of social investing. "It's an important model for shareholder activism," says Conrad McKerron of the As You Sow Foundation in San Francisco, which co-filed the resolution. In fact, he added, "it's as close to a perfect model as you can get. You need the impact of a grassroots campaign, and then you have shareholders adding a different element of pressure."

---

of any profits from their management fee to environmental programs. This adds an extra 0.55 percent to the yearly management cost, making it a bit more expensive to own than Domini.

The Citizen Core Growth Fund is another index fund that has flexed its shareholder rights. The environmental screens of the Citizens index are a bit stricter than Domini's, but it holds fewer stocks and is more weighted in technology companies, making it a bit more volatile than Domini.

Calvert has a wide array of socially screened, shareholder-proactive funds pursuing a variety of investing styles—from those specializing in small companies to foreign conglomerates. One downside to Calvert funds is that most have a 4.75 percent up front "sales load." (All the other funds mentioned in these pages are no-load funds, which means you pay no immediate sales charges to buy the fund—though, like all funds, there is a range in the annual management and administration fees deducted from assets held.)

Pax World Balanced Fund, which was the first SRI mutual, has been monitoring corporate behavior since 1971 and using shareholder voting to influence business practices. Pax World believes that it can often be more effective advocating for policy changes of the companies it owns, rather than simply selling a company's stock without making any noise. Over the years, Pax World has been a solid performer, often landing in the top tier for funds that own both stocks and bonds. (The fund can't put more than 75 percent of its holdings in stocks.)

WHAT YOU CAN DO

Frugality: The Eco-Money Connection

Since "reduce" is the first "R" in the environmentalist's mantra, "reduce, reuse, recycle," most environmentalists know that "doing without" is good for the planet. But they may not realize just how good it is for their savings account. In *The Millionaire Next Door*, Thomas Stanley and William Danko write that "being frugal is the cornerstone of wealth-building." After all, money one might spend on an impressive SUV, a large engagement ring, or even a regular habit of junk food snacks, leaves you with less money to invest or give away.

Think such choices can hardly matter to one's retirement fund? Then you're overlooking how "little" costs add up—and can then take off with the power of compounded returns. If, for example, from the ages of twenty-three to sixty-seven you bypassed the popular American habit of buying a new mid-size car every two years (say, a Toyota Camry) and instead bought a used one and invested your savings, you'd end up with an extra $869,638. Manage without a car altogether, invest the savings, and that money alone can make you a millionaire.

Sure, you say, but who can afford a new car every two years? Well, even small, everyday acts of frugality can make a big difference. According to Dwight Lee and Richard McKenzie's book *Getting Rich in America*, if from the ages of eighteen to sixty-seven you save $1.50 a day by cutting out junk food or a takeout cup of java from the corner store, and then invest the difference, you'll end up with an extra $290,363 at retirement time. And of course along the way, you'd have saved the Earth the cost of extracting petroleum, cutting down trees, and then landfilling all those plastic wrappers, coffee cups, and lids.

The No-Sweat Change That Makes a Big Difference

About the easiest way to make a difference with your money is to move your checking and savings accounts to a green bank or credit union. With electronic banking, automatic deposits, and ATM machines never far away, you can often use an out-of-town eco-friendly bank even for your day-to-day needs (though if your area has a good socially conscious bank, stick with them as you'll be strengthening your area's economy and the institution's responsiveness to local issues).

Simple as progressive banking sounds, only a small minority of socially concerned investors do it. According to 2003 survey done by the nonprofit Social Investment Forum (SIF), only two thirds of 1 percent—or $14 billion of the $2.1 trillion invested by socially conscious investors—is spent on community investing. To boost this important sector, SIF and Co-op America have developed an initiative to get 1 percent of SRI assets into community development financial institutions (CDFIs) over the next few years. To help support this effort, SIF has developed a community investing logo (a half-circle of human figures holding hands, connected to a house) that identifies members of SIF with at least 1 percent of managed assets in community investments. Consider this as criteria when selecting a fund or money manager.

Remember, Numbers Don't Tell Everything

When choosing a stock fund or money manager, don't limit yourself to its investing track record. Select one that takes advantage of the shareholder rights you entrust them with. The ideal money management firms not only vote the right way, but also initiate shareholder actions and resolutions.

Some funds and most money managers who handle individual SRI portfolios don't do any shareholder activism at all. "Some of these funds are what I call 'SRI Lite,'" says First Affirmative Financial Network President Steve Schueth. For instance, TIAA-CREF, which handles roughly $291 billion in pension funds for teachers and nonprofits, manages more than $5.4 billion in its Social Choice account, the country's biggest socially screened portfolio. But Schueth adds, "TIAA-CREF only avoids the worst of the worst; it does not seek actively to bring about social change. Vanguard is another one; its new social index emulates one from Calvert, but this is not a fund that will do shareholder activism or community development."

The funds mentioned above—such as Domini's Social Equity Fund, Pax World, Portfolio 21, or the Sierra Club funds—are all examples of mutual funds that engage in shareholder activism.

Don't Fret the Bet

Exhaustive studies on the performance of financial assets indicate that lots of fussing (i.e., trading) doesn't help, and actually tends to hurt your returns (through the bite of transaction costs). So while it makes good sense to have a solid investment plan in place, it doesn't make sense to be glued to your Palm Pilot checking stock or mutual fund quotes. For those who plan well, time is your friend. Once you have an appropriate mix of stocks, bonds, real estate, or other investments set up, most folks only need an annual rebalancing. In many cases this can take under an hour, leaving you freed up the rest of the year to advocate for stronger environmental laws or enjoy hikes in the woods.

Making Your Donations Go Further

Donating Appreciated Assets

Stocks, bonds, mutual funds, and real estate that have appreciated in value make great charitable gifts because you get to write off their current market value and sidestep capital gains taxes. So if you have $5,000 worth of Ben and Jerry's stock that cost you $1,000, you could give the shares to the charity of your choice and take the full $5,000 deduction—without paying the taxes due on the $4,000 profit.

There are two caveats to remember, however: First, the asset must be considered a long-term gain, which means you must have held it for at least a year. Second, give the shares to the charity and have *them* sell it. Otherwise the gain—and IRS tax—will still be in your name.

Setting Up a Poor Man's Foundation

You no longer have to be rich to establish the equivalent of your own foundation. Instead you can use a *gift fund* for a shrewd way to make substantial donations.

Traditionally, wealthy philanthropists established foundations for tax write-offs and the legacy of having their name live on connected with largess. The income and appreciation from their foundation's investments could theoretically fund charitable disbursements in perpetuity. The problems with setting up a private foundation are you need to be giving away *at least* $250,000 to create one, the initial setup costs are from $2,000 to $5,000, and your foundation will incur ongoing administrative and investment management fees, including a 2 percent annual excise tax.

With a charitable gift fund, you can essentially create the same institution with as little as $10,000 (subsequent contributions must be $2,500 or more)—and get better benefits. Since gift funds are considered public charities, you get advantages private foundations don't: You can write off more of your donations against your income; you don't have to give away a minimum of 5 percent every year; you don't have to keep books and file foundation tax returns; you pay no setup charges; and you pay only a 1 percent (as opposed to 2 percent) administrative fee. It won't even cost your ego much: Even though you aren't setting up your own freestanding institution, you can name your gift fund account whatever you'd like so that your charitable recipients can know who their benefactor is.

Gift funds also work well for anyone who is ready to make a big gift, but isn't yet sure who they want to give it to. In other words, you can be generous when the spirit moves you and then concern yourself with the details later.

To set up one of these gift funds, you need to contact one of the half dozen (and growing) mutual fund companies that offer them, including

Calvert Giving Fund, Vanguard Charitable Endowment Program, and Charles Schwab's Charitable Giving Fund.

Where There's a Will There's a Way

Since we can't take it with us, about the most painless and powerful way our money can help the Earth is by making an environmental organization a benefactor in our will. Since most wills are reasonably simple documents, you probably don't even need a lawyer. Computer software and three witnesses can create a competent will for most basic estates.

To donate money to nonprofit groups or foundations through your will, simply state in the document (or add to it, if you already have an established one) "I give, devise, and bequeath to _____ (put name and address of charitable organization) the sum of $_____ to be used for its general purposes (or whatever particular program you're interested in supporting)." Instead of indicating an exact dollar amount to donate, consider putting it as a percentage of your assets. That way should late-in-life medical costs greatly diminish your estate, a charity won't end up with $20,000 while your spouse or beloved niece gets $2,000. Some people make their gift contingent on other beneficiaries predeceasing them. Any monies willed to a tax-exempt charity reduces the value of your estate—a real consideration when your assets are over $1.5 million, since federal and possibly state taxes will take a big chunk anyhow.

If you have substantial assets (in 2004, that was more than $1.5 million) or your life, financial or otherwise, is slightly complicated, or your beneficiaries' needs are, check with a lawyer who has experience drawing wills.

Helping to Move SRI to the Next Level

Some funds, like the already mentioned TIAA-CREF Social Choice, don't seem to understand the importance of shareholder activism. Other money management firms are too small to make activist efforts. The net result is billions of dollars invested by socially concerned investors don't make the impact they could.

Ideally, there should be some certification or indicator that shows our financial managers are devoting some part of their fees toward economic

The Real Estate Option

If you know what you're doing, have the inspiration, time, and cash to invest in rental property, by all means do so. You can construct, renovate, and repair buildings with eco-friendly materials, make your properties energy-efficient, and be a humane landlord. In short, you'll have more control over the effect of your investment than you would with stocks and bonds, plus you'll have a hedge against inflation with additional tax benefits. If that's the route you go, feel free to substitute part or even almost all of the money you'd allocate to investing in stocks to real estate.

Of course, the downside to all that control is that managing your own real estate properties is like taking on a second job or even full-time job. There aren't many options for social investors who want to turn this task over to others—unless you have a large portfolio and can hire your own manager. For most investors with an eco-bent, about the only thing available is the Canadian Hotel Income Properties Real Estate Investment Trust (symbol on the Toronto stock exchange: HOT._u.TO). This Vancouver-based company encourages its visitors to reduce their impact on the environment and is the first hotel chain in Canada to have all its hotel properties receive a national eco-friendly certification.

activism. So a small SRI money management firm could either pool resources with other companies and share shareholder activist coordinators or perhaps they could contract with an independent nonprofit to do it for them. This outside agent could coordinate their efforts with other social investors and nonprofit groups who use grassroots nonfinancial tactics. The most obvious candidates for such a coordinator would be the Social Investment Forum, As You Sow, or the Interfaith Center for Corporate Responsibility (ICCR), which has thirty-plus years of experience waging shareholder advocacy campaigns and orchestrating coalitions of investors.

Similarly, it's important to remember that screening and shareholder activism alone can't make corporate America sustainable. Right now, even the CEOs of most of the most powerful corporations in the world are limited in their choices to do the right thing. Consider Ford Motor Company. Can its management really close down the SUV division if those cars are making huge profits? As the company's financial caretaker, a CEO that did that would be ignoring his or her legal responsibilities. This literal bottom-line pressure accounts for the schizoid behavior of companies like Ford, which will sign on to environmental pledges such as the eco-friendly CERES principles while also making the huge Excursion, a 12-mile-per-

gallon SUV. Creating true sustainability will require changing political and economic rules. To support such efforts, SRI money managers could allocate a small percentage of their fees or levy a tiny "tax" on their clients' assets, earmarked for supporting nonprofits that work at a structural level, such as Redefining Progress, an economic think-tank and advocacy group.

Ironically, the SRI industry is unlikely to adopt such a scenario unless individual ethical investors create a grassroots effort to let money managers and industry organizations (such as the Social Investment Forum) know these issues matter to them—and then vote with their dollars by supporting firms that are willing to move in that direction.

Resources

The "category killer" website for socially responsible investing is SRI World (sriworld.com), which is the parent company of the better known socialfunds.com. "At this point, we have more than 10,000 pages of articles on or related to social investing," says Jay Falk, SRI World president. SRI World offers one-stop viewing on everything from shareholder activism news to ordering prospectuses for mutual funds.

The Social Investment Forum (www.socialinvest.org) also offers a comprehensive SRI site and includes a listing of SRI professionals—helpful for anyone who wants (and can afford) a money manager to work with their individual financial and social concerns.

The largest socially responsible mutual fund companies, Domini (www.domini.com), Calvert (www.calvergroup.com), and Citizens (www.citizenfunds.com) all have extensive sites which offer information beyond their own products.

Green Money Journal (www.greenmoneyjournal.com), has both a popular website and a quarterly newsletter largely devoted to SRI.

Published since 1988, the bimonthly *Business Ethics* magazine (www.business-ethics.com), is the oldest and still-leading chronicler of the socially responsible business movement. It offers regular columns and articles devoted to social investing.

Books

The Mindful Money Guide by Marshall Glickman (Ballantine Books, $13). Written for investors interested in integrating their values and aspirations with their finances.

Investing with Your Values by Jack and Hal Brill and Cliff Feigenbaum (Bloomberg, $23.95). The best title devoted solely to SRI. Feigenbaum is publisher of *Green Money Journal*.

The SRI Advantage: Why Socially Responsible Investing Has Outperformed Financially by Peter Camejo (New Society, $29.95). The book is comprised of articles from a variety of perspectives, written by SRI experts.

Organizations

Watchdog and Research Organizations

As You Sow. A nonprofit organization dedicated to promoting corporate social responsibility. 311 California Street, Suite 510, San Francisco, CA 94104-2602, (415)391-3212, www.asyousow.org.

Coalition for Environmentally Responsible Economies. CERES is a coalition of investment funds, environmental organizations, and public interest groups. 99 Chauncy Street, 6th Floor, Boston, MA 02111, (617)247-0700, www.ceres.org.

Interfaith Center on Corporate Responsibility. A coalition of religious investors working to promote corporate responsibility through dialogue with management, combined with public pressure, research, and publication of materials; shareholder resolutions; and social screening. Membership includes more than 275 Roman Catholic, Jewish, and Protestant orders, dioceses, health care institutions, and agencies. ICCR assists investors wanting to co-file resolutions. 475 Riverside Drive, Room 550, New York, NY 10115-0079, (212)870-2295, www.iccr.org.

Investor Responsibility Research Center. IRRC offers an array of services for portfolio screening and corporate benchmarking. Provides information on shareholder activism and guidance on proxy voting worldwide. With *Portfolio$creener* software, users can query a company's involvement in up to sixteen issues and review details on why a company passed or failed a requirement. 1350 Connecticut Avenue NW, Suite 700, Washington, DC 20036-1734, (202)833-0700, www.irrc.org.

KLD Research & Analytics, Inc. Compiles social profiles on 3,000 U.S. companies, and global lists on controversial industry involvement. Maintains SRI benchmark indexes, including the Domini 400 Social Index. 250 Summer Street, 4th Floor, Boston, MA 02210, (617)426-5270, www.kld.com.

Social Investment Forum. SIF is a national nonprofit membership organization promoting the concept, practice, and growth of socially responsible investing. SIF does periodic surveys of the social investing universe. 1612 K Street NW, Suite 650, Washington, DC 20006, (202)872-5319, www.socialinvest.org.

SRI Publishing—Websites

Business Ethics. A quarterly newsletter covering corporate responsibility and SRI investing. 2845 Harriet Avenue Suite 207, P.O. Box 8439, Minneapolis MN 55408, (612)879-0695, www.business-ethics.com.

Co-op America. Publishes the *Real Money* bimonthly newsletter. The newsletter is about "taking control of your financial future with socially responsible investing, and living a life with more meaning and less stuff." Subscriptions are $15 per year. www.realmoney.com.

SRI World Group. A comprehensive website on SRI, with more than 10,000 pages of content. Includes updated and extensive SRI mutual fund information at their site, www.socialfunds.com. 74 Cotton Mill Hill—A255, Brattleboro, VT 05301, (802)251-0500, www.sriworld.com.

SustainableBusiness.com. Publishes *Progressive Investor*, a monthly newsletter that guides investors and advisors toward sustainable investments. Its online trade journal, *Sustainable Business Insider*, reports on the latest developments and trends. According to President Rona Fried, "To us, sustainable businesses are companies that unabashedly embrace the goal of enhancing life on Earth as an integral part of their business strategy." www.sustainablebusiness.com.

Green Money Journal. A quarterly newsletter covering SRI and green consumer issues, P.O. Box 67, Santa Fe, NM 87504, (505)988-7423, www.green moneyjournal.com.

Banks

Chittenden Bank. A well-rounded socially conscious bank, within a traditional bank. P.O. Box 804, Brattleboro, VT 05302, (800)772-3863, www.sociallyresponsible.chittenden.com.

ShoreBank Pacific. The most environmentally focused bank in the country. P.O. Box 400, Ilwaco, WA 98624, (888)326-2265, www.eco-bank.com.

Self-Help Credit Union. A credit union that concentrates on the economically disadvantaged; likes supporting sustainably focused enterprises. P.O. Box 3619, Durham, NC 27702, (800)966-SELF, www.self-help.org.

Mutual Funds

- **Calvert Financial Group.** 4550 Montgomery Avenue, Bethesda, MD 20814, (800)248-0337, www.calvertfoundation.org.

- **Domini Social Investments.** P.O. Box 9785, Providence, RI 02940, (800)225-3863, www.domini.com.

- **Citizens Funds.** 230 Commerce Way, Suite 300, Portsmouth, NH 03801, (800)223-7010, www.citizensfunds.com.

- **Green Century Funds.** 29 Temple Street, Suite 200, Boston, MA 02111, (800)934-7336, www.greencentury.com.

- **Neuberger Berman Mutual Funds.** 605 Third Avenue, 2nd Floor, New York, NY 10158, (800)877-9700, www.nb.com.

- **New Alternatives Fund.** 150 Broadhollow Road, Suite 306, Melville, NY 11747, (800)423-8383, www.newalternativesfund.com.

- **Parnassus Investments.** One Market-Stewart Tower, #1600, San Francisco, CA 94105, (800)999-3505, www.parnassus.com.

- **PAX World Fund.** 14 Wall Street, Suite 1702, New York, NY 10005, (800)229-1172, www.paxworldcapital.com.

- **Portfolio 21.** 721 NW Ninth Avenue, Suite 250, Portland, OR 97209, (877)351-4115, www.Portfolio21.com.

- **Sierra Club Mutual Funds.** 433 California Street, 11th Floor, San Francisco, CA 94104, (415)863-6300. www.sierraclubfunds.com.

- **Winslow Green Growth Fund.** P.O. Box 446, Portland, ME 04112, (888)314-9049, www.winslowgreen.com.

Money Managers/Financial Consultants

- **Clean Yield.** P.O. Box 117, Greensboro, VT 05841, (800)809-6439, www.cleanyield.com.

- **First Affirmative Financial Network.** 1040 South 8th Street, Suite 100, Colorado Springs, CO 80906, (800)422-7284, www.firstaffirmative.com.

- **Principle Profits.** P.O. Box 2323, Amherst, MA 10114, (800)972-3289, www.PrincipleProfits.com.

- **Progressive Asset Management Network.** 1730 Franklin Street, Suite 201, Oakland, CA 94612, (800)786-2998, www.progressiveasset management.com.

- **Trillium Asset Management.** (800)548-5684, www.trilliuminvest.com.

Environmental Tax Policy

- **Clean Water Action.** www.cleanwateraction.org.

- **Friends of the Earth.** www.foe.org.

- **Redefining Progress.** www.rprogress.org.

- **Resources for the Future.** www.rff.org.

- **Sustainable America.** www.sanetwork.org.

- **Tellus Institute.** www.tellus.org.

- **World Resources Institute.** www.wri.org.

The Healthy Home

From Cellar to Attic

O ver the past few years, Americans have rediscovered nesting. We're staying at home more, spending time with our families, cooking, gardening, and puttering with the tools we buy at home-improvement centers. Unfortunately, many conventional home products may be hurting our health rather than improving our quality of life.

While we think of our homes as safe and comforting havens, the pollutants they contain can put our health and well-being at risk. Indeed, your indoor air may be dangerously similar to that which surrounds you during a rush-hour commute. Fumes emitted by many everyday household products—including carpets, cleansers, cosmetics, plywood, finishes, and paints—are "the same stuff that comes out of a tailpipe or a smokestack," a spokesman for the California Air Resources Board told the *Los Angeles Times*.

Household products are the second greatest source of outdoor air pollution in the Los Angeles region. Think, then, of their impact indoors, where they're used. Levels of pollutants can be from two to five times higher inside than outdoors, according to the Environmental Protection Agency (EPA). The largely petrochemical fumes emitted from many of these products are known as volatile organic compounds (VOCs). "These VOCs can evaporate, or 'offgas' into the air we breathe," says John Bowers of the Healthy House Institute, publisher of the useful, comprehensive *Healthy House* green building books.

VOCs in daily household products can build up for months and years in the enclosed space of your home (especially if it's a post-1970 dwelling, well-sealed to conserve energy), sinking into carpets and upholstered furniture, from which, each time we take a step or plump down, they puff back up into the air. In the short term, VOCs can cause headaches, dizziness, watery eyes, respiratory problems, rashes, sneezing, and other allergic reactions. In the long term or in very high exposures, many of these chemicals have been linked to nervous system damage, hormone disruption, and cancer. Plus, in the enclosed environment of the home, we are breathing in a mixture of chemicals rather than just one exposure at a time.

In greening your home, you may start with a simple, easy step such as changing a cleaning product because fumes have provoked an allergy. As needs evolve—the teenager goes to college, the upstairs neighbor causes a flood—you'll have ample opportunities to refinish and repaint, or install new wallboard and flooring, using healthier products. Sometimes a green addition leads the way for giving the rest of the house an eco retrofit. This can include detecting and neutralizing such hazards as radon gas that naturally seeps from the ground in some areas; carbon monoxide from leaking boilers or poorly vented gas stoves; asbestos in old insulation; lead in old paint and water pipes; and mildews and mold.

Another major issue in green homes is conservation of natural resources, such as forests and clean water, and nonrenewable resources such as fossil fuels. Energy efficiency in design, building features, fixtures, and appliances is key.

Remember, it's not a race. You will breathe easier, and here's why:

- You'll have cleaner indoor air (worth investing in, as most of us spend 90 percent of our time indoors);

- You'll save on electric bills and quite probably on health costs;

- You'll have a clean conscience, knowing that your dwelling place is leaving a gentler footprint on the Earth.

Plus there's an aesthetic bonus: Many green and natural materials, such as sustainably harvested wood or bamboo (a fast-replenishing grass), are radiantly beautiful and shown off to their best effect in the natural daylighting that is a fundamental feature of green homes.

This chapter will specify the least toxic, most environmentally sound products and practices you can use for your green home project, whether it's a gradual eco-upgrade, a complete renovation, or building a whole new eco-dream home from scratch.

CURRENT EVENTS/LEGISLATIVE/POLITICAL

Green homes—built to consume fewer natural resources, produce less waste, and provide healthier indoor air quality—are catching on across the United States. "An increasing number of home buyers are demanding that environmental issues become a top priority in new construction and re-modeling efforts," Ray Tonjes of the National Association of Home Builders (NAHB) told *The Christian Science Monitor*. Some 13,224 green homes were built in the United States in 2002, as compared with a total of 18,887 in the previous decade.

About twenty cities and states now have green building programs, and NAHB is planning to release national guidelines this year. The EPA and the U.S. Green Building Council are also working on certification standards for green homes. This is good news for the environment and for those who are seeking more environmentally sound building products and design. For specific examples of new green homes, see page 141.

In another positive development, state and federal legislators and agencies have been moving in recent years to restrict the use of health-threatening chemicals across a broad spectrum of everyday home products. Here are some examples:

- The EPA phased out the residential use of two common insecticides between 2001 and 2003: chlorpyrifos (known as Dursban) and diazinon. These organophosphate pesticides are potent neurotoxins that have been linked to low birth weights and can harm the development of fetuses and children.

- The EPA ordered that pressure-treated wood, preserved with chromium copper arsenic (CCA), stop being produced for residential uses, such as decking and playsets, by the end of 2003. The federal Consumer Product Safety Commission has warned that exposure to CCA, which can rub off the greenish-tinted wood onto hands and leach into soil, can increase the risk of bladder and lung cancers, particularly in children.

- By 2008, flame-retardant chemicals known as polybrominated diphenyl ethers (PBDEs) may no longer be used in upholstered furniture and computer and television casings in California. (The European Union has already banned the chemicals.) PBDEs, similar in structure to some banned neurotoxins and widely used in polyurethane furniture, have been found in animal tests to slow brain development, disrupt hormone levels, and have carcinogenic properties. According to studies published in 2002 and 2003, PBDEs are appearing at high levels in the breast milk of North American women as well as in umbilical cord blood, posing threats to breastfeeding infants and fetuses in the womb.

- In an example that could be followed by more locales, New York City has just passed a law making landlords more responsible for detecting and cleaning up lead paint in households with children younger than six.

GREEN PRODUCTS

Taking a problem/solution approach, this section provides a room-by-room, product-by-product look at how to make a greener, healthier home, plus checklists of safety issues and building supplies. Personal and environmental health will both be served by avoiding and removing toxic substances and buying locally and sustainably produced materials.

Products used throughout the house are divided into structural and home maintenance categories.

Building Materials

Wood

According to the Worldwatch Institute, nearly half of the world's original forests—about 7.5 billion acres—have been lost to human development since our species started clearing land. And every year, Americans alone consume 27 percent of wood commercially harvested worldwide. The solution: Products from certified sustainably managed forests bear the Forest Stewardship Council (FSC) label, which also covers some "reclaimed" or recycled wood (see sidebar on sustainable wood, page 139).

Recycled wood, including doors and window frames, can also be found through salvage companies (see your local Yellow Pages). Before buying, however, examine boards for stray nails and bolts, structural flaws, and old lead paint that could pose a danger. For vintage wood furniture, check antique and flea markets.

Tree-Free Wood Substitutes. To spare forests, choose materials that have not directly caused living trees to be cut. Beams of engineered wood, made from recycled newsprint, straw or wood chips, can now be found in the marketplace. Bamboo, a fast-growing grass, provides the warm look of hardwood at a comparable cost ($7 to $8 per yard). For more options, see Flooring, below.

Health Problems of Composite Woods. Composite woods such as particleboard and plywood cost less than hardwoods but can emit, or "offgas," formaldehyde, warns Paul Novack, owner of Environmental Construction Outfitters (ECO), a consulting and green retailing firm in New York. Formaldehyde can cause headaches, nausea, allergic reactions, and a burning sensation in eyes, nose, and mouth and is classified by the EPA as a probable human carcinogen.

It is the glues used in pressed woods that are the primary source of VOCs, says John Bowers of the Healthy House Institute. Look for low-VOC options certified by Scientific Certification Systems. If you find these too costly (they can average about 20 percent more than conventional products), you can coat conventional pressed woods with an appropriate low-VOC sealant.

Flooring

There are many alternative flooring options. The safest bets are natural (not vinyl) linoleum and cork, hardwood, bamboo, ceramic tile, marble, stone, concrete, and slate. If you can use locally produced materials, such as stone or slate from a nearby quarry, you'll save shipping costs and energy while making your house truly of its region. To prevent offgassing from any floor, stains, finishes, and glues—including tile adhesive and grout— should be low-VOC. These products are readily available.

Hardwood remains the most popular material, and it can be found either new or recycled in sustainably certified forms. A good low-VOC finish for a wood floor is Polyureseal BP, made by AFM Safecoat. Milled bamboo is installed just like a traditional hardwood floor. You can also get low-VOC, pressed-bamboo "plyboo."

Sub-flooring, laid between your foundation and interior floor, is usually made of exterior-grade plywood. Although this emits fewer VOCs than interior-grade plywood, it's still worth it to apply sealant to keep fumes in.

From a health and environmental standpoint, one of the worst materials for a floor is vinyl, also known as polyvinyl chloride, or PVC. Widely used in flooring, wall coverings, countertops, mini blinds, water pipes, and window frames, vinyl is toxic throughout its life cycle. Its manufacture and incineration create dioxins, which are known human carcinogens and also linked to reproductive and immune disorders. Because exposure to a single PVC fire can cause respiratory disease, the International Association of Fire Fighters says it supports "alternative building materials that do not pose as much risk as PVC to fire fighters, building occupants or communities."

In your home, PVC surfaces can offgas plasticizing chemicals known as phthalates, added to soften vinyl and make it more flexible. In animal tests, some phthalates have been found to harm the heart, liver, kidneys, and reproductive systems. As for respiratory systems, a 1997 study by the National Institute of Public Health in Norway showed that children with PVC flooring in their homes had an 89 percent higher risk of bronchial obstruction than children in PVC-free homes. The phthalates migrated from the PVC to minute particles of house dust that were inhaled.

In fall 2000 and early 2003, the U.S. Centers for Disease Control and Prevention's *National Report on Human Exposure to Environmental Chemicals* found higher-than-expected levels of phthalates in American bodies, but could not specify the source. In addition to soft vinyl products, phthalates are commonly used as fragrancing agents in everything from perfumes to cleaning products.

If you want resilient, sound-absorptive flooring, try natural linoleum, made of sawdust, linseed oils, pigments, and a jute backing. Also forgiving underfoot is cork, the substance with which Marcel Proust, a writer often incapacitated by asthma, lined his bedroom walls. Cork is harvested in Europe without cutting the trees; only their outer bark is taken, once every ten years. Before buying cork tiles, however, examine them and make sure they are not the inferior kind that use only a thin veneer of cork on a vinyl backing.

For kitchens, laundry rooms, exercise areas, baths, and those steep back stairs, recycled rubber flooring makes a bouncy, easy-to-clean and non-skid surface. It can be found bearing no-formaldehyde, no-vinyl, and other low-VOC credentials.

Room by Room

The Kitchen

Because heat and humidity makes VOCs vaporize more quickly and in greater amounts from any surface, you may be inhaling toxins along with the wholesome odors of cooking in your kitchen's steamy air. These VOCs may be coming from all around you: cabinets and countertops, vinyl flooring, and cleaning products. Carbon monoxide may also be leaking from a poorly ventilated or maintained gas oven and range.

Kitchen cabinets and countertops are typically made of particleboard, fiberboard, pressed wood, and interior-grade plywood, all of which can off-gas formaldehyde for years. Laminated surfaces such as melamine, while they haven't been found to be toxic, often surround composite wood cores. This can easily be determined by looking at any unfinished edges, where you can see layered pressed wood sandwiched between white laminate. The problem can also be easily cured by sealing these raw edges, preferably before installing, with a low-VOC sealant that blocks formaldehyde fumes.

Alternative materials for kitchen cabinetry include formaldehyde-free medium density fiberboard or particleboard substitutes, such as strawboard or wheatboard. If you use solid wood, you can save money by installing open shelving. That way, things are easier to see and reach, and in the frenzy of preparing that four-course gourmet meal for eight, you won't hit your head on open cabinet doors.

Don't spoil your shelves, whether open or enclosed, with vinyl shelf liner that can offgas phthalates. Instead, apply a hardy least-toxic finish or enamel paint that can be wiped clean with a damp sponge.

For countertops or floors, tiles made from recycled glass or ceramics cost about the same as conventional mid-price tile, according to the Green Resource Center in Berkeley, California. In addition to new porcelain stone tiles made from local clay and minerals, there are products made from recycled ceramic or glass tile.

For appliances that will save you energy and water (and money) in the kitchen, see below. While gas stoves cook with less energy than electric ones, they can pose a health risk if improperly ventilated or maintained. Carbon monoxide (CO), a colorless, odorless gas, can cause symptoms such as headaches, nausea, and fatigue, and is fatal in high doses. Nitrogen dioxide (NO2), a sharp-smelling gas, can cause coughing and trigger asthma attacks. If you have a gas stove, make sure that the pilot light is working and that you can ventilate the kitchen by opening windows or that the stove has an exhaust fan and flue that are vented to the outdoors. Because blockages or leaks can occur, have the system examined yearly by a professional. Make sure to install carbon monoxide alarms and fire/smoke alarms in hallways outside bedrooms.

The Natural Bedroom

Mattresses and Bedding. Untreated (no stain/water/fire repellants) certified organic cotton mattresses, sheets, blankets, and comforter covers may cost more money than conventional products, but they come with far-fewer environmental costs. Conventional cotton accounts for up to 25 percent of the insecticides used worldwide, and seven of the top fifteen pesticides used on cotton are classified as at least possible human carcinogens. Nitrogen-spiked synthetic fertilizers are also used, so that cotton field runoff can create aquatic "dead zones" in waterways.

Additionally, cotton is often bleached (sometimes with sodium hypochlorite, the manufacture of which releases dioxin), and treated with dyes and color fixers (heavy metals such as chromium, copper and zinc). Roughly half the chemicals used as dyes or fixers on cotton end up as waste in rivers and soil.

Synthetic fillings and fabrics, such as polyurethane foam, polyester, and nylon, are environmentally unsound because they are made from petroleum, a nonrenewable resource. Also, for our personal health, natural fillings and fibers—not necessarily organic, but free of toxic treatments—are best.

To comply with federal regulations, mattresses and pads must be treated with fire-retardants. Some of these can emit formaldehyde; others use polybrominated diphenyl ethers (PBDEs), which have been rapidly accumulating in humans and pose potentially significant health risks. Many mattress cores contain polyurethane foam (which may also be treated with PBDEs) that can emit VOCs associated with upper respiratory problems and skin irritation. Finally, some less-expensive bed frames, including box spring containers, use plywood or particleboard, both of which commonly contain formaldehyde. Some plywood manufacturers also use pentachlorophenol, a probable human carcinogen, as a preservative.

In addition to fire-retardant chemicals, sheets and blankets, no matter what they're made of, can be treated with permanent-press and stain- and water-repellent finishes, which can offgas formaldehyde and perfluoro-chemicals (PFCs). One variety of PFCs, known as PFOA, is associated with testicular and bladder cancers and has been found in the blood of children tested at more than twice adult levels.

The Solution

If you want an untreated mattress or futon, you can fulfill U.S. standards by choosing one wrapped in wool, which is naturally fire-resistant. Otherwise, to purchase an untreated mattress you'll have to present a doctor's prescription stating that you have chemical sensitivities to fire retardants. These are not difficult to get. But for safety's sake, do not do so before making sure that you have working fire/smoke alarms outside your bedrooms; and promise yourself that you'll regularly check that the batteries are fresh.

Organic or natural cotton mattresses may also have steel springs or a filling of natural latex rubber instead of polyurethane foam. Springless, rubber-free options can be found.

No matter what kind of mattress and bedding you have, you may still be vulnerable to asthma and allergies unless dust mites are contained. These microscopic mites, which ingest our shed skin, multiply in both foam- and cotton-stuffed furniture and thrive in warm, humid conditions and wherever dust accumulates—in carpets, for instance. The droppings of dust mites are one of the most potent allergens and asthma triggers around.

To kill mites, wash bedding every two weeks in hot water. It's also a good idea to encase your mattress in a tightly woven barrier cloth that prevents mites from reaching your skin. A washable organic cotton encasement is the most environmentally sound; while vinyl is commonplace, it does not breathe, making it uncomfortable to lie on, and can offgas VOCs.

Wood Furniture. Most conventional furniture is made not of solid wood, but veneers glued to a core of plywood or particleboard. These offgas formaldehyde.

Although preferable from the standpoint of your personal health, solid wood furniture needs a further vetting for its environmental impact. Steer clear of products made from old-growth or endangered forests. Look for Forest Stewardship Council (FSC)–certified wood dining tables, chairs, and other pieces. Also look for Scientific Certification Systems (SCS)–certified, composite wood furniture that is formaldehyde-free or uses recycled or reclaimed wood. (See the sidebar on page 139.) Wood furniture finishes, like those for wood floors, can emit unhealthy VOCs. These are available in no- and low-VOC products.

Forgoing Foam. Many couches, armchairs and other upholstered furnishings are stuffed with polyurethane foam, an unpleasant substance made of petrochemicals that eventually crumbles into a yellow dust, adding lung-congesting particles to the air you breathe. Polyurethane furniture foam is also typically treated with fire-retardant, and potentially toxic, polybrominated diphenyl ether (PBDEs).

PBDEs can best be avoided by buying furniture stuffed with natural fibers such as cotton, wool, and old-fashioned horsehair. Flat cotton or wool cushions can be secured with ties to the seat and back of a wood-frame sofa. Less-toxic fire retardants can be used on foam.

You'll breathe easiest if you pick furniture covered in untreated fabric. Permanent press, fire retardant, and water- and stain-repellant finishes may create headaches or worse by releasing formaldehydes or perfluorochemicals (PFCs.) Select removable, washable slip covers and you won't have to worry about stains or dust mites. The same goes for window treatments.

Decorating/Maintenance

Paints

Unfortunately, the heady "clean" smell we associate with fresh paint is really the evaporation, or offgassing, of toxic petrochemical solvents known as volatile organic compounds (VOCs). These include benzene, formaldehyde, toluene, and xylene, which are known carcinogens or neurotoxins. The strong odors can also bother asthmatics and those with allergies. Both conventional oil-based and water-based, or latex, paints can contain petrochemical-based solvents that control drying time; latex paints also use fungicides and preservatives to prevent mold and mildew.

Happily, much cleaner and less malodorous paints are available. Look on labels for "no-VOC," or "low-VOC." If you don't mind a strong natural fragrance, what's best for the environment—but often more expensive—are all-natural and even certified organic plant-based paints. These use aromatic solvents made from citrus and other plant oils, and can release natural VOCs, so use with caution. And read labels carefully: Some natural paints do contain small amounts of petrochemical solvents. For the most chemical-sensitive people, natural, old-fashioned milk paints and whitewashes are VOC-free and virtually odorless. Natural milk paints must be used quickly after mixing. And remember, water-based paint without fungicides may not be long-lasting, and can be a rich habitat for mold and mildew, so don't use in areas exposed to dampness.

When painting interiors, throw open windows to let out fumes. It takes most paints at least six weeks to fully dry and offgas. Pregnant women and people with asthma or allergies should not do the painting, and should stay out of the area until after paint has dried. Patch-test any paint and have sensitive family members give it a sniff.

Cleaning and Laundry Products

Many conventional cleaning products, rather than producing pristine homes as advertised, actually leave indoor air polluted with a toxic smog of petrochemical VOCs and the synthetic fragrances used to mask them.

Think, then, what damage cleaning products used on a regular basis year-round can do in the enclosed space of a home, where VOCs can build up for months. "When they evaporate, they are transported directly to the brain, where they can be as intoxicating as ether or chloroform. These are palpably dangerous to health," says Kaye Kilburn, professor of internal medicine at the University of Southern California medical school. In other words, when someone complains of being knocked out after cleaning house, it's likely more than just a turn of phrase.

Cleaning product VOCs, many of which are neurotoxins and known or suspected carcinogens and/or hormone disruptors, have been implicated in headaches, dizziness, watery eyes, skin rashes, and respiratory problems. A Spanish study published in 2003 surveyed more than 4,000 women and found that 25 percent of asthma cases in the group were attributable to domestic cleaning work.

Here are some ingredients to avoid in cleaning products, and safer, simpler alternatives.

- **Detergents for Dishes, Clothes, Floors, and Countertops.** Most conventional soaps are made from petroleum, a nonrenewable resource. Some contain alkyphenol ethoxylates (APEs), suspected hormone disruptors that can threaten wildlife after they go down the drain. Inhalation of vapors from butyl cellosolve, used as a solvent to dissolve grease, may irritate the respiratory tract and cause nausea, headaches, dizziness, and unconsciousness. The synthetic fragrances in these products can make you sneeze and wheeze. "Fragrances are common allergens and repeated exposures can lead to onset of allergies, including symptoms such as skin and respiratory tract irritation, headache and watery eyes," says Dr. Harvey Karp, a Los Angeles pediatrician and assistant professor of medicine at UCLA. A family of chemicals known as phthalates, used in synthetic fragrances, have been found to produce cancer of the liver and birth defects in lab animals. Look on labels for safer and more eco-friendly ingredients such as grain alcohol as a solvent, and natural plant oils (olive, palm, pine, coconut, eucalyptus, citrus, peppermint, or lavender) as a soap base. Choose soaps and detergents labeled "fragrance free."

- **Chlorine Bleach.** Also known as sodium hypochlorite and sodium hydroxide, this common disinfectant, found in liquid bleach, drain cleaners, and oven cleaners (combined with caustic lye), can burn skin and eyes and be fatal if swallowed. When it goes down the drain, it can produce organochlorines, which are suspected carcinogens as well as reproductive, neurological and immune-system toxins. Instead, use non-chlorine bleaches based on hydrogen peroxide, sodium percarbonate, or sodium perborate. Borax, washing soda, or white vinegar in water can also clean and remove stains. For ovens, coat surfaces in a paste of water and baking or washing soda and let stand overnight, then scrub off while wearing gloves.

- **Glass and Bathroom Cleaners.** Ammonia, the main ingredient in many window, tub, toilet, and tile cleaners, is caustic and poisonous if ingested—and, if combined with chlorine, present in many scouring products, produces toxic chlorine gas! Instead, use chlorine-free scouring powders or baking soda. For windows and mirrors, mix white vinegar with water. Safer toilet bowl and other cleaning solutions are sold by Seventh Generation, Earth-Friendly Products, Ecover, and others.

Do not put old cleaning products down the drain. Call your local solid waste department to learn how to dispose of safely. And keep all cleaning products, even least-toxic ones, well out of children's reach.

WHAT YOU CAN DO

For an Existing House

Take an inventory of your house or apartment, looking for the dangerous substances discussed in this chapter, which should be safely disposed of or stored elsewhere. High on the suspect list are drain and oven cleaners (see above), pesticides, and paints (especially leftover lead-based paint, discussed below).

In addition, to give your home a clean bill of health, go through this checklist of toxins and what to do about them.

- **Asbestos.** Asbestos, another hazard appearing in pre-1970s homes—in insulation around steampipes, boilers, and furnace ducts; vinyl floor tile; roofing, shingles, and siding; and dry-wall joint compound—should be removed only by professionals.

- **Mold.** Notice a musty smell? Mildews and molds, potent allergens, can be exposed during renovations. Although the underlying problem, usually a leak, will need to be fixed, light infestations of mold can be scrubbed from wood or plaster with a nontoxic detergent or non-chlorine bleach mixed with water. In cases of pervasive contamination, contact a certified contractor—and be sure to ask for references from previous clients.

Lead Paint

If you are renovating a dwelling built earlier than 1978, when lead in interior house paints was limited to the safe level of 0.06 percent, you need to test paint for lead. This potent neurotoxin persists in an estimated 39 million homes, or more than 80 percent of those built before 1978. Lead can be inhaled or ingested in paint dust and chips and causes developmental harm and brain damage. Fetuses and young children are especially at risk of lead poisoning.

Under federal law, disclosure of any known lead paint in a dwelling, has, since December 1996, been required of all home sellers and landlords. However, what they don't know may still hurt you.

Although blood lead levels in children have dropped dramatically since the metal's reduction in paint and gasoline, the U.S. Centers for Disease Control and Prevention have found that 4.4 percent of American children under the age of six have levels higher than the current safety threshold of 10 micrograms per deciliter (10 mcg/dl). This signifies an ongoing public health crisis, according to Dr. Herbert Needleman, a professor at the University of Pittsburgh Medical Center. Needleman's studies have shown that, "As bone lead levels rise, so do aggression, delinquency, and attention problems." It cannot be emphasized enough, Needleman says, that our primary exposure to lead still comes from old lead-based paint.

Before doing any renovations that can disturb old paint, have it tested by an EPA-certified lab. Find a certified lab near you through the National Lead Information Center, (800)424-LEAD or www.epa.gov/opptintr/lead/nlic.htm. Hire a certified lead paint removal specialist—never remove it yourself.

Pressure-Treated Wood: Often used for outdoor structures such as decks and playgrounds, wood treated with chromated copper arsenate (CCA) is another renovation concern. Although it is no longer being produced for home uses, some CCA wood remains in the marketplace and should be

Greening Hollywood: One House at a Time

The actress Julia Louis-Dreyfus (*Seinfeld*) and her husband Brad Hall (a writer-producer and former *Saturday Night Live* cast member), are lifelong environmentalists who have been actively involved with nearly a dozen green groups, including the Natural Resources Defense Council, Heal the Bay, National Parks Conservation Association, Trust for Public Land, and the Waterkeeper Alliance. They both drive Toyota Priuses. Here, they talk with writer Amanda Griscom about the design and building of their oceanfront bungalow just north of Santa Barbara, California, a showcase of green design and state-of-the-art energy efficiency mechanisms.

Brad Hall: I grew up in Santa Barbara in the 1970s, and learned how to surf as soon as I could walk. When I was about twelve years old, one of the oil derricks then located off the coast of Santa Barbara exploded because of a drilling pressure problem. I'll never forget seeing all the beaches I'd grown up with coated with black sludge. The fish were belly-up, the birds were completely slimed. It was incredibly disturbing, but also, I suppose, a turning point for me politically.

Julia Louis-Dreyfus: I never had any kind of defining experience like that—no specific turning point or activist rite of passage. I grew up spending a lot of time hiking in Wyoming, so I certainly had an early appreciation for the natural world. I was made aware of the idea of being a part of something bigger than you. That impulse is defi-nitely what now drives my environmental work. It's certainly part of what compelled me to want to live efficiently and build our new house, which incorporates environmentally sensitive materials and building techniques, including net-metered rooftop solar panels, sustainably harvested tropical woods, a natural ventilation system, and insulation made of recycled newspaper.

Hall: We didn't plan on making this house a model of green building; it was just going to be a small addition of two bedrooms and a bathroom. But then we met architect David Hertz, who runs the Santa Monica–based architecture firm Syndesis and is a green-building visionary. His own home is essentially a laboratory for green design.

Louis-Dreyfus: My favorite thing is the retractable roof. It functions as a "thermal chimney" that exhausts hot air upward and draws ocean breezes through the windows. All the rooms are connected by transoms so that the air is constantly circulating and there's no need for air conditioning, which dramatically diminishes energy demand. It also does wonders to integrate the outside world—the gulls and pelicans and weather patterns circling overhead.

Hall: There's generous use of glass, which means there's minimal need for electric lighting. The window glass is laminated with a "heat mirror," so warmth is not lost when it's cool outside, or let in when it's hot. The lighting is energy-efficient halogen, and the kitchen appliances and washer/dryer are all Energy Star–certified. The rooftop solar thermal panels produce hot water that flows through radiant tubing in the floors to heat the house; the rooftop photovoltaic panels are net-metered so that during the week when we're in L.A. and the house is empty and the energy goes unused, it's pumped directly back into the grid and creates a credit at the local utility. Also, we asked our Santa Barbara–based contractor, Jed Hirsch, to be sure that all the lumber, doors, windows, plumbing, and electrical fixtures gutted from the original house were salvaged and donated to a builder's exchange for reuse.

Let's face it: Having a second home is itself a sort of appalling excess. We figured if we're going to do it, we better be as responsible as we can. We were diligent about keeping the scale small and trying to get as many of our materials and labor locally, so they didn't have to travel long distances.

There are a few items, like the Jacuzzi, that kick up the energy load, but we make up for it with efficiencies elsewhere. The larger point is that living efficiently is not about asceticism, it's about balance.

Louis-Dreyfus: As Americans we are incredibly fortunate. We are 5 percent of the world's population and consume a third of the total resources. We should all feel guilty relative to the world. So for me, these lifestyle decisions are a way of having control and feeling less guilty. I walk around feeling a sort of existential guilt all the time; for me this house is a way of feeling less guilty about the universe.

This excerpt is published with permission from *Grist Magazine* (www.grist.org). The full story can be read at www.grist.org/news/powers/2003/07/31/griscom-house. For more environmental news and humor, sign up for *Grist*'s free e-mail dispatches at www.grist.org/signup.

avoided. It has a greenish tint and can be easily tested and safely sealed with a brush-on coating. If you have CCA wood, avoid breathing the sawdust, and wash hands after touching it.

Radon: This naturally occurring, radioactive gas is produced by the decay of uranium and radium in soil and rock and can enter basements and build up in a home. It can damage lung tissues and cause lung cancer. Colorless and odorless, radon is worth testing for. National Safety Council Radon Hotline: (800)767-7236.

Carbon Monoxide (CO): This colorless, odorless and very deadly gas is produced by combustion. It is most commonly present in automobile exhaust but can also be produced by fireplaces and gas stoves, water heaters, clothes dryers, and furnaces, all of which should be vented to the outdoors. Every home should have a CO alarm. *Consumer Reports* recommends plug-in detectors, such as those in the Nighthawk 900 series, American Sensors' CO920, and Lifesaver FYCO-6N.

BUILDING A NEW GREEN HOME

To help you start planning a new green home, here's a list of basics to address.

Green Design and Building Checklist

Foundations

To make cement more eco-friendly, it can reuse waste in the form of fly ash, the residue from coal-fired power plants. Fly ash in cement is specified by the U.S. Green Building Council's Leadership in Energy and Design (LEED) certification program. As an alternative to cinder blocks, there are Faswall blocks made of 85 percent sawdust and 15 percent cement, and Rastra blocks made from recycled polystyrene plastic and cement.

In a slab-on-grade foundation, a concrete slab can be poured over a bed of gravel on graded soil to form the ground floor, in place of a wood-framed floor. This has to be done in areas where the soil doesn't freeze, or where the structure will be heated. See www.concretenetwork.com/concrete/foundations.htm. If you live in an area prone to hurricanes, you might consider an all-concrete home.

Framework, Walls, and Beams

Ninety percent of the 1.2 million single-family houses built annually in the United States use wood-framed construction. Happily, in a green home this can be done using wood-saving framing techniques, also known as "optimum value engineering," recommended by the National Association of Home Builders Research Center.

By framing walls with 2×6 studs separated by twenty-four inches rather than sixteen inches, for example, wood use can be reduced by 19 percent, writes Jennifer Roberts in her beautiful and useful book, *Good Green Homes* (Gibbs Smith, 2003), which is filled with photographs of different regional examples. Box headers, usually made from smaller trees, are preferable to standard headers, which tend to be taken from old-growth trees, Roberts adds. She notes that up to 30 percent less wood can be used without sacrificing structural integrity in a traditional "stick" framed house. Another option is "in-line" framing, which aligns studs with roof rafters and puts windows between studs, writes veteran home designer, builder, and materials expert Dan Chiras in *The New Ecological Home*. Even such a simple deduction as using two-stud rather than three-stud corners adds up to a substantial wood savings, Chiras notes.

In addition to framing techniques, wood can be saved by specifying pre-made trusses, made of wood and metal plates, for rafters and ceiling and floor joists. Hayward Truss of California makes prefab ones from certified lumber. Stronger, straighter, and cheaper beams can be made from "green" engineered wood (made from recycled materials such as newsprint, straw, or wood chips taken from small trees rather than old growth, and bound with low-VOC adhesives). If using hardwood beams, you can conserve wood by using cut-away "I" joists for roofs (they resemble Lincoln logs), Chiras notes.

If you've saved money on the amount of wood needed for the job, you may be better able to afford a framework made from FSC-certified wood from sustainably managed forests.

For framework, steel makes a practical wood substitute. It is a recyclable material, and about 35 percent of steel is made from a combination of industrial scrap and post-consumer waste. It can't be eaten by insects, which makes it popular in termite-plagued places like Hawaii. Light-gauge steel frames can replace the average 400 wood studs used in a new home, Chiras notes. However, it remains an industrial product, using energy and creating waste in its manufacture.

For walls, roofs, and floors, both authors highly recommend prefabricated Structural Insulated Panels (SIPs), which utilize rigid foam insulation between panels of engineered wood. SIPs can "nearly eliminate framing required to build exterior walls," Chiras writes. Recycled gypsum board, or dry wall, can also be used. If you need replastering, Paul Novak of

Seeking Sustainable Wood

Choose Wood Products Bearing the FSC label

When starting a home-improvement project, remember that all building wood is not created equal. The label of the Forest Stewardship Council (FSC), endorsed by a majority of environmental groups, certifies that the wood in a product has been sustainably produced. Key FSC principles include: the protection of forest watersheds, soil, and indigenous species; restricted chemical use and limits on genetic engineering; and fair-labor policies.

The FSC operates by accrediting individual certifiers. In the United States, labels to look for are those of the SmartWood Program of the Rainforest Alliance (RA) and Scientific Certification Systems (SCS). Some FSC policies have been criticized. While noting that there's a potential for conflict of interest because some industry representatives sit on FSC's board, and that requirements limiting herbicides and protecting old-growth forests could be more specifically stated, Consumers Union rates FSC's as by far the most meaningful certification for sustainable wood products available.

RA's SmartWood Rediscovered Wood Program certifies wood that would otherwise rot, get chipped up, or be carted to a landfill. Sources include dilapidated buildings, "nuisance" or fallen trees on urban or suburban land, and unproductive trees in orchards.

"An old warehouse with one million board feet of reusable lumber can offset the need to harvest one thousand acres of forest, while yielding the kind of weathered beams and boards that homeowners prize," says Laura Terral, a SmartWood chain-of-custody specialist. Look for the "SmartWood Rediscovered" label on finished products from furniture to cutting boards.

Composite Woods

As a general rule, composite woods use less tree feet than hardwoods, which is why they're cheaper, says Dan Chiras, author of *The New Ecological Home* (Chelsea Green, 2004). Look for FSC/SCS certified sustainable, low-VOC veneers, plywoods, and other composite woods if you decide to go this route.

A Greenwashing Label

The timber industry has developed a competing labeling program called the Sustainable Forestry Initiative (SFI). The Consumers Union (CU) eco-labels website (www.ecolabels.org) notes that the SFI fails to meet some basic criteria, such as checks on conflict of interest, and "has no standard for chemical management—leaving that up to the individual foresters—and no definition of 'old growth.'"

—Adapted by permission from *The Green Guide Newsletter*, May 2003.

Environmental Construction Outfitters (ECO) notes that "premixed plasters will have preservatives, latex, and other VOCs, so put the primer over it fast to seal and prevent offgassing." Or find craftspeople who will mix traditional plaster—made of gypsum, rock, and sand—with water. "That's basically no-VOC," Novack says.

Look for local and traditional materials to use in building your walls. For example, in Austin, Texas, architect Pliny Fisk uses straw and clay from the area. Similar earthen materials include rammed earth, made of clay and sand. The earth is packed into wood or steel wall forms, which are then peeled off.

A variation, and a solution to an overwhelming waste problem, is the rammed earth tire home. Earth is tamped into the tires, which are stacked in walls and covered with stucco, a no-VOC mix of Portland cement, lime, sand, and water. Earth walls are also fireproof.

Another fascinating and rather romantic material is the straw bale, whose provenance in this country blows back to the windy plains of Nebraska. It is the most popular natural building technique, according to Chiras, and involves stacking rectangular bales into walls. The environmental plus is that straw, i.e., grass, grows in most locales and therefore doesn't have to be shipped long distances. Those with hay fever allergies need not worry, as the walls are coated with plaster. Mold and mildew love straw, however, so it must be rigorously defended from the damp.

Windows and Insulation

Alex Wilson, editor of the invaluable green building publication *Environmental Building News*, recommends positioning windows to maximize daylight and reduce the need for electric light. For further energy efficiency, he advises that homeowners "put in tightly sealed, coated windows and increase insulation in attics, walls and floors." Double-glazed windows insulate almost twice as well as single-glazed glass (see Chapter Eleven).

When choosing window frames, beware of vinyl (see the "Flooring" section). Unless certified by SCS, prefabricated wood frame windows may contain pesticides and glues and should be allowed to offgas VOCs before installation.

Insulation poses numerous challenges, from petrochemical foam to fiberglass that offgasses formaldehydes and releases particulates. If using fiberglass, which can release fine pollutants that can irritate the lungs and

Real Green Dream Homes

Small Is Beautiful—and Leaves a Lighter Footprint on the Land

In the oak-forested hills of California's Napa Valley, two families share a 1,200-square-foot, earth-wall country home built near, but out of the sight of, their father's house. Designed by Okamoto Saijo Architecture, with its dynamic, multi-angled roofs in different heights and its walls in colors that blend with the golds and greys of the landscape, the Rubissow farmhouse looks much bigger than it is.

Also in Sonoma County, using exactly the same square footage, architect Henry Siegel designed a gable-roofed dwelling in the style of local farmhouses, following the hillside contours and removing as few trees as possible. Made of straw bales and stucco, the thick walls are filled with cellulose insulation that, along with a "breezeway" running down the center of the house, keeps it cool in the region's hot summers. The kitchen and children's rooms are set in glass-walled bays at opposite ends of the house that let daylight fall through. In the nearby town of Emeryville, California, Siegel's firm designed a compact house with many green features, including the use of 20 percent less wood due to techniques such as placing wall studs twenty-four inches rather than the standard sixteen inches apart.

A 1,555-square-foot, two-story stucco house in Palm Beach Gardens has been given the 2004 "greenest house" award by the Florida Green Building Coalition. It has bamboo floors and low-VOC paints and finishes throughout, carpeting made from plastic soda bottles and energy-efficient CFL light bulbs that automatically switch off when people leave the room. These and other features should save the home $431 per year in energy bills, according to the Florida Solar Energy Center. Sensors also switch off faucets in the bathroom, where dual-flush toilets can save more than 2,000 gallons of water a year. Kitchen food waste goes into compost bins; there is no garbage disposal. Builders hope that the prototype, nicknamed "Geni-G" for Generation Green, will be used as a model nationwide.

Eco-Apartments

The Solaire, the new, twenty-seven-floor green apartment tower in Manhattan's Battery Park City, opened in 2003. Built-in eco features include photovoltaic cells built into the building facade and high-performance, floor-to-ceiling windows that allow 100 percent more daylight into bedrooms and 200 percent more into living rooms than required by the city code. Centralized HVAC systems filter 85 percent of particulate matter out of the air—a primary concern in lower Manhattan following the dust and toxic pollution residents struggled with after the WTC collapse and subsequent demolition and construction work.

All apartments were supplied with Energy

stimulate asthma attacks and migraines, walls should be carefully sealed with an airtight barrier such as Tyvek or Typar. Among other options, spray-on polyurethane foam is a common choice.

Paul Novak of ECO recommends recycled cotton insulation. Because either cotton or foam is treated with fire-retardant chemicals, you might want to use a non-VOC sealant on the walls to keep chemicals in. Cellulose insulation, made from ground-up newspaper, can be extremely dusty unless applied wet.

In addition to readymade SIP wall panels (see the "Walls" section) you might want to look into low-E radiant barrier insulation, made of microcell polyethylene core sandwiched between sheets of reinforced aluminum foil. There is also an expandable insulation known as Icylene that can be sprayed in the attic.

Roofing Materials

The safest roofs are probably natural slate, ceramic tile, cedar shingle, or metal, according to ECO. You can also use aluminum made from recycled beverage cans. Recycled asphalt shingles may offgas petrochemicals downwards (as well as up), but again, one can keep out fumes by using sealants. Modified bitumen, made from recycled tires, is a similar option.

Home Climate and Conservation

Whole-house Heating Ventilation and Cooling (HVAC) systems are basically central heat and air, which are piped through ducts into every room in the house. You might want to look into a geothermal pump to provide energy from the Earth's core (see Chapter Eleven). At the very least, you should consider an Energy Star boiler, which uses 10 percent less fuel.

It's important to remember, however, that your home's "passive" siting and orientation on the land can make a great difference in energy needs. Keep your region's climate in mind. Planting trees can do much to keep a house cool. South-facing windows and roofs will maximize solar heat in a cold climate.

One great way to direct heat where it's needed rather than force it through the air in ducts is to install radiant heating in which heated water runs through pipes under the floor. Heat rises, so such floors are efficient.

In hot and humid Honolulu, architect Philip White has found that proper ventilation saves energy. "We design homes with high attics and cross ventilation to make sure the air conditioner is used as rarely as possible," White says.

If you're buying room air conditioners rather than going for an HVAC, choose Energy Star. In hot but not humid climates, an evaporative cooler uses up to 75 percent less electricity annually than an air conditioner and can cost half as much.

Your house should be well-ventilated. To stave off mold, mildew, and asthma-inducing dust mites, keep relative humidity at 30 to 50 percent (in the middle of rooms). If necessary, install a dehumidifier in the basement—and empty the water regularly.

The U.S. Department of Energy (DOE) estimates that if a typical home more than ten years old were to install the energy- and water-efficient toilets, dishwashers, and clothes washers that are on the market today, this could save $200 in utility bills and 18,600 gallons of water a year. Most energy-efficient appliances will pay for themselves in energy savings over the life of the product, according to the American Council for an Energy-Efficient Economy (ACEEE). And, if every American household switched to energy-saving appliances today, we'd reduce $CO2$ emissions from power plants by over 175 million tons in one year.

Fixtures

Aerators mix air into the water stream, maintaining water pressure while using less water. A variety of low-flow shower and sink fixtures, inexpensive to install, can reduce water consumption by 50 percent. For sinks and tubs, look for models rated at 2.75 gallons per minute (gmp) or below. For showers, look for models rated at 2.5 gmp.

As toilets consume up to 45 percent of a household's water, you may want to choose a low-flow model that uses 1.6 gallons of water per flush, saving 1.9 gallons or more each flush. If you have an older toilet, a brick (or water-filled jug) in the tank will also reduce water waste.

Many cities have voucher and exchange programs for upgrading to water-efficient appliances, sold in places such as Sears. Recently, California became the first state to approve efficiency rules for washing machines. (See Chapter Eleven for information on energy-efficient water heaters.)

To irrigate the yard and flush toilets, it's worth considering a gray-water system to reuse the water from clothes washers, bathtubs, showers, and sinks (50 to 80 percent of total wastewater from U.S. households). Gray-water systems (which cost up to $1,000) use automated pumps and sand, gravel, mechanical, or biological filters that clean water and prevent the growth of anaerobic bacteria.

Small and Eco-Sound

It seems obvious: One of the simplest ways to build a house that leaves a smaller footprint on the Earth is to make it smaller. If all else is equal, a small house will use fewer raw materials, and will require less energy to cool and heat. Yet the average new American home, at 2,250 square feet, is more than twice the size it was in 1950. And that figure quadrupled from 1993 to 2000 in affluent areas such as California's San Mateo County, where the average home is now 10,000 square feet. "These mega-homes pose a significant threat to our open space and agricultural lands," the Committee for Green Foothills newsletter wrote in 2002. Meanwhile, specimens upward of 21,000 square feet are ballooning throughout the United States.

Resources

For General Information on Green, Least-Toxic Home Products

Environmental Building News. The professional builder's source on the latest green building techniques. Also invaluable for hands-on homeowners. www.buildinggreen.com.

The Green Guide. Specializing in the simplest and most stress-free solutions to environmental home problems, this is the green consumer's reliable source for the healthiest, most ecologically sound products and practices for everyday life. Visit for Web-only articles and comprehensive product reports on appliances, home goods, cleaning supplies, and more. Published every two months by the Green Guide Institute, P.O. Box, 567 Prince Street Station, New York, NY 10012, (212)598-4910, www.thegreenguide.com.

Healthy House Institute. An independent resource center offering books and videos containing practical information for designers, architects, contractors, and homeowners interested in making houses healthy places in which to live. 430 North Sewell Road, Bloomington, IN 47408, (812)332-5073, www.hhinst.com.

Sources for Green Home Building and Decorating Materials

Environmental Construction Outfitters (ECO). Specializing in least-toxic, allergen-free as well as green materials. 901 East 134th Street, Bronx, NY 10454, (800)238-5008, www.environproducts.com.

Environmental Home Center. The green building product line includes nontoxic paint, natural carpets, sustainable wood products, energy-efficient insulation, and cleaning supplies. 1724 Fourth Avenue South, Seattle, WA 98134, (206)682-7332, www.environmentalhomecenter.com.

HealthyHome.com. The site was launched in 1993 as an online store selling allergy control products, environmentally safe building materials and air and water filters. 2435 Dr. Martin Luther King Jr. Street North, St. Petersburg, FL 33704, (800)583-9523, www.healthyhome.com.

Finding a Green Architect or Contractor

For architects and contractors certified by the U.S. Green Building Council's Leadership in Energy and Environmental Design (LEED) program, see

accredited professional directories at www.usgbc.org and at www
.greenbuilder.org, which can help you find them in your area.

No- and Low-VOC Paints, Sealants, Grouts, and Finishes

AFM Enterprises. For all varieties of VOC-free paints and finishes, plus Safe Seal low-VOC sealants and MexeSeal, Paver Seal, and Watershield water- and stain-proofing. 3251 Third Avenue, San Diego, CA 92103, (619)239-0321, (619)239-0565, www.afmsafecoat.com.

Antique Drapery Rod Company. Offers Walker Paints, made from a minimum of 85 percent food-grade ingredients and no VOCs. 140 Glass Street, Dallas, TX 75207, (214)653-1733, www.antiquedraperyrod.com.

Auro. For organic natural paints and finishes, 1340 Industrial Avenue, Suite G, Petaluma, CA 94952, (888)302-9352, www.aurousa.com.

BioShield Paint Company. Eco-friendly paints, stains, and finishes. (505)438-3448, www.bioshieldpaint.com.

Miller Paint Company. One hundred-year-old paint company with many product lines, some of which are eco-friendly. Portland, OR, office: 12812 NE Whitaker Way, Portland, OR 97230, (503)255-0190. Seattle, WA, office: 1550 NW Leary Way, Seattle, WA 98107, (206)784-7878, www.millerpaint.com.

Old-Fashioned Milk Paint Company. Organic, VOC-free paint that is also biodegradable. 436 Main Street, Groton, MA 01450, (978)448-6336, www.milkpaint.com.

Detecting and "Curing" Problems with Lead Paint, Asbestos, Radon, and Carbon Monoxide

For information on detection and certified lead removal specialists, or a pamphlet on "Reducing Lead Hazards When Remodeling Your Home," call EPA's National Lead Information Center, (800)424-LEAD, www.epa.gov/opptintr/lead.

For information on asbestos, see www.epa.gov/asbestos.

For the latest on radon, call the National Safety Council Radon Hotline, (800)767-7236.

Cleaning Products

Bi-O-Kleen. P.O. Box 82066, Portland, OR 97282, (503)557-0216, www.naturallysafecleaning.com.

Citra-Solv. 188 Shadow Lake Road, Ridgefield, CT 06877, (800)343-6588, www.citra-solv.com.

Ecover. P.O. Box 911058, Commerce, CA 90091, (323)720-5730, www.ecover.com.

Earth-Friendly Products. 44 Green Bay Road, Winnetka, IL 60093, (847)446-4441, www.ecos.com.

Mountain Green. 7956 East Via Costa, Scottsdale, AZ 85258, (866)686-4733, www.mtngreen.com.

Seventh Generation. 212 Battery Street, Suite A, Burlington, VT 05401, (802)658-3773, www.seventhgeneration.com.

Carpets

Bonded Logic. Offers 100 percent recycled cotton carpet pads. (480)812-9114, www.bondedlogic.com.

Earth Weave Carpet Mills. P.O. Box 6120, Dalton, GA 30722, (706)278-8200, www.earthweave.com.

Natural Carpet Company. (310)447-7965, www.naturalcarpetcompany.com.

Natural Home Products. Makers of Naturlich Carpeting. P.O. Box 1677, Sebastopol, CA 95473, (707)824-0914, www.naturalhomeproducts.com.

Bedding, Mattresses, and Linens

AbundantEarth.com. 762 West Park Avenue, Port Townsend, WA 98368, (888)513-2784, www.abundantearth.com.

Coyuchi. P.O. Box 845, Point Reyes Station, CA 94956, (415)663-8077, www.coyuchi.com.

EcoPlanet/EcoChoices Natural Living. P.O. Box 1491, Glendora, CA 91740, (626)969-3707, www.ecochoices.com.

Gaiam. 360 Interlocken Boulevard, Broomfield, CO 80026, (303)222-3665, www.gaiam.com.

GreenSleep. 50 Colonnade Road, Ottawa, ON K2E 7J6, Canada, (613)727-5337, www.greensleep.com.

Heart of Vermont. P.O. Box 612, Barre, VT 05641, (802)476-3098, www.heartofvermont.com.

Lifekind Products. P.O. Box 1744, Grass Valley, CA 95945, (530)477-5395, www.lifekind.com.

Nirvana Safe Haven. 3441 Golden Rain Road, #3, Walnut Creek, CA 94595, (800)968-9355, www.nontoxic.com.

Tribal Fiber. P.O. Box 707, Nederland, CO 80466, (303)258-9166, www.tribalfiber.com.

White Lotus Home. 191 Hamilton Street, New Brunswick, NJ 08901, (877)426-3623, www.whitelotus.net.

For comprehensive lists of companies making furniture and structural wood products from certified sustainably managed forests, see the Forest Stewardship Council website at www.certifiedwood.org. For certified no-formaldehyde pressed woods, see Scientific Certification Systems at www.scs.com. For furniture and building wood that's made from recycled/reclaimed sources, see Rainforest Alliance's www.smartwood.org. For Consumers Union's criteria and ratings of green label claims, including certified wood programs, go to www.ecolabels.org. Some manufacturers:

EcoTimber. 1611 Fourth Street, San Rafael, CA 94901, (415)258-8454, www.ecotimber.com.

Expanko. Cork and recycled rubber flooring. (800)345-6202, www.expanko.com.

Forbo Linoleum North America. Natural linoleum. (800)842-7839.

Furnature. 86 Coolidge Avenue, Watertown, MA 02472, (800)326-4895, www.furnature.com.

Globus Cork. Cork flooring. (718)742-7264, www.corkfloor.com.

Goodwin Heart Pine Company. (800)336-3118, heartpine.com.

Greenfloors.com. Recycled commercial and residential eco-carpeting, padding, flooring, and linoleum. 3170-7 Draper Drive, Fairfax, VA 22031, (703)691-1616, www.greenfloors.com.

Jefferson Recycled Woodworks. P.O. Box 696, McCloud, CA 96057, (530)964-2740, www.ecowood.com.

NorthWest Builders Network. Sells recycled plastic picnic tables. (888) 810-8296, www.nwbuildnet.com.

Smith & Fong. Bamboo products. (866)835-9859, www.plyboo.com.

Tamalpais Natureworks. Sustainable furniture and furniture kits. P.O. Box 3353, (415)454-9948, San Rafael, CA 94912, www.tamalpais.com.

Technologies Inc. Recycled plastic outdoor benches. (413)789-0067, mbp tech.com.

Cabinets

Ecoproducts.com. Strawboard and wheatboard cabinets. www .ecoproducts.com.

Sierra Pine Co. Sells formaldehyde-free, medium-density fiberboard called Medite II. (800)676-3339, www.sierrapine.com.

Insulation

See "Is Polyurethane Foam Insulation Safe?" at www.thegreenguide.com.

Bonded Logic. (480)812-9114, www.bondedlogic.com.

International Cellulose Corporation. (800)444-1252, www.spray-on .com.

Palmer Industries. Air Krete. (800)545-7383, www.palmerindustriesinc .com.

Water-Saving Appliances

For specific models see product reports at www.thegreenguide.com.

Windows

Lowen. Wood windows. www.lowen.com.

Marvin. (888)537-8268, www.marvin.com.

Paramount Windows. Wood and metal-clad windows. (204)233-4966, www.paramountwindows.com.

Thermal Line. Non-PVC thermoplastic windows. (800)662-1832, www.tl windows.com.

Weather Shield. (800)477-6808, www.weathershield.com.

chapter eight

Baby Basics

From Organic Feet Pajamas to Pesticide-Free Food

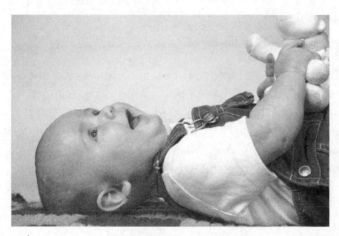

Taking steps to live a healthier life makes sense for adults, but for children it's crucial. For one thing, the accelerated growth rate of childhood boosts the absorption and toxicity of the hazardous chemicals in their surroundings.

"Children are not small adults," says John Peterson Myers, spokesperson for www.EnvironmentalHealthNews.org and www.OurStolenFuture.org. Children have developing systems that undergo great changes, especially in their first years. So, their bodies are more vulnerable to the effects of certain environmental contaminants than their parents' fully matured systems might be."

Also at issue is the average child's consumption. By weight, children drink and eat more than adults—and with less variety. So, the health risks associated with certain foods impact them to a greater degree.

Kids make intimate contact with pollutants every day. They crawl on floors, with eyes, hands, and mouths close to the surfaces that collect much of the fallout from toxins. And with their tendency to place everything in their mouths, children provide contaminants direct access to their vulnerable systems.

SIDS: Still a Threat

"For children from one month to one year, the leading cause of death is Sudden Infant Death Syndrome (SIDS)," says Betty McEntire, executive director of the American SIDS Institute. SIDS strikes most often between two and four months of age. Although many questions about this killer remain unanswered, McEntire points to a triple-risk model. First, the child must have a subtle nervous-system defect; second, the child enters a vulnerable stage in development; and third, the child is exposed to an unknown environmental factor or factors.

The good news is that the total of SIDS deaths has declined since the 1970s, when this syndrome claimed 11,000 infants. Today, that number hovers around 2,500.

To outsmart this killer, McEntire advises parents to purchase firm crib mattresses, strip the bed of blankets, pillows, and stuffed animals, and dress babies in just enough clothing for comfort. A recent addition to McEntire's "do" list involves moving cribs into parents' rooms. Although it's unclear why, several European studies have found this strategy decreases crib deaths.

"We know maternal smoking increases the occurrence of SIDS, as does secondhand smoke," says McEntire. Tummy sleeping is verboten, and children with colds bear special watching, too. Some recent evidence points to pacifiers as possible deterrents.

Jane Sheppard, editor and publisher of Healthy Child Online and the *Healthy Child E-Newsletter*, wants parents to know that the most prevalent, toxic, and overlooked environmental hazard for children is toxic gases in mattresses. Although Sheppard admits that the connection between mattresses laced with chemicals and SIDS needs more study, she says the evidence so far is very compelling. Links may also exist with autism and ADD.

"The fact is, in over nine years, not one baby who has slept on a properly wrapped mattress has ever died of crib death," says Sheppard. "This is the only crib death prevention advice that has ever been 100 percent successful. And the solution is simply purchasing a simple inexpensive cover." With this small investment in linen, everyone will sleep easier.

Young children spend more time indoors than even an adult's whopping 90 percent. As mentioned in Chapter Eight, indoor air quality is five to ten times worse than outside. Add to that children's higher breathing rates, and the damaging effects of the typical home's air pollutants are greatly enhanced.

Chemical exposure limits are determined by adult reactions. The majority of the information about reaction to chemicals has been compiled solely by the immediate effects of accidental on-the-job exposures. The specific effect on young systems remains largely a mystery.

In addition, scientific methods demand that only one contaminant at a time be studied. That means that, by their nature, investigations neglect to examine the effects of multiple compounds—which may have a synergy.

"There remain many questions surrounding the 'layering' of environmental components," says Kagan Owens, a program director at Beyond Pesticides, a national network committed to pesticide safety and the adoption of alternative pest management strategies.

When children develop asthma, the cause can be hard to pinpoint. Was it the power plant a mile away? The vegetables laced with pesticides? The ozone created when sunlight heated freshly painted walls?

The latest news is even more disturbing. "News coming down the pipeline is that even low-level exposures—those amounts that were previously thought safe—are more harmful than ever suspected," says Elizabeth Sword, executive director of the Children's Health Environmental Coalition (CHEC).

The body of evidence linking environmental toxins and the degrading health of our youngest generations is growing. Among the leading culprits: volatile organic compounds (VOCs), pesticides, polybrominated diphenyl ethers (PBDEs), bisphenol A, phthalates, mercury, lead, arsenic, and anti-germicidals.

The environmental onslaught begins even before babies are born. According to the National Institute of Environmental Health Sciences (NIEHS), birth defects affect more than 150,000 babies each year, but the causes of 60 percent of the abnormalities are unknown. And many birth defects are now believed to be caused by exposure of a genetically susceptible embryo or fetus to environmental toxins.

The most common birth defect in U.S.-born children is cardiovascular malformations (CVMs). Affecting almost 1 percent of births, their cause remains a mystery. But NIEHS studies are looking at certain environmental chemicals as possible culprits.

Sounds dismal for the health of the youngest generation, doesn't it? But power is embedded in knowledge. And there are many strategies and solutions that concerned adults can employ to mitigate children's exposure to unsavory chemicals.

From changing the way you clean the house to shopping differently at the supermarket and furniture store, you can ensure your baby gets a good nontoxic start in life.

CURRENT EVENTS/LEGISLATIVE/POLITICAL

Efforts to guarantee environmental health for children have met with mixed results. For instance, U.S. federal law has not followed Europe's lead in barring harmful chemicals from being added to cosmetics and personal-care products. A landmark state effort failed in the California legislature. Federal law has also lagged behind the Europeans in regulating chemical flame retardants (most notably, polybrominated diphenyl ethers, or PBDEs).

There is no current directive for manufacturers to even disclose the ingredients of these products to consumers. Nor are state and federal agencies currently obliged to test the ingredients in personal-care products for safety. So, in the case of personal-care product chemicals—such as phthalates, acrylamide, ethylene oxide, and formaldehyde—buyers should be careful.

A direct challenge to children's health still exists in the form of a poison and known carcinogen that is embedded in outdoor play equipment, as well as decks, fences, and walkways. An Environmental Working Group and Healthy Building Network study found that an area of arsenic-treated wood the size of a four-year-old's hand contains an average of 120 times the amount of arsenic allowed by the EPA in a six-ounce glass of water. While the industry "voluntarily" phased-out arsenic-treated wood at the end of 2003, these wood products are still widely available. And legislative efforts to enact laws to order the elimination of this treated lumber have not been successful.

A few vaccines given to children still use thimerosal as a preservative, despite its mercury content, and many parents remain unaware of non-toxic alternatives. Many parents remain concerned about these vaccines, though an Institute of Medicine review panel in 2004 found no convincing evidence linking them to autism. Some states are trying to implement legislation to protect women of childbearing years and children from other sources of mercury exposures. For instance, a pending Alabama bill would prohibit the use of mercury alloys in dental amalgams on children less than 18 years of age, as well as pregnant or lactating women. The bill also provides that all consumers be warned that the product contains mercury.

There have been some victories in the fight to safeguard children's environmental health. Guidelines recently finalized by the California Environmental Protection Agency (EPA) call on regulatory agencies to look at cumulative exposure to pollutants, rather than merely examining the effects of one contaminant at a time.

In Washington State, the governor signed an executive order focusing on reducing persistent toxic chemicals. Citing contaminants that bio-accumulate—including mercury, dioxin, and polychlorinated biphenyl (PCBs)—he directed that the action plan be put on a fast track.

The Environmental Health Coalition (EHC) is developing guidelines for local land-use planners that will create buffers to segregate facilities using hazardous materials from homes and schools, says Joy Williams, EHC research director. "For example, we've argued that a proposed school site that has soil contaminated with lead and arsenic should be cleaned up to a higher degree than standard health risk assessment would require," she says. "These guidelines also mandate public participation in environmental decisions, so that the people who are exposed to toxins—or may be exposed—have a say in those determinations."

The challenge of protecting children's environment remains complex and crammed with loopholes. For instance, the fragrance industry remains completely unregulated. Sweet-smelling pesticides are used in many fragrances. The fact that 800 of the chemicals commonly used in scented products are neurotoxins is a testament to the influence of that industry.

Nonprofit organizations may test vitamin and mineral supplements, or analyze the quality of drinking water, but few are targeted specifically toward children. Cohesive, collated information regarding children and prospective moms is at a premium. Because conflicting convictions abound, parents become the main advocates for their children.

GREEN PRODUCTS

There is more than one reason to support environmentally friendly businesses. Besides their organic offerings, most "green" vendors also track environmental trends, cut down on wasteful packaging, and offer fair and equitable workplaces. And, when baby products are the focus of the vendor, companies encourage similar nurturing and nourishing habits for the family, the community and the world.

Baby Bee. The Burt's Bees line of natural, personal-care products for babies, including baby oils, diaper ointments, buttermilk bath products, skin creams, and dusting powders, is available in health food stores. P.O. Box

The Diaper Debate: Cloth or Plastic?

While there are heated arguments as to whether cloth or disposable diapers are more environmentally friendly, there are natural options for both.

According to *Mothering* magazine, 18 billion disposable diapers are thrown in landfills each year, and they can take as long as 500 years to decompose. After newspapers and food or beverage containers, they're the largest source of solid waste in landfills. A 1990 study concluded that cloth diapers used twice as much energy and four times as much water as disposables, and created greater air and water pollution than disposables. Another 1990 study, commissioned by Procter & Gamble, claimed that laundering a cloth diaper over its lifetime consumes up to six times the water used to make a single-use diaper, and that washing cloth diapers produced almost 10 times the water pollution of disposables.

Once staunch defenders of reusables, green groups now argue that competing social and ecological concerns make it difficult to evaluate the environmentally correct position. "We've come to appreciate that downstream solid waste is only one of many public health and resource use issues associated with diaper technology," says Allen Hershkowitz, a senior scientist at the Natural Resources Defense Council. He adds that these issues include pediatric dermatology, adult incontinence, upstream resources, manufacturing impacts, an increase in women in the work force, and more out-of-home child care.

While the debate rages, the retailers are refining their products. "Cloth diapers come in contoured, pre-folded, and fitted varieties," says Lisa Rae Oshesky, owner of the green marketing company Organic Bebe. "One type even impersonates its disposable counterparts." And contemporary cloth diapers come in sizes, unlike those available during grandma's time.

"Another textile choice for diapers is hemp," says Susie Little, founder of What's Hempenin' Baby. She notes that sailors have long exploited this fiber for its durability and absorbency—two qualities that make it an excellent option for other soggy situations. The company's signature product, Hempers ($28), shares a website with hemp clothing for mom and baby, as well as hemp-based powders and salves.

The up-front investment for cloth diapering is substantial, but the people at Indigenous Babies offer a fiscal compromise. Through their exchange program, clients can swap outgrown diapers for larger-sized used diapers or trade in used for new. Tushies diapers ($7.99) are chlorine-free and gel-free disposables made without latex or perfume. And the same company manufactures disposable diaper wipes sans scents and alcohol.

Dressing babies in organic cotton clothing has less to do with inspiring infant fashionistas and more to do with children receiving positive attention, says Lynda Fassa, co-owner of Green Babies. "A happy, healthy baby generates a great deal of affirmation from adoring adults." Organic cotton forms longer fibers, which makes a softer cloth. Fassa's most popular seller is a romper ($32) with the slogan "Give Peas a Chance" printed across the front.

13489, 701 Distribution Drive, Durham, NC 27709, (800)849-7112), www.burtsbees.com.

Baby's Only Organic. By avoiding genetically modified seeds, bovine growth hormones, steroids, antibiotics, synthetic herbicides, and harsh chemical processes, while also ensuring that cows are fed only organic grains and grasses, Nature's One manufactures one of the few organic baby formula product lines available in the United States. 818 Busch Court, Columbus, OH 43229, (888)227-7122, www.naturesone.com.

Babyworks. The focus of this vendor is on products that support healthy lifestyles, including but not limited to organic cotton diapers, clothes, toys, blankets, bedding, and bibs, as well as natural body-care products, such as vapor creams and bug repellents. 2537 A NW Upshur Street, Portland, OR 97210, (800)422-2910, www.babyworks.com.

California Baby. This company offers a nice assortment of natural health care, skin care, and hair products for babies ranging from calendula cream, diaper rash ointment, a non-talc powder, and cold and flu remedies. A line of calming baby items, a completely safe bubble bath, and sun-care products complete the product line. 3349 La Cienega Place, Los Angeles, CA (877)576-2825, www.californiababy.com.

Diaper Pin. This site started as a how-to cloth diapering page, but quickly expanded into an everything-diaper project. Product reviews, a diaper savings calculator, and vendor directory guide parents through the confusion of the cloth-diapering world. www.diaperpin.com.

Earth's Best Baby Food. Part of Hain-Celestial Group, this line of organic baby foods, cereal bars, cookies, and juices can be found in most grocery stores. The site's Doctor's Corner presents information about pregnancy, morning sickness, and nutrition, as well as links to infant, environmental, natural, and organic sites, while the Store Locator leads parents to local outlets that stock this brand. 734 Franklin Avenue #444, Garden City, NY 11530, (800)434-4246, www.earthsbest.com.

Ecobaby Organics. Huge site featuring organic cotton clothes, diapers, bassinets, bedding, towels, toys—including outdoor gear and fantasy wear. 332 Coogan Way, El Cajon, CA 92020, (800)596-7450, www.ecobaby.com.

Fresh Baby. The company's Fresh Start Kit contains all the supplies needed to make homemade, all-natural baby food in less than thirty minutes per week. Also available on the website are Mama Jewels, a breastfeeding reminder item, and the All About Me Diary, a keepsake album. Visitors may peruse monthly nutrition advice and tips for healthy eating. 616 Petoskey Street, Suite 202, Petoskey, MI 49770, (866)403-7374, www.my freshbaby.com.

Gerber's Tender Harvest. Gerber's line of certified organic baby food with first-, second-, and third-stage foods for a baby's graduating sense of taste and texture. 445 State St., Fremont, MI 49413, (800)443-7237, www.tender harvest.com, www.gerber.com.

Green Babies. This company introduces new collections of chic organic cotton clothes for babies from six through twenty-four months, and girls from 2T through 6X every spring and fall. Visitors can find a neighborhood vendor with the site's zip code locator. 28 Spring Street, Tarrytown, NY 10591, (800)603-7508, www.greenbabies.com.

Healthy Times Organic Baby Products. The only family-owned baby food business in the country, featuring four fully supplemented baby cereals; a wide variety of jarred foods, including tropical fruits; teething biscuits; cookies; and puff cereal. Because the company avoids soy, dairy, and wheat whenever possible, pediatricians often recommend this product line. All-natural soaps, lotions, and shampoos are offered at this site as well. 13200 Kirkham Way No. 104, Poway, CA 92064, (858)513-1550, www.healthytimes.com.

Heart of Vermont. Among its home, family, and baby merchandise, this site highlights organic bassinets, futon mattresses, and receiving and baby blankets made with materials grown and processed without pesticides or other chemicals. P.O. Box 612, 131 South Main Street, Barre, VT 05641, (800)639-4123, www.heartofvermont.com.

Indigenous Babies. Natural products and a sustainable philosophy are the focus of this company, which sells moccasins, diaper gear, wooden toys and games, potty-training supplies, and children's furniture. A unique component of Indigenous Babies is their exchange program, which allows clients to swap outgrown diapers for larger-sized diapers, or trade in used diapers for new. 455 Hillside Terrace, Vista, CA 92084, (877)695-8369, www.indigenousbabies.com.

Little Merry Fellows. The unique organic clothing, toys, and bedding for babies and children displayed on this website are hand assembled in the United States. P.O. Box 3637, Newtown, CT 06482, (203)270-1820, www.littlemerryfellows.com.

Lifekind Products. This site combines information and products to help reduce daily exposures to unnecessary and hazardous elements in the bathroom, bedroom, and playroom. The chemical glossary, database links, and suggested readings present parents with an array of resources for combating chemical contact. P.O. Box 1774, Grass Valley, CA 95945, (800)284-4983, www.lifekind.com.

Made 2 Matche. This company designs clothing made exclusively in the United States from organic cotton, as well as other natural fibers and low-impact fabrics. Visitors may purchase maternity fashions, nursing supplies, bath and body products, and natural toys at this site. Return any used Made 2 Matche clothing for a percentage off the next purchase. 182 Cherokee Drive, Abita Springs, LA 70420, (877)255-2217, www.made2matche.com.

Mama's Earth: The Environmental General Store. Mama's Earth provides reasonably priced, Earth-friendly basic goods and apparel for the home and family. Its children's items include organic stuffed animals, toys, towels, sheets, blankets, and diapers. To spur loved ones' indulgence in a greener philosophy, a free baby registry is available. This website is also an important information resource and clearinghouse devoted to natural and sustainable living. P.O. Box 786, Housatonic, MA 01236, (800)620-7388, www.mamasearth.com.

Mother's Nature. Proponents of attachment parenting, breast-feeding, and cloth-diapering, this site's creators also highlight vendors for baby and maternity clothing toys and gear. For the ultimate recycling experience, visitors can register at no charge to join the auctions, where parents buy and sell used and new items. 620 Meadow Drive, McKinney, TX 75069, www.mothersnature.com.

New Native Baby. These makers of 100 percent organic cotton baby carriers also offer diaper bags, hooded and receiving blankets, doll carriers, T-shirts, and an assortment of native American herbals. P.O. Box 218, Soquel, CA 95073, (800)646-1682, www.newnativebaby.com.

Organic Bebe. Everything parents need for stocking a nursery—including music for babies and kids, parenting books and videos, clothing, skin care, nursery supplies, toys, strollers, diapering and feeding supplies, and a gift registry for expecting moms and dads. 233 Harvard Boulevard, Lynn Haven, FL 32444, (866)734-2634, www.organicbebe.com.

Organic Cotton Alternatives. This site's Natural Nursery concentrates on organic products, such as Moses baskets, crib mattresses, and linens. Yoga and pet supplies also available. 3120 Central Avenue SE, Albuquerque, NM 87106, (888)645-4452, www.organiccottonalts.com.

Seventh Generation. One of the nation's leading brands of nontoxic and environmentally safe household products. Chlorine-free diapers, extra-gentle laundry liquid for baby clothing, baby wipes, and nontoxic household cleaners are available at health food stores. Guests to the website may enroll to receive the free *Non-Toxic Times*. 212 Battery Street, Suite A, Burlington, VT 05401, (800)456-1191, www.seventhgeneration.com.

Tushies and Mother Nature Diapers. Both brands of disposable diapers are gel-free, latex-free, perfume-free, and dye-free as well as available in preemie sizes. The natural baby wipes are hypoallergenic and alcohol-free. Automatic front-door delivery can be arranged through the website or toll-free numbers. 675 Industrial Boulevard, Delta, CO 81416, (800)344-6379 or (800)569-1462, www.tushies.com or www.tendercarediapers.com.

Under the Nile. The apparel, diapers, and toys from this vendor are made from 100-percent certified organic Egyptian cotton. 2070 San Benito Drive, Fremont, CA 94539, (800)883-4402, www.underthenile.com.

What's Hempenin' Baby (Baby Hemp). As one of the most absorbent textiles, hemp is the focus of this site's selection of diapers and diaper accessories. BabyHemp clothing and Mama Hemp wear for pregnancy and nursing join a new line of vegan bath and body products for baby—including hemp baby powder, baby wash, oil, lotion, and bar soap. P.O. Box 21, Fredericktown, OH 43019, (740)694-4442, www.babyhemp.com.

White Lotus Home. This vendor specializes in mattresses manufactured without chemical flame retardants, plastics, and steel. Also offered are beautiful, sustainably harvested, chemical-free wood cribs made from only North American trees, as well as organic bedding, furniture, and meditation pillows. 191 Hamilton Street, New Brunswick, NJ 08901, (877)426-3623, www.whitelotus.net.

WHAT YOU CAN DO

It may be comforting to think that any baby product on the market has been proven safe, but that's unlikely to be true. Parents need to educate themselves about the common chemicals that, for example, make pajamas fire-retardant, or preserve baby foods for long shelf lives. In many cases, natural alternatives exist that may cost slightly more, but are well worth the extra investment—for your child, your family, and your community. Beyond baby items, it's time to look at the entire house and how it can be made safer for your baby. Below, we lay out a strategy to consider, looking room by room.

Home Entrance

Ask visitors to kindly remove shoes, a practice that keeps contaminants—such as lead—from dropping onto the very floors upon which your baby crawls. Vacuum regularly throughout the house with a HEPA vacuum cleaner to pick up lead and other contaminants. Lead can be found in any home—usually not in the much-publicized form of paint chips—but as dust. Windows, coated with lead paint in years past, sliding open and shut will generate minute metal particles.

"Ninety percent of houses built before 1940 contain lead paint," says Pierre Erville, spokesperson for the National Safety Council (NSC). "Any house constructed before 1978—the year this paint additive was banned—should be tested for lead."

The irreversible brain damage this metal causes in children endures. In a case of upside-down logic, low lead levels can cause more harm than higher readings. Clinical trials of lead-lowering drugs intended to reverse the IQ damage have been disappointing. And this toxic metal leaves an especially harmful heritage for females. "Girls exposed to lead during childhood," Erville says, "will release it during pregnancy and menopause."

Living Areas

Use flooring made of natural materials such as wool, bamboo, or wood. When it comes time to buy furniture, opt for secondhand solid furniture, antiques, new furniture made of solid wood (a controversial idea in some circles), or other furniture found to emit no or low amounts of airborne chemicals. In short, don't willy nilly buy carpet or bargain furniture that is made of particleboard and covered with thin veneers that look like woods such as cherry or oak.

Your goal is to avoid items that contain volatile organic compounds (VOCs), which have been implicated in auditory abnormalities such as speech discrimination problems and hearing loss, as well as developmental defects and abnormal hormone "mimicking." Federal researchers are beginning to explore how exposures that take place in the womb may cause permanent damage that manifests later in life. Some health issues that the investigators have been examining include reproductive and hormonal disorders, cardiopulmonary diseases, and brain and central nervous system diseases, such as Parkinson's and Alzheimer's.

"By their nature, all of these compounds are potentially harmful," says Dr. Harold E. Buttram, a fellow of the American Academy of Environmental Medicine. "They are found in thousands of commercial products using petrochemicals, such as cleaning solutions, solvents, synthetic fragrances and perfumes.

"Fresh paint, carpeting and wallpaper all offgas volatile organic compounds," says Buttram. One VOC, formaldehyde—a suspected carcinogen—is found in such diverse products as perfume, permanent-press textiles, and particleboard.

So, use low-emitting paints, natural cleaning solutions, and fragrances containing natural oils.

Bathroom

Consider ditching the plastic shower curtain in favor of a glass door. That's because soft plastic shower curtains tend to contain phthalates, a chemical also found in bath and beauty products, nail polish, and fragrances (limit use of those). Scientists have found evidence that this chemical is associated with premature breast development in females, which alludes to links between youthful exposures and puberty. A recent Centers for Disease Control (CDC) assessment of phthalate exposure in the general population recorded high amounts in women of childbearing age. One study confirms the presence of phthalates in samples of blood taken from newborns.

Opt for glass baby bottles, not plastic. When heated, clear plastic bottles made of polycarbonate have been found to leach a chemical called bisphenol A into baby formula at forty times the safe limits (see sidebar, page 161). Bisphenol A disrupts the endocrine system. By its nature, this chemical mimics the female hormone, estrogen. And it has been linked to reduced sperm production, increased prostate weight, and endometriosis, even at very low doses. Studies link breast and prostate cancer, miscarriage, and even obesity to the bisphenol A running through our systems.

Newborn babies and unborn babies pay the highest price when this element is in their lives. Imbalances of hormones have pronounced—but sometimes delayed—effects when they occur early in life. And polycarbonate water bottles have been associated with chromosomal damage.

"Scientific studies now highlight possible, indeed likely, negative health effects," says Myers. We should take every step possible to avoid putting polycarbonate plastic in contact with food and water."

Another nursery issue: Don't use anti-germicidal soap, chemical air fresheners, and commercial carpet cleaners, which often contain pesticides. Use nontoxic alternatives (see sidebar, page 170). Even when parents are meticulous about keeping baby's spaces free of labeled pesticides, they may be unintentionally introducing these highly toxic elements indirectly into their baby's breathing zones.

Also, buy nontoxic sleepwear for the baby and growing child. Some acrylics and natural materials with tight weaves and heavy weights pass flame retardancy standards without the use of polybrominated diphenyl ethers (PBDEs), which virtually saturate our environments and can be found in electronics, carpets, furniture, clothing, and, most predominantly, polyurethane foam. The chemicals are rapidly accumulating in humans and wildlife. Although the means by which such fire retardants get into the environment is largely still a mystery, the chemicals are now found worldwide in house dust, indoor and outdoor air, and waterways.

According to the Environmental Working Group, the EPA has set no safety standards or other regulations for their manufacture, use or disposal. Only California has banned some chemical fire retardants with the phase-out to be complete by 2008. If current trends continue, many watchdog organizations predict that the average person will have levels of PBDEs shown to cause developmental damage within ten years.

"PBDEs interrupt brain and organ development, affect thyroid hor-

Focus on Formula

While most American women realize that breastfeeding is best for their baby, lifestyle choices and job realities can dictate the use of formula instead. When your baby is allergic to cow's milk formula, it can be a relief to find there's a widely available alternative: soy-based powders and liquids.

Soy formula, used for centuries in Asia, but only since 1909 in the West, has become enormously popular, capturing 25 percent of the formula market. Soy's good reputation makes it the healthy choice, right? Unfortunately, it's not that simple. Research on thyroid and reproductive disorders, as well as rising concerns over genetically engineered (GE) soybeans, suggest soy-based infant formula could be setting up your baby for a triple whammy.

What's good for adults isn't always good for babies. Infants react differently than adults to the high levels of disease-fighting phytoestrogens in soy. In 1996, Dr. Kenneth Setchell of the Children's Hospital Medical Center in Cincinnati studied five leading brands of soy-based baby milk. He found the products contain the phytoestrogen level of several contraceptive pills every day,

about six to eleven times the amount that alters the menstrual cycle. But, in a 2002 interview, Dr. Setchell added that soy formula has an established safety record, and that any phytoestrogen effects may not be detrimental.

"Infants on soy formula are two to three times more likely to develop thyroid disease than if they were drinking cow formula or breast milk," Dr. Naomi Baumslag, clinical professor of pediatrics at Georgetown University Medical School, said in a 1999 interview.

But before you throw out your miso soup and Tofutti ice cream, remember that soy has many positive benefits—at least for adults. Eating moderate levels of natural, organic soy is a time-tested health benefit. But because the milk source makes up nearly the entire diet of infants, soy babies are at an increased risk for harm.

The Infant Formula Council (now known as the International Formula Council) said as long ago as 1998 that studies "have not indicated any harmful effect" from phytoestrogen.

mones, and are suspected of causing cancer," says Renee Sharp, a senior EWG analyst. "And PBDEs can cause permanent neurological and developmental damage and delays at surprisingly low levels." Those most at risk for PBDE contamination are pregnant women, developing fetuses, infants, and young children. "Scientists have found this chemical present in both placental blood and breast milk," says Sharp.

The Green Shower

By their nature, baby showers are wasteful events. Typically, mountains of wrapping paper, single-use cardboard decorations, and forgotten plastic favors litter the host's house after the party. But these environmentally depleting celebrations can be transformed into eco-events with just a few simple alterations.

"Encourage guests to create wrapping from reusable items, such as receiving blankets or cloth diapers," says Lynda Fassa, co-owner of Green Babies. That way, she says, your baby's first effect on the planet will not be a negative one. At Baby Shower Central, an "Earth First" theme calls for hosts to give seed packages and baby trees as prizes. "As for gifts, I suggest cloth diapering and breastfeeding supplies," says Marsha Roberts, owner of Baby Shower Central. "Diaper cakes (not the edible kind) are practical, reusable, and much nicer to look at than paper banners and streamers." Constructed with diapers, pacifiers, burp cloths, bibs, bottles, shoes, pins, and receiving blankets, the multiple tiers present prospective parents with plenty of child-centered paraphernalia.

"Diaper wreaths and sock rose bouquets are popular recyclable decorations, also," says Roberts. A how-to page leads virtual visitors through the simple process of creating these practical decorations and includes links for ordering ready-made versions.

"A wonderful alternative to throwaway party favors is our set of Party! Bubble Baths ($3.49)," says Sue Farr, spokesperson for California Baby. "The bubbling agent in almost all of the commercial bubble baths strips the mucous membranes and thus promotes yeast or bladder infections," she adds. "Because we use a gentle, noninvasive bubbling agent, women and little girls of all ages can safely enjoy bubble baths again."

California Baby produces other lotions and potions for babies and people with sensitive skin, including a wide assortment of sun protectants and aromatherapy spritzers. "A great eco-baby shower game is to blindfold guests and offer them spoonfuls of three different traditional jarred baby foods," says Fassa. Participants then guess the flavors. Next, guests taste test three organic meal selections. The flavorful results usually surprise even enviro-skeptics.

Kitchen

Grandma was right. Baking soda, vinegar and water are powerful nontoxic cleaners (see sidebar on page 170 for better cleaning methods). As for tableware, Grandma never used plastic, and tests suggest that's a good strategy. Tests on polycarbonate tableware used in Japanese primary schools indicated that bisphenol A will leach into hot liquids from plastic containers and confirmed that worn, scratched polycarbonate leaches at a higher rate.

Consumers Union and FDA studies duplicate the Japanese results regarding the positive correlation between high temperatures and leaching, but also noted that significant leaching occurred at room temperatures, too.

Foodwise, buy organic varieties or, second best, wash conventionally grown produce diligently (see more strategies in Chapter One).

Many popular fruits and vegetables—including common baby food staples such as peaches, green beans, and apples—contain pesticide residues that exceed the government's "safe dose" for children by a factor of one hundred or more, according to tests by Environmental Working Group, a watchdog organization specializing in green-themed investigations.

Play Area

Opt for toys made of wood, cloth, and rubber—not soft pliable plastic, such as that found in inflatable toys, squeeze toys, dolls, or in items elsewhere in the home, such as the plastic shower curtain. These soft plastics can contain hazardous chemicals called phthalates, which can leach out of the very toys chewed by investigative babies. According to the Our Stolen Future website, about one billion pounds of this substance is produced every year. Some phthalates affect male reproductive development, especially when exposed in utero. The Food and Drug Administration (FDA) concluded that exposure during gestation of a male fetus to one particular phthalate could harm the fetus's testicles.

Young children come directly into contact with phthalates during play. Toys containing phthalates cause a wide range of toxic effects in laboratory mammals, including effects on organ development, cancer incidence, and reproductive capabilities. And, when Greenpeace tested sixty-three plastic toys for children under three, scientists found that almost all contained between 10 and 40 percent of these hazardous softening additives by weight. Best bet: Opt for old-fashioned cloth Raggedy Ann and Andy dolls, wooden blocks, wood puzzles, wood trains.

Make It Yourself

Did you know that the commercial cleaners stored under your kitchen sink are considered "household hazardous waste" to lots of government agencies? So is that drain cleaner, the bug killer, that chemical fertilizer, that toilet bowl cleaner, and several other items. Below, find nontoxic alternatives—which coincidentally save money.

AROUND THE HOUSE

All-Purpose Cleaners

Mix three tablespoons washing soda in one quart of warm water, or use baking soda and a small amount of water.

Kitchen Countertop Sanitizer and Vegetable or Fruit Spray

According to *Science News* and a NASA newsletter, a food scientist at Virginia Polytechnic Institute and State University came up with this recipe: Spritz countertops, cutting boards, vegetables, or fruit with vinegar (white or apple cider vinegar), then spritz with ordinary 3 percent hydrogen peroxide. Rinse produce with water. No, there's no lingering aftertaste. Tests found that the two mists killed virtually all salmonella, shigella, or *E. coli* bacteria—making it more effective than chlorine bleach.

Kitchen/Bathroom Surfaces

Use baking soda on a damp sponge to clean and deodorize. Toss sponge into clothes washer or dishwasher to kill germs.

Room Deodorizer

At least 2 to 4 tablespoons of baking soda, or ½ to 1 cup of cat litter used in trash cans, or 1 cup of vinegar in a dish will absorb odors. Cross-ventilation and fragrant potpourri will also help to freshen air. Replace every three months.

Floor Cleaner

Wash slate, ceramic tile, and no-wax floors with ½ cup of white vinegar mixed in ½ gallon of warm water.

Laundry

Eliminate soap residue by adding 1 cup of white vinegar to the final rinse water. DO NOT use chlorine bleach and vinegar together—you will produce harmful vapors. Add ¼ to ½ cup of baking soda to the rinse cycle to make clothes feel soft and smell fresh.

Rug and Upholstery Cleaner

Clean immediately with soda water and baking soda paste. Vacuum.

Glass Cleaner

Mix 2 tablespoons white vinegar with 1 quart water. Increasing the vinegar will deepen the cleaning action. Put into labeled spray bottle. To remove stubborn hard water spots and streaks, use undiluted vinegar.

IN THE BATHROOM

Disinfectant

Sponge on isopropyl alcohol. Allow to dry to ensure effectiveness. Be sure to use in a well-ventilated area.

Drain Cleaner/Opener

Pour about ½ cup of baking soda down the drain. Add ½ cup of vinegar and cover drain opening, if possible. Let stand for a few minutes, then pour boiling water down the drain to unclog and deodorize drains. A mechanical snake or plunger will manually unclog drains. This is safer than commercial cleaners; some can burn skin.

Tub and Tile Cleaner

Use white vinegar full-strength on mold and mildew stains. Add ¼ cup (or more) of vinegar to 1 gallon of warm water to clean most dirt. To remove film buildup on tubs, wipe full-strength vinegar on with a sponge, then use baking soda or borax as you would scouring powder. Rub with a damp sponge; rinse with water. To prevent soap scum and mildew buildup in the shower, wipe walls dry after every use.

Toilet Bowl Cleaner

Sprinkle baking soda in bowl, then drizzle with vinegar and scour with toilet brush.

Sources: University of Maryland College of Agriculture and Natural Resources, New Mexico State University Cooperative Extension Service, City of Albuquerque Solid Waste Management Department, Solid Waste Authority of Central Ohio.

Backyard and Deck

When building a deck or play set, don't use ordinary pressure-treated wood, which is treated with cancer-promoting arsenic; instead inquire about the wide range of safer wood options, such as composites made from recycled plastic or wood treated with borate. Recent studies point toward a relationship between arsenic and type II diabetes, as well as immunological and cardiovascular problems.

The consequences of combining children and arsenic present ample incentives to use precautions once your toddler is old enough to toddle outside. Children are less efficient than adults at converting arsenic into a less toxic substance. And according to an EPA risk assessment, 90 percent of all children face a greater than one in one million cancer risk from their exposure to arsenic-treated wood. In southern states, 10 percent of all children face a cancer risk that is one hundred times higher, according to EWG.

While manufacturers began phasing out arsenic-treated woods for residential use in 2004, decades will pass before all playground equipment, decks and fencing containing arsenic are replaced. Even then, the chemical will be embedded in the soil and foliage around this poisonous wood's former home for generations.

In the end, parents need to cultivate a global perspective to defend their children from environmental threats. First, adults need to learn to identify the most significant dangers to their offspring. Phillip Landrigan's seminal work, *Raising Healthy Children in a Toxic World: 101 Smart Solutions for Every Family* is a good starting point for concerned parents.

A clear grasp of the scope of various governmental bodies is vital. For instance, knowing what issues fall under the jurisdiction of the EPA, the Consumer Product Safety Commission (CPSC) and the FDA will be invaluable when parents choose to take a proactive stance.

A University of California study recommends that the state form an interagency Office of Environmental Health Tracking under the auspices of the Department of Health and the EPA to collect and collate data regarding environmentally caused diseases and disorders. Because toxins are believed to be causing 10 percent of the neurodevelopmental problems in children, researchers believe this would be an effective way to detect and diminish risky elements. Parents from other states might propose the same type of program to their own state legislators.

"Many of the risks of environmental pollutants can be reduced by individual actions . . . choices that parents or parents-to-be make about what they eat and how they live," says Myers. "Some, however, depend upon changes in public health protections. People should look for ways to support efforts that advance health standards, and let their voices be heard. A good starting point is the Collaborative for Health and the Environment, www.CHEforHealth.org and www.ProtectingOurHealth.org."

Prospective and new parents can monitor the ingredients in baby products, encourage vendors to stock organic goods, and register their concerns with watchdog organizations and government regulatory groups as well as local and national legislators.

Parents can also depend on the wisdom of their forebears and rely on the basics when protecting their children. Good hygiene, clean homes, organic foods, and fresh air will go a long way toward helping our young ones live healthy and long lives.

Striving to give your baby the best of all beginnings and choosing an environmentally aware attitude are symbiotic. And there is great comfort in the fact that your children's environmental footprints will remain as small as the ones on their birth certificate because of your actions.

Getting Involved with Children's Environments

Parents can consult these nonprofit and government resources for an array of perspectives, information, and guidance about creating healthy surroundings for children of all ages.

Agency for Toxic Substances and Disease Registry. Monitors relevant children's health issues and stimulates new projects to benefit kids. 1600 Clifton Road, E42, Atlanta, GA 30333, (888)422-8737, www.atsdr.cdc.gov/child.

America's Children and the Environment. Collects quantitative information about environmental contaminants in air, water, food, and soil, concentrations of contaminants in the bodies of mothers and children, and childhood diseases that may be influenced by environmental factors. EPA Headquarters, Ariel Rios Building, 1200 Pennsylvania Avenue NW, Washington, DC 20460, (202)272-0167, www.epa.gov/envirohealth/children/index.htm.

BAM! Body and Mind. An online destination for kids created by the Centers for Disease Control and Prevention focusing on healthy lifestyle choices and using kid-friendly language, games, quizzes, and other interactive features. Centers for Disease Control and Prevention, 1600 Clifton Road, MS C-04, Atlanta, GA 30333, www.bam.gov.

Center for Children's Health and the Environment. The nation's first academic research and policy center to examine the links between exposure to toxic pollutants and childhood illness. Mount Sinai School of Medicine, P.O. Box 1043, One Gustave Levy Place, New York, NY 10029, (212)241-7840, www.childenvironment.org.

Children's Environmental Health Network. A national multidisciplinary organization whose mission is to protect the fetus and the child from environmental health hazards. This site's Resource Guide offers one-stop shopping to find any and all organizations involved in children's health. 110 Maryland Avenue NE, Suite 511, Washington, DC 20002, (202)543-4033, www.cehn.org.

Children's Environmental Health Occupational Environmental Health Unit. A newly designed and updated website by the World Health Organization geared specifically to children's environmental health. Department for the Protection of Human Environment, World Health Organization, Avenue Appia, 1211—Geneva 27, Switzerland, www.who.int/ceh/en.

Children's Health Environmental Coalition. The single best source of up-to-date, pertinent information, CHEC's clearinghouse and resource center keep close watch on topics geared toward kids' well-being. Among its many resources, prospective parents can learn more about constructing safe home environments month-by-month with the First Steps e-newsletter, free with registration, from the CHEC website. The agency's Virtual House leads visitors through a room-by-room audit of less-than-healthy substances found in the typical American home. P.O. Box 1540, Princeton, NJ 08542, (609)252-1915, www.checnet.org.

Collaborative on Health and the Environment. Health-affected groups, scientists, health professionals, and environmental organizations formed this coalition to serve as a resource to help reduce public exposure to environmental toxicants. c/o Commonweal, P.O. Box 316, Bolinas, CA 94924, (415)868-0970, www.cheforhealth.org.

Environmental Health Perspectives Online. A peer-reviewed journal of the National Institutes of Health with a monthly section devoted to children's health and environmental medicine. Field notes, breaking news and searchable archives by topic or term make this site a first-stop research must. www.ehp.niehs.nih.gov.

Environmental Health News. Published daily by Environmental Health Sciences, a not-for-profit organization founded in 2002 to help increase public understanding of emerging scientific links between environmental exposures and human health. www.EnvironmentalHealthNews.org.

The Germ-Fighting Paradox

Scrubbing nurseries with germ-killing products is a common practice among parents mindful of microorganisms. And spending money on antibacterial agents may give adults a sense of security, but it's only a false one.

"Using antigerm products is a bad idea, especially around children," says Elizabeth Sword, executive director of the Children's Health Environmental Coalition. "During their first years, kids have to develop immune systems to fight off basic colds and flus. And, when parents use these products, they kill the good bacteria with the bad bacteria. A common ingredient, triclosan, actually mutates genes of the bacteria, raising concerns over the eventual creation of superbugs and antibiotic resistances."

"Germ-killing" soaps are unnecessary and even risky. Most antibacterials contain pesticides and, sometimes, even formaldehyde. More than 200 parents called the Chemical Injury and Illness Network (CIIN) for advice on coping with nerve damage after bathing young children with antibacterial soap during the 1990s, according to Cynthia Wilson, CIIN executive director. Companies eventually lightened up on the amount of pesticide in their products—but these toxic chemicals are still part of the formula in many antibacterial soaps.

Seventy-six percent of all liquid soaps and 29 percent of bar soaps have bacteria-killing chemicals, according to CHEC. Some hand soaps, shoe inserts, cutting boards, knives, socks, and toothpastes may include this element. For a time, manufacturers even added this element to highchairs and toys, lauding its anti-germ characteristics but neglecting to mention that the equipment would still need to be sanitized, essentially negating the purpose of its germ-killing properties.

Environmental Health Watch. Provides information, assistance and advocacy, including telephone consultation, group presentations, fact sheets, data mapping, and news links. Cleveland Environmental Center, 3500 Lorain Avenue, #302, Cleveland, OH 44113, (216)961-4646, www.ehw.org.

Environmental Working Group. A watchdog group that conducts and tracks environmental investigations, as well as furnishes practical pointers on how to minimize chemically induced threats to children. 1436 U Street NW, Suite 100, Washington, DC 20009, (202)667-6982, www.ewg.org.

Healthy Child Online. A comprehensive electronic resource that provides parents and caregivers with free information and newsletters about holistic alternatives to promote natural health. www.healthychild.com.

Household Products Database. A feature of the National Institutes of Health website that allows visitors to search for health and safety information by product type, ingredient, or effect, such as headache or dizziness. www.householdproducts.nlm.nih.gov.

The National Institute of Child Health and Human Development Information Resource Center. Provides information on health issues within the organization's research domain to the public. Through its research center, callers receive access to trained information specialists, health information and support organizations. P.O. Box 3006, Rockville, MD 20847, (800)370-2943.

The Noise Pollution Clearinghouse. The NPC is a national nonprofit organization with a mission to raise awareness, distribute information and strengthen laws regarding noise pollution. P.O. Box 1137, Montpelier, VT 05601-1137, (888)200-8332, www.nonoise.org.

Office of Children's Health Protection. The EPA's gateway to information about environmental risks to children from everyday hazards—including pesticides, carbon monoxide, and lead. U.S. Environmental Protection Agency, 1200 Pennsylvania Avenue NW, Mail Code 1107A, Room 2512, Ariel Rios North, Washington, DC 20004, (202)564-2188, yosemite.epa.gov/ochp/ochpweb.nsf/homepage.

Pediatric Environmental Health Specialty Units. This toll-free number connects parents to specialists for referrals to one of eleven PEHSU regional centers involved in education, training, and outreach as well as clinical consultations and evaluations for children who may have been exposed to hazardous environmental substances. 1010 Vermont Avenue NW, Suite 513, Washington, DC 20005, (888)347-2632, www.aoec.org/pehsu.htm.

Pesticide Action Network North America. Works to replace pesticide use with ecologically sound and socially just alternatives, while the Pesticide Database and the Pesticide Advisor present the latest facts to visitors. 49

Powell Street, Suite 500, San Francisco, CA 94102, (415)981-1771, www.panna.org.

Preventing Harm. The Clean Water Fund's resource and action center for children and the environment, which interweaves current initiatives, critical hotlines, and up-to-the-minute alerts with practical advice, discussions and forums. 4455 Connecticut Avenue NW, Suite A300-16, Washington, DC 20008-2328, (202)895-0432, www.preventingharm.org.

chapter nine

Kids' Stuff

Starting Them Young, from the Nursery to the Bookshelf

$\mathcal{T}$he song lyric tells us that children are our future, but when it comes to the environment, they have a lot to learn from our mistakes. You've heard the grim statistics about global warming, deforestation, air and water pollution, and the toxic chemicals we are all carrying around in our bodies. Even native people living near the North Pole have high levels of cancer-causing dioxin stored in their fat tissue. But changes can be made, and they start with parents and kids recognizing the problems and doing something about them.

The good news is that toxic exposure can be limited by making a few smart choices for your kids, and teaching them about the hazards and wonders of their environments has never been easier. Environmental education, a mere toddler in the 1970s, is now a respected educational field with numerous resources, from books to websites to local nature centers and camps that just didn't exist forty years ago. And teaching your kids about the natural world around them and why it's important may help you learn a thing or two as well. As a parent, educating your children to be savvy consumers is one of the best things you can do to help the planet. One big lesson is that commercials are not objective truth, and that corporations, whether they produce food, video games,

Green Babies "Give Peas a Chance" romper, www.greenbabies.com

sneakers, or news, are more concerned with making a sale than doing what's best for you or your family.

Even young children can understand how to read food labels or think about wasteful packaging. They can grasp the simple truth that if they take care with their toys they will be less easily broken, and that many of the things they own can be repaired instead of replaced.

Other lessons will come with time. You can't expect elementary-age kids to make the connection between their plastic toys and factory waste (even if you point it out to them), and they're not likely to go on the Internet to research a company's social and environmental practices before making that big purchase.

Perhaps the most difficult lesson for many parents to teach is the simplest: If you want environmentally conscious children, set a good example. That means incorporating "green living" into your everyday life. While many companies use misleading advertising to hide wasteful or environmentally destructive practices, there are also hundreds of companies selling organic foods just for kids; pesticide-free clothing; or green-themed music, movies, and books, which help parents educate their children about their health and the environment in age-appropriate ways.

CURRENT EVENTS/LEGISLATIVE/POLITICAL

Kids and the Media

Even the savviest child will fall prey to new-toy lust, since kids are even more conscious of fitting in and having the right "stuff" than adults are. Advertising companies spend billions to buy kids' brand loyalty, inundating the average American child with more than 20,000 commercials a year—about fifty-five per day. All this because, according to *The Kids Market: Myths and Realities*, by James McNeil, children's spending (independent from parents) has doubled every ten years for the past three decades, and tripled in the 1990s. Kids' direct buying power is expected to exceed $51 billion by 2006. Among older kids, from twelve to nineteen, spending topped out at $115 billion of their own money in 2001, up from $63 billion just four years earlier. And when it comes to kids' influence on family purchases, that number grows to $500 billion.

According to *Children's Business*, a marketing magazine, brand loyalty can begin by age two, so teaching your kids about advertisers' real mission is important, since children under the age of eight "absorb information without any screens—meaning that a child that age doesn't understand that a commercial may not be true," according to Betsy Taylor, president of the nonprofit Center for a New American Dream (CNAD), and author of *What Kids Really Want That Money Can't Buy: Tips for Parenting in a Commercial World*.

CNAD is working with the nonprofit group Commercial Alert to ask Congress to repeal a 1980 law that removes any limits from advertising aimed at children. Sweden allows no advertising to children, a stance these activists would like the United States to emulate, especially limiting advertising to very young children.

The term "greenwashing" is now found in the *Oxford English Dictionary*, defined as "disinformation disseminated by an organization so as to present an environmentally responsible image." Misleading ads can easily fool busy parents, and for kids it may be especially hard to discern when a company is hiding bad practices behind a green banner. Recent winners of the "Don't be Fooled" award by Earth Resources for Living Green are good examples of how these ads work. Simply Orange juice's tag line reads, "Do not disturb nature at work" over a close-up of an orange—but the company uses pesticides on its fruit. Tyson Chicken advertises that its poultry is "all natural," even though the chickens live quite artificially, as millions of debeaked birds live in cramped cages piled from floor to ceiling, encouraging disease and resulting in widespread antibiotic use. Neither company changed its ad after receiving the "award," though Tyson Chicken announced it is cutting back on antibiotic use due to public pressure. A commitment to ending antibiotic use would be a real step toward all-natural chicken. Deconstructing these ads can be difficult, requiring research and critical thinking for kids and parents alike.

McSchools?

As recently as fifteen years ago, schools were relatively free from the commercial influence of corporations. But now Channel One, featuring ten minutes of news and two minutes of commercials daily, is compulsory viewing in 40 percent of U.S. middle and high schools. Channel One hooks its Board of Education customers by giving video equipment free to schools that agree to air its daily program. Companies pay up to $195,000 for a thirty-second ad, which is shown to a captive audience of eight million students. The ads reinforce consumerism and a taste for junk food; food product promotions make up half of all advertising aimed at kids.

"Marketers have come to realize that all roads eventually lead to schools," Ed Winter, cofounder of Channel One, told *Business Week*. Since Channel One opened the door in 1990, corporations have found struggling school systems receptive to advertising on school buses, lockers, along school corridors, and even on textbook covers and inside them.

Ostensibly a fund-raising promotion, McDonald's restaurants in Washington State get teachers to work shifts at a local McDonald's restaurant on the slowest night of the week—Tuesdays. Promotional signs are put up in hallways and on the marquee in front of schools encouraging kids to eat at the fast food purveyor and see their teachers taking orders and bussing tables. McDonald's then donates part of the profits from that night to the school.

Coca-Cola sponsors Parent-Teacher Association (PTA) events, even as the website for the National PTA decries advertising to kids in school. Box top programs net schools very small amounts of money, yet the sponsors get lots of free promotion for the five or ten cents that is donated to the school per top.

One posting on the bulletin board of the Citizens' Campaign for Commercial-Free Schools tells the following sobering story (the name of the child involved has been changed): "When our daughter, Sarah, was in the second grade we encountered the Pizza Hut reading program. If the child read a certain amount each month, he/she received a coupon for a personal pan pizza. Sarah loved to read, so not thinking much about the long-range impact, our family participated. Then summer came and Pizza Hut pizza was the only type of pizza Sarah wanted to order. Yikes, I fell for it!

"In the third grade, we opted out of the Pizza Hut reading program. I told Sarah's teacher we wanted Sarah to learn to read for the love of reading, not for the love of eating. She said fine, it was an optional program. I explained our reasons to Sarah and she said, 'Oh, you mean they are bribing kids to read?'

"All was well until the end of the year when Pizza Hut put on a party for Sarah's class. Sarah wasn't allowed to eat any pizza because she was the only child who didn't participate in the program. She had to sit in the corner while other kids ate pizza and partied. Sarah came home crying that day."

Some cash-strapped school cafeterias now serve junk foods during the lunch hour, and advertising can be found everywhere from the lunchroom to the gym. Because young people and kids spend so much of their disposable money on food, that's where the most significant marketing is directed.

An amazing 71 percent of California high schools serve fast food, half of which is branded. Taco Bell, Subway, Domino's, and Pizza Hut are the most popular brands, according to the 2000 California High School Fast Food Survey. In Fayette County, Georgia, selling pizza, hamburgers, and French fries—even supersizing them—has been a cash-cow for the school cafeterias. Kids who can pay will buy more expensive, fattier foods instead of the meals designed to meet federal nutrition standards.

Some school systems are fighting back; starting in the fall of 2003, New York City schools have banned candy, soda, and sweet snacks from vending machines and replaced them with pretzels, energy bars, water, 100 percent fruit juices, and low-fat, low-salt chips. Sugar, fat, and salt will also be trimmed from the lunch program, which serves 800,000 students.

Home Toxin Hazards

American parents spend billions of dollars a year on products to keep kids healthy and safe. From baby seats in ever-safer minivans to electric outlet covers, no price is too high when it comes to protecting children.

But it turns out that parents have been overlooking a significant threat to children's health. Environmental toxins pose numerous risks to growing children's hormone systems, developing brains, immune systems, and major organs. These toxic risks aren't only found near major industrial sites; they are common in our homes and schools where our children spend the majority of their time.

More than 80,000 new synthetic chemical compounds have been developed and released into the environment since World War II. Fewer than half of these have been tested for their potential toxicity to humans, and fewer still have been assessed for their particular toxicity to children, according to the Children's Health and Environmental Coalition (CHEC). Many of these chemicals can be found in products used daily around the house and in schools or daycare facilities.

For many years the scientific community treated children like "little adults," but in 1993 the National Academy of Sciences recognized that children need a higher level of protection from chemical exposure. In 1996, the Environmental Protection Agency (EPA) introduced the "National Agenda to Protect Children's Health from Environmental Threats," which announced that special risk assessments of childhood chemical exposure must be undertaken as a matter of urgent national priority.

It turns out that not only are children proportionally exposed to more toxins—they drink more water and breathe more air in proportion to their body size—but those bodies are much less able to process and remove chemicals than adults. Kids' bodies are so busy growing it is difficult for them to process many chemicals.

Children are exposed to more pesticides since they consume more fruits and vegetables than adults, and live closer to the floor where toxins that are heavier than air settle. Elizabeth Sword, executive director of CHEC adds, "It's the additive exposure of the variety of chemicals that creates the problem for kids. It's not always one thing; it's the window cleaner, it's what comes in on your shoes, the smoker who visited yesterday, and the unventilated home, beating on a small developing organism, battering it constantly." CHEC has launched a national campaign to let people know that it's this chemical soup that we all live around that needs to be studied.

Reading, Writing—and Toxins

Unfortunately, no matter how well you teach your children, or how toxin-free you make your home, by the time they reach school age, kids face some serious chemical hazards at their schools and on their playgrounds. The start of the academic year arrives with both new clothes and a round of illness, which is usually attributed to common germs. However, sickness may be caused or exacerbated by offgassing from wall paints, carpet, sealants, cleaning supplies, pesticides, and herbicides, not to mention molds. A daunting list of common chemicals, including volatile organic compounds (VOCs), polyvinyl chloride (PVC), chromated copper arsenate (CCA), radon, lead, and carbon monoxide, have been implicated in making children ill.

New school buildings, newly painted classrooms and even brightly colored "fun" carpets can have especially high levels of VOCs (formaldehyde, benzene, and tolulene are some), as they "offgas" into the surrounding air. Energy efficient buildings that are tightly sealed off from outside air can accumulate harmful vapors, and ventilation systems can circulate these vapors continually if not properly set up.

Fortunately, there are great alternatives to the paints, particleboard, cleaning supplies, glues, and carpeting that are VOC culprits. Because VOCs can be emitted for years, can cause cancer and damage to the central nervous system, and can cause short-term health problems like sore throats, headaches, nausea, dizziness, and fatigue, it is worth the time for school districts to find alternative products that are low or free of these chemicals.

Although the asbestos threat has been well covered in the media, some schools are still riddled with the toxin, which can cause lung cancer after being released into the air. Molds produce allergens, irritants and sometimes mycotoxins (produced by fungi). Mycotoxins can trigger a wide variety of reactions, including difficulty breathing, irritated skin, aggravation of asthma, bloody noses, and irritated eyes, according to a 2001 EPA report. PVC is used in piping, flooring, carpets, blinds, and wall coverings, and according to a study in the *American Journal of Public Health*, can cause immune system damage, reproductive problems, and cancer, due to offgassing of plasticizers.

Even on the ride to school, kids are exposed to harmful diesel fuels on the school bus. Diesel exhaust is composed of fine particles of carbon and a mix of toxic gases that federal agencies have classified as a probable human carcinogen. There is no known safe level of exposure to diesel exhaust for kids, who collectively spend three billion hours on school buses every year, according to Environment and Human Health, Inc. (EHHI). Queued idling buses, which are often directly outside entrances and exits to schools, emit the most toxic chemicals. Although some new regulations will go into effect in 2006 to regulate diesel emissions, the EPA has set those standards lower than many advocacy organizations would like to see. The EHHI suggests phasing in natural gas buses, which emit 60 to 98 percent less carbon than diesel-powered buses.

WHAT YOU CAN DO

If all the hazards to kids seem daunting, it's important to know that there are resources at your disposal. Help can come from other knowledgeable parents, or from the many nonprofit groups, small and large, that are on your side. Some organizations will provide you with resources, information, and tactics to challenge local or state legislation, while others will show you how to put together a group of parents and kids to tackle planting trees or cleaning a waterway. Some groups are even formed or inspired by kids, so your child will be getting advice from peers.

Kids and Advertising

Fortunately, teaching kids about advertising can be simple and fun if you make it into a game. Betsy Taylor of the Center for a New American Dream (CNAD) recommends, "Start at age four or five by explaining what a commercial is, in simple language. For three weeks (too long and it won't be a game), teach media literacy proactively; when you see or hear an ad, ask your child simple questions like, 'What is this company trying to sell? How are they selling it?' Explain how a famous person is paid to say a product is great, whether it is or not. Their first reaction to ads after that makes them critical of advertising. This way you empower your child to deconstruct the ads."

Taylor also recommends setting up limits around media. Forty-seven percent of American kids have a TV in their bedrooms—removing the TV is a good start to limiting media exposure. Because of the fact that young kids aren't good at filtering information, Taylor suggests that kids under eight shouldn't even be watching commercial television. One to two hours of movies and educational programs a day is sufficient for younger children. The American Academy of Pediatrics suggests that for children of less than two years, TV viewing should be replaced by interactive activities that will promote brain development, like talking, playing, singing, and reading.

While you might feel like a "bad guy" for saying no to a favorite program, you can say yes to something non-commercial. Taylor says that after surveying kids of all ages, number one on their list of "things they want that can't be bought" is "more time with parents," and number two is "more time to spend with friends, just hanging out or playing."

Children are increasingly overscheduled with competitive activities. In March 2004, the *Washington Post* reported that even the idea of naps for pre-school children is disappearing, in order to "take advantage of this early stage where they grasp everything." The idea is to let kids be kids.

Showing your children what you loved to do as a child is a good way to slow them down. Some fun, noncommercial activities can include art projects, biking, neighborhood walks, or getting kids to work with their hands, learning a craft like woodworking or pottery. Young teens can be put in

Kids and Commercialism

- Expose kids to other media besides TV: intelligent films, art exhibits (carefully selected), gatherings of interesting adult friends with non-mainstream stories to tell.

- Remove logos from clothes—theirs and yours. Talk with kids about why you're doing this. Suggest kids design their own, personal logos.

- Teach children to be doers and creators rather than shoppers and buyers.

- Talk about where things come from, who made them and what they're made of.

- Teach kids empathy for others. Instead of buying toys, suggest they spend the money bringing some groceries to the local food bank.

Tips from Center for a New American Dream's "Kids and Commercialism" campaign.

charge of putting meals on the table, and even young kids can help with the cooking.

Here are some personal stories from CNAD of thinking parents in action:

- Turn off the TV if a commercial is not muted. Not only does this keep kids from hearing the "hype," many times they lose interest in the TV and go do something else before the show is over if they don't have the "entertainment" from the commercial.

- Next birthday, give a special child in your life a "happening" instead of a toy. A "happening" is a card redeemable for a fun outing just for the child. They may choose a movie, a sports event, a play, a trip to the art museum, and so on.

- Exposure to the natural world has been shown to enhance the development of kids' brains, so gardening, even if it's just beans growing on a shelf in an apartment building, is educational, teaches a child to nurture, and is a real-world example of how much time and energy goes into the food that appears in the fridge. Keeping track of celestial events—a passing comet, an eclipse, or a meteor shower—is a way for suburban kids to feel connected to the universe around them.

Environmental Education

After-school and summer programs can be an ideal way to immerse urban or suburban children in the outside world for a more holistic natural experience. But kids don't have to leave the city to learn about the outside world. Dawn Chavez, education program director for the Urban Ecology Institute in Boston, which is part of the Natural Cities Program, works with teachers within urban schools and assists with long-term ecological studies in the urban environment. "Any outdoor experience is a great entrée to broaden a kid's perspective beyond themselves and learn about the natural world," says Chavez.

Chavez recommends looking into introductory programs at your local park or environmental organization, which may offer activities designed for kids and adults; in this way both you and your child can learn about what is unique to your local environment and a shared experience can be that much more powerful.

"Parents shouldn't be expected to know everything, and it's great if there's a process of discovery for both the adult and child. It's a good example for your kids to show you are interested in learning new things and that these are issues that you care about," says Chavez.

Kids can form their own environmental groups within school or outside of class. There are lots of resources they can draw from, including Earth Force, which has three programs: CAPS: Community Action and Problem Solving, which enables youth to implement positive environmental changes in their communites; GREEN: Global Rivers Environmental Education Network, which gives resources to educators and parents so they can form local water-protection alliances organized by kids; and Earth Force After School, which involves using after-school time to learn about and help the local environment. Earth Force has a national and local Youth Advisory Board system to provide assistance to local projects.

Middle-school student Melissa Poe founded Kids F.A.C.E. (Kids for a Clean Environment) in 1989 in Nashville, Tennessee. The organization has spread throughout the United States, involving thousands of kids in an on-going reforestation project (they've planted more than one million trees). Kids are encouraged to start a local chapter and work on one of three issues: recycling, planting, or building wildlife habitats.

The legendary animal behaviorist Jane Goodall's Roots and Shoots Program encourages young people to be active locally in activities that pro-

Green Flags

At Lewis Cass Technical High in Detroit, Michigan, a pest problem, including infestations of mice, roaches, and rats, motivated teachers and students to find alternatives to hazardous pesticides. Larry Swain, a pest manager with the Michigan Department of Agriculture, helped students run "The Roach Patrol," whose aim was to rid Cass Tech of unwanted pests. "I wanted to prove that pesticides alone weren't doing the job," he says. "I also wanted kids to learn about environmental issues and about taking control . . . things they could apply in life."

After training the kids in detection and teaching them about a pest-control kit that uses biological controls for pests, the students had enough knowledge to tackle the initial pest problem and subsequent recur-rences over the next five years. The students keep track of what works and what doesn't, and pass information on from one year to the next. Michael Jones, a science teacher at the school, explains that there are benefits beyond getting rid of rats and roaches: "The students learn a higher order of thinking. They see the problems, put a plan together, analyze it, and decide what to do based on scientific knowledge. It's a process they can use in the real world."

The Lewis Cass program was a 2003 winner in the Green Flag Program of the Center for Health, Environment and Justice. The Childproofing Our Communities Campaign works with communities to reduce environmental health hazards in schools.

mote concern for the environment, especially in relation to animals. Toddler to pre-K groups can get age-appropriate curriculum and project ideas when signed up as an early childhood group, and older kids can get advice and learn from Goodall.

Most kids are Web-savvy these days, and great environmental websites abound just for them. Many of the major environmental and animal-advocacy groups have great information and activities for children of all ages through their websites or can be ordered for free or low-cost directly through the mail. World Wildlife Fund, the Rainforest Action Network, and Defenders of Wildlife are just a few. The U.S. Environmental Protection Agency (EPA) also has separate, comprehensive websites for young kids, preteens, and teenagers.

In-school environmental education programs can also be a good jumping-off point for learning and feeling more comfortable in a natural environment, especially for urban kids. According to a survey done by The North American Association of Environmental Educators (NAAEE), almost 90 percent of teachers surveyed in grades K to 4 covered environmental topics, but only 58 percent of teachers in grades 5 to 9 and 44 percent of high school teachers did.

Encourage your child's teacher to incorporate an environmental issue like alternative energy, extinction, or water quality into the curriculum. All of these topics can fit into state-mandated science curricula. The NAAEE can connect you with different programs in your area, as well as national programs for kids from kindergarten through college, including an extensive listing of educational materials.

The EPA has an Environmental Education Program with resources and contacts for both parents and teachers available in each region. By using real-world problems and solutions, an environmental lesson in the classroom will be that much more relevant to a child. Combining a background class with a field trip to see an environmental issue firsthand is a simple way to get kids interested in natural processes.

If your child has an interest in environmental issues, or if you think he or she would benefit from immersion in natural education, there are hundreds of camps and summer programs that include traditional outdoor activities like nature hikes, canoeing, and educational games. Some are more science-based and may give a child a leg up once the school year begins. Other camps are oriented toward adventure sports or leadership (some of these may have little environmental content; outdoor doesn't always equal environmental).

Chavez suggests looking at a schedule of a typical day for a good idea of what kids will be doing regularly, and asking about environmental curricula specifically. Accreditation may be important to consider, such as that given out by the American Camping Association, but smaller camps and programs often don't have it, and they needn't be unnecessarily excluded.

You can check a few basics for yourself, including inquiring about background checks on teachers or counselors, looking for a low staff-to-student ratio, and ensuring the program has basic safety certifications. If there's a waterfront area, the appropriate life guarding certifications are required by law. Allen's Guide (www.allensguide.com) is a good way to search for camps with environmental programs in your state, as are Camp Page (www.camppage.com) and the comprehensive American Camping Association website (www.acacamps.org).

The Appalachian Mountain Club in the Northeast runs summer excursions for teens and families. Whether you and your children go camping or hiking on your own or with a program, the Leave No Trace ideals should be followed. The concept is to leave a minimal footprint when you're enjoying outdoor activities, and is important in both wilderness areas and in state and national parks that may receive a lot of traffic. Both the Boy and Girl Scouts of America also have summer camps and programs—check with your local branch to see what kinds of environmental lessons are taught.

Home Toxins

There are ways to get toxins out of your home without completely starting over. CHEC's list of the top five conduits that bring toxins to your home includes ways to reduce air, water, and other pollutants while still maintaining your life and your sanity.

- **Air.** Outdoor air is generally healthier than indoor air, so make sure your home is well-ventilated. Open windows once a day, and look at what is influencing your indoor air quality—smoking in the house, a leaky gas stove or furnace, and bug killers are just some of the many trouble areas.

- **Water.** Check the quality of your home's water supply. Forty million people in the United States have wells, in which case it's necessary to independently test your own water. If you are on a public water supply, you should still test what comes out of your faucets; water contamination may occur between the water filtering plants and your home.

- **Food.** Pesticide residues are a particular risk to kids. It's recommended that a family buy as much organic food as they can afford. "Pick and choose," says Elizabeth Sword of CHEC. "Find the foods that your child eats a lot of and buy those organic." Systemic pesticides (those that you can't wash off with water) like those found in broccoli can be avoided by eating local foods in season, since produce that is shipped across borders requires more pesticides. "Co-ops are also good, because you can talk to the farmer that's growing your food directly," says Sword.

- **Consumer products.** "Buy responsibly and use responsibly; don't be fooled by seemingly natural products," says Sword. Cleaning products are one of the largest contributors to toxins in the home. "If you know

School Food: Organic Changes

In Berkeley, California, a chef has dedicated time and money to fight the childhood obesity epidemic and environmental devastation that have been fueled by fast food, giving parents a good idea of how to change an unhealthy system. Alice Waters of Chez Panisse restaurant took what she learned from running the extremely successful restaurant—organic ingredients, fresh local food, and mouth-watering combinations—and helped create the Edible Schoolyard program at Martin Luther King Jr. Middle School. Waters also has a hand in creating the Sustainable Food Project at Yale, her daughter Fanny's alma mater. "There is a degree of consciousness with this generation of kids," Waters says. "They want to buy fair trade coffee, and they want vegan options."

Starting with just one angry parent who didn't like the way the school lunch program was running, the Berkeley school district soon realized that it wasn't practicing what it was teaching in its nutrition classes. Working with the Center for Ecoliteracy and a federal pilot program that links local farms to schools, the Edible Schoolyard program at the middle school has converted a former abandoned lot into a garden where kids are responsible for growing vegetables. With a kitchen-classroom next to the garden, a compost heap, and an outside pizza oven, kids learn about how food is grown and prepared, how buying locally saves resources and supports local farmers, and how good fresh meals taste.

Other schools around the country are catching on. The state of North Carolina gives schools grants to purchase local farm produce. In Chicago, the local Slow Food group (a branch of an Italian organization that encourages the savoring of gourmet meals made with wholesome ingredients) brings schoolchildren to the city's Green City Sprouts Farmers' Market and treats kids to salads made entirely with local produce. While parents often think kids don't want to eat their vegetables, all these programs have had to increase the amount of produce they order or grow, as students have cultivated connections with what's on their plates.

To learn about these programs, get in touch with the Edible Schoolyard. A group of parents will be more effective than just one or two. Working through the PTA can be helpful, as can finding allies on the school board. Challenging both the cafeteria and the curriculum in a school is a big undertaking, possibly involving the government agencies that make sure low-income kids get fed.

you should keep a product out of reach of children, ask yourself if you need it in your house. Once you take it out of that locked cupboard and use it, you expose your child." Nontoxic products are available for almost every cleaning problem, and one of the easiest ways to learn what's in cleaners is to make your own. Pesticides and herbicides are very toxic, so if a chemical company puts a sign on your lawn that you shouldn't let people or animals on it, it's going to put an added stress on your child's system. Remember that wild animals don't know how to read, so birds, small mammals, and beneficial insects can be sickened along with your kids.

- **Soil.** "People assume pesticides stay where you spray them," says Sword. "That's a fallacy. Soil is a major conduit for heavy metals and pesticides." Arsenic-drenched playground equipment and decking renders the soil beneath it toxic for many years to come, so be wary of what soil was exposed to when renovating. Most houses built before 1978 have lead paint dust contamination in about a three-foot radius from the house, so be careful when siting a vegetable garden or future play area.

School Toxins

Keeping VOCs or other toxins out of your home is up to you, but making changes within a school district is more difficult. If you're concerned with the chemicals and toxins that may be present in your child's school, you're not alone.

The Center for Health, Environment and Justice (CHEJ), founded in 1981 by Lois Gibbs, who emerged as an environmental leader through Love Canal, gives parents guidelines, information, and action plans to change individual schools' and districts' consumption of potentially toxic products, from pesticides to cleaning products.

Through the Childproofing our Communities project, CHEJ works on several levels to make schools healthier environments for kids and teachers.

Patrick Masterson of CHEJ says the top five environmental hazards that make kids sick at school are pesticides, poor indoor air quality, mold, building materials, and, most significantly, school siting.

"We examined five states, and found that 1,000 schools—attended by more than 600,000 kids—were within a half-mile of Superfund sites," says Masterson. Because school budgets are always tight, new schools sometimes sit on the cheapest land in town. These properties can be brownfields (old industrial sites), old landfills, or former incinerator locations.

"Sites that one couldn't build a house on, one can build a school on," says Masterson. "There is virtually no legislation surrounding school siting, except in California. People forget that the land under a school was once a hazardous waste dump, and later, when new construction occurs, toxic substances are kicked up into the environment where kids spend eight hours a day."

The Green Flag Program at CHEJ encourages kids to get directly involved in making their own schools healthier. By organizing around one of a set of topics, including indoor air quality, nontoxic products and recycling, kids get involved in their own school's environment, and they learn about the topic and also how to make change. Masterson explains, "Green Flags gets people together engaging in environmental education, and gives them the tools to do something about it."

GREEN PRODUCTS

Food at Home

Limiting processed foods, like white flours and especially partially hydrogenated oils and high-fructose corn syrup (both of which are available in a majority of packaged cookies, crackers, and other kids' favorites) as well as artificial flavors and colors can be tricky, especially if "all the other kids are eating it." How do these guidelines translate into day-to-day living for parents?

Children have high calorie and nutrient needs, but their stomachs are small. Offer your child snacks regularly; peanut butter (vary with other nut butters) and jelly sandwiches, vegetarian hot dogs, veggies cut into fun shapes, muffins, and crackers with bean dips like hummus are all filling and healthy for kids, and won't be so different from what their friends are used to eating.

Normalizing the eating of whole, natural foods within your household (you have to eat them too!) means that kids will grow up with a strong defense against disease and also a knowledge that their parents truly care about their health, an invaluable lesson that will counteract the "ewww" factor of new and different tastes. The website of the Physicians Committee for Responsible Medicine (PCRM) has a listing of nutritionist-recommended meal plans and snacks for kids of all ages.

As they get to school, it's important to discuss your child's diet with his or her teacher. Lactose intolerance, ethnic preferences, allergies, and religious dietary restrictions are all common. You will not be the only parent to set rules for your child's eating, so be upfront with what is and is not acceptable. PCRM recommends you meet with your child's teacher, explaining their diet and finding out if there are any rules that the teacher has made for their classroom—like no sweets or no sodas. Donating books on vegetarianism or organics to the school library can help, and finding like-minded parents can help influence whether vegetarian lunch options are available, for example.

A host of health and organic food companies make kid-sized portions or foods that are especially appealing to younger palates. Stony-field Farms Squeezables yogurt is packaged in tubes for easy eating and smaller stomachs; Nature's Path Foods makes Envirokidz foods including snack bars, cereals, and waffles; and Lightlife makes kid-sized soy hot dogs. Pamela's Products include all-natural wheat- and gluten-free baking mixes and cookies. Veggie burgers, from the "meatier" Boca brand, to the more grain-centered Gardenburger, are always popular with kids.

Other great resources for parents include the Consumers Union website on product labels, which can help you dissect what exactly is in an Oreo. Healthy Child Online is an online resource and forum on children's natural health. Laptop Lunches teaches kids about portion control while saving Earth's resources, and promotes reusable lunch containers to reduce waste.

Consumer Goods

After you've detoxified your home, don't forget that many toxins get into the environment through manufacture of consumer goods. Consider buying organic cotton clothing and bedding for your kids at:

Garden Kids Clothing. Organic clothing for babies and kids. 275 Hambletonian Drive, Eugene, OR 97401, (541)465-4544, www.gardenkids clothing.com.

A Happy Planet. Organic-fiber clothes and bedding. 884 46th Avenue, San Francisco, CA 94121, (888)424-2779, www.ahappyplanet.com/ahpstore/ clothing/prclkids.html.

Rawganique. Cotton and hemp clothes, kids' section listed under "Ecokidswear." 270 Marin Boulevard, Suite #4P, Jersey City, NJ 07302, (877)729-4367, www.rawganique.com.

Natural, Nontoxic Toys

Garden for Kids. Includes gardening utensils for smaller hands and lots of links to agriculture sites. 11035 NE 14th Street, Bellevue, WA 98004, (800)574-7248, www.mastergardenproducts.com/kidsgarden.

Heirloom Wooden Toys. Makes kids' wooden furniture, dollhouses, and train sets. P.O. Box 2201, Pittsfield, MA 01201, (866)202-8073, www .heirloomwoodentoys.com.

Nature Toys/Knowledge Tree Products. The Santa Cruz Waldorf School's toy line. 135 Royal Oak Court, Scotts Valley, CA 95066, (800)847-7570, www.naturetoys.com.

Prang Soy Crayons. 195 International Parkway, Heathrow, FL 32746, (800)829-9000, www.prangpower.com.

Think Button. "Knowledge Products for Growing Children." P.O. Box 471493, Charlotte, NC 28247, (704)572-5161, www.thinkbutton.com.

Kids' Environmental Media

There are some great sources for positive media out there. You can feel good about sharing some of them with your kids.

Music

Earthsongs. A collection of environmental songs, albums, and songbooks with lyrics that promote the love and protection of the Earth, and links to related resources. (The site is a reference tool that does not support online ordering.) www.planetaryexploration.net/patriot/earth_songs.html.

A Gentle Wind. Award-winning children's recordings make car rides fun and educational for you and your child. Call for a catalog. (888)FUN-SONG, www.gentlewind.com.

Books

Childsake. Hundreds of environmentally themed children's books, and all commissions go to Jane Goodall's Roots and Shoots program. #1090 1733 H Street, Suite 330, Blaine, WA 98230, www.childsake.com.

Film and TV

The Environmental Media Association. Gives out awards for children's animated and live action television and film. Nominees have included *The Simpsons, The Wild Thornberrys, Whale Rider, Malcolm in the Middle,* and *Everwood.* 10780 Santa Monica Boulevard, Suite 210, Los Angeles, CA 90025, (310)446-6244, www.ema-online.org.

Teach with Movies. 1717 Fourth Street, Third Floor, Santa Monica, CA 90401, www.teachwithmovies.com.

Video Games

Star Wars Episode 1: The Gungan Frontier (at www.download.com), and *Sim City* (at retail stores) are great for older kids. Middle-school children will probably like *Steer Madness* from Veggie Games (the world's first environmentally themed gaming company) and young kids will enjoy *The Living Sea* from Montparnasse Media (direct order) and *Jumpstart Animal Adventures,* available online and in retail stores.

Resources

Toxin Resource Information

Center for Children's Health and the Environment. Mount Sinai School of Medicine, Box 1043, One Gustave Levy Place, New York, NY 10029, (212)241-7840, www.childenvironment.org.

Center for Health, Environment and Justice. P.O. Box 6806, Falls Church, VA 22040, (703)237-2249, www.childproofing.org.

Children's Environmental Health Network. 110 Maryland Avenue NE, Suite 511, Washington, DC 20002, (202)543-4033, www.cehn.org.

Children's Health Environmental Coalition. P.O. Box 1540, Princeton, NJ 08542, (609)252-1915, www.checnet.org.

The Collaborative on Health and the Environment. Includes database of two hundred human conditions and cross-references with disease risk; click on "Overview of chemical exposures linked to human disease." Commonweal, P.O. Box 316, Bolinas, CA 94924, www.protectingourhealth.org.

Environmental Protection Agency. Ariel Rios Building 1200 Pennsylvania Avenue, NW, Washington, DC 20460, (202)272-0167. Site for kids at www.epa.gov/kids. Also, call and ask about your region's pediatric environmental health special unit, or PEHSU.

Natural Resources Defense Council. 40 West 20th Street, New York, NY 10011, (212)727-2700. Toxic chemicals and health section at www.nrdc.org/health/default.asp.

Media Literacy Sites

Citizens' Campaign for Commercial-Free Schools. A Washington State–based organization with information and action tips on how to change school policy. www.scn.org/cccs.

Commercial Alert. Nonprofit aimed at protecting kids from advertising. 4110 SE Hawthorne Boulevard, #123, Portland, OR 97214-5426, (503)235-8012, www.commercialalert.org.

Corpwatch. Keeps track of what corporations are doing and how they're doing it. 1611 Telegraph Avenue, #702, Oakland, CA 94612, (510)271-8080, www.Corpwatch.org.

Dissect an Ad. Though it hasn't been updated since 1996, this site sponsored by the Corporation for Public Broadcasting shows how to dissect a political ad; the questions provided can be used on any kind of commercial. www.pbs.org/pov/pov1996/takingonthekennedys/dissect.html.

Information Literacy Standards for Student Learning. American Library Organization, 50 East Huron, Chicago, IL 60611, (800)545-2433, www.ala.org.

Media Awareness Network. Media and information literacy for young people. 1500 Merivale Road, 3rd Floor, Ottawa, ON K2E 6Z5, Canada, (613)224-7721, www.media-awareness.ca/english/index.cfm.

The Media Literacy Online Project. Maintained by the University of Oregon Department of Education, this site provides a comprehensive collection of links to media literacy resources. University of Oregon, Eugene, OR 97403, http://interact.uoregon.edu/MediaLit/mlr/home/index.html.

Project Look Smart. www.ithaca.edu/looksharp/library/edulist.html.

Taking Charge of Your TV: A Guide to Critical Viewing for Parents and Children. Videos, articles, and audiocassettes from the New Media Center at Ithaca College, including a breakdown of subjects by age and medium. Links to additional media literacy sites and a guide for parents. 1724 Massachusetts Avenue NW, Washington, DC 20036, (202)775-1040, www.ciconline.com/Enrichment/MediaLiteracy/TakingCharge/default.htm.

Center for Ecoliteracy. Founded in 1995 by Fritjof Capra, Peter Buckley, and Zenobia Barlow, brings the ideas of sustainability to the dinner table. 2528 San Pablo Avenue, Berkeley, CA 94702, (510)845-4595, www.ecoliteracy.org.

Community Food Security Coalition. With more than 250 member organizations, CFSC seeks to create a system of growing and selling food that is regionally based and grounded in the principles of justice and sustainability. P.O. Box 209, Venice, CA 90294, (310)822-5410, www.foodsecurity.org.

The Edible Schoolyard. Martin Luther King Jr. Middle School, 1781 Rose Street, Berkeley, CA 94703, (510)558-1335, www.edibleschoolyard.org.

Healthy Child Online. Resource and forum on children's natural health. www.healthychild.com.

No Junk Food. Online resource for those who wish to create a healthier learning environment for our youth. www.nojunkfood.org.

Organic Consumers Association. OCA's Safeguard Our Schools Campaign works to make school-lunch programs healthy and sustainable. 6101 Cliff Estate Road, Little Marais, MN 55614, (218)226-4164, www.organicconsumers.org/sos.htm.

Organic Lunchbox. Dr. Alan R. Greene gives advice on what to put in your child's lunchbox, and you can ask him questions online. 9000 Crow Canyon Road, Suite S220, Danville, CA 94506, (925)964-1793, www.drgreene.org/body.cfm?id=21&action=detail&ref=1670.

Prevention Institute. A nonprofit national center dedicated to improving community health and well-being by building momentum for effective primary prevention. 265 29th Street, Oakland, CA 94611, (510)444-7738, www.preventioninstitute.org.

Stonyfield Farms. The yogurt maker promotes "Menu for Change: Getting Healthy Foods into Schools Parent Action Kit." Ten Burton Drive,

Londonderry, NH 03053, (800)PRO-COWS, www.stonyfield.com/menufor change.

Environmental Education

Action for Nature. Answers environmental questions and encourages young people to take personal action to make this world a better place for humans and animals. 2269 Chestnut Street, #263, San Francisco, CA 94123, www.actionfornature.org.

American Camping Association. Links to many environmental or outdoor-themed summer programs. 5000 State Road 67, North Martinsville, IN 46151, (765)342-8456, www.acacamps.org.

Appalachian Mountain Club. Kids and teens outdoor adventure and environmental education programs in the Northeast. 5 Joy Street, Boston, MA 02108, (617)523-0636, www.outdoors.org.

Boy Scouts of America. P.O. Box 152079, Irving, TX 75015-2079, www.scouting.org.

Earth Force. Kids discover and put into place lasting solutions to environmental change in their communities. 1908 Vernon Avenue, Second Floor, Alexandria, VA 22301, www.earthforce.org.

EPA. Websites packed with detailed information from ecosystems to water, from waste to conservation, and links to EPA-sponsored careers, internships and scholarships. Kids' site at www.epa.gov/kids and teen site at www.epa.gov/highschool.

Girls Scouts of America. 420 Fifth Avenue, New York, NY 10018-2798, (800)478-7248, www.girlscouts.org.

Kids For A Clean Environment (FACE). Started as a club in Nashville in 1989, with just six members, including founder Melissa Poe. Now its mission is to provide information on environmental issues to children, to encourage involvement with effective environmental action, and to recognize and celebrate efforts that result in the improvement of nature. (615)331-7381, www.kidsface.org.

Kids' Planet. Sponsored by Defenders of Wildlife, this is a website for kids to go to for information and games about animals and their habitats. www.kidsplanet.org.

Leave No Trace. The "leave no trace" philosophy is part of any environmentally conscious camper's responsibility code. P.O. Box 997, Boulder, CO 80306, (800)332-4100, www.lnt.org.

North American Association of Environmental Educators. Hundreds of environmental education links for teachers and parents. 2000 P Street NW, Suite 540, Washington, DC 20036, (202)419-0412, www.naaee.org.

Rainforest Action Network Kid's Corner. Steps kids can take for the environment, letter-writing for kids, activities, and games. 221 Pine Street, Suite 500, San Francisco, CA 94104, (415)398-4404, www.ran.org/kidsaction.

Roots and Shoots Program. Jane Goodall's organization to empower local communities to work on behalf of animals and the environment. 8700 Georgia Avenue, Suite 500, Silver Spring, MD 20910, (800)592-JANE, www.rootsandshoots.org.

Windows on the Wild by World Wildlife Fund. Kids can learn about biodiversity, animals and endangered species, and play games. www.worldwildlife.org.

Food Resources

Boca Foods. Makes tasty "meaty" vegan burgers. 910 Mayer Avenue, Madison, WI 53704, (847)646-6761, www.bocaburger.com.

Consumers Union. Products label website can help you dissect what is in your favorite foods. www.eco-labels.org/home.cfm.

Envirokidz. Nature's Path Foods, 7453 Progress Way Delta, BC V4G 1E8 Canada, (604)940-0505, www.envirokidz.org.

Gardenburger. Grain-based veggie burgers. Authentic Foods Company, 1411 SW Morrison Street, Suite 400, Portland, OR 97205, www.garden burger.com.

Laptop Lunches. Teaches children portion control while saving the Earth's resources: Reusable lunch containers promote waste-free lunches. 849 Almar, Suite C-323, Santa Cruz, CA 95060, (831)457-0301, www.lap toplunches.com.

Lightlife Tofu Pups. Kids' soy hot dogs. 153 Industrial Boulevard, Turner's Falls, MA 01376, (413)863-8500.

Pamela's Products. Makes all-natural wheat- and gluten-free baking mixes and cookies. (650)952-4546, www.pamelasproducts.com.

Solae Wonderdogs. Veggie hot dogs for kids. P.O. Box 88940, St. Louis, MO 63188, (800)325-7108.

chapter ten

Organic Gardening

Nature's Way Offers Bountiful Harvests Without Pesticides

Gardening is arguably the most popular activity on the planet, and certainly one of the most enduring. It puts you in touch with the Earth and out in fresh air. It rewards you with bright flowers, luscious fruits and vegetables, and visiting birds and butterflies. Gardening offers time for quiet introspection, gives you a healthy workout, and feeds your soul and aesthetic senses.

But gardening—as taught by most home centers and master gardener programs—can also be one of the biggest sources of pollution coming from your home. Gas-powered lawnmowers and leaf blowers billow soot and ozone-causing chemicals into the air. Pesticides and herbicides pollute the waterways after killing dandelions and bugs—and can even harm your health. Chemical fertilizers may boost plant growth for an initial period, but organic advocates say they ultimately bankrupt the soil life that supports natural fertility.

The good news is that it doesn't have to be that way. Organic gardening can quickly reverse your toxic toll and make your garden time a way to improve your own health and that of the air, water, and land around you. Organic gardening eliminates chemical pesticides and fertilizers and uses ecological thinking to plan and maintain your garden. By choosing plants that do well in your climate, recycling kitchen and yard wastes as compost, encouraging beneficial ladybugs and other insects, and feeding the microscopic life within the soil, your garden will be just as lush and much more healthy for all the life it supports.

CURRENT EVENTS/LEGISLATIVE/POLITICAL

Before 1940, almost all agriculture was organic. Farmers and gardeners used time-tested methods and crop varieties to make sure they had enough food to feed those depending on the harvest. They had no other choice. Family farms proliferated, maintaining diversity of foodstuffs.

As science and industrialization rose, chemists identified what they believed to be the most important nutrients in the soil: nitrogen, phosphorous, and potassium (chemically denoted "K"), the now-famous "NPK" that appears on fertilizer containers.

The era of chemical agriculture took root at the end of World War II, when factories manufacturing nitrates for bombs converted to a peacetime job of making nitrates for crops. At first, the new fertilizers were a tremendous success. The chemicals were cheap and plentiful, and farmers saw yields they never had before. But after the initial explosion of fertility, the effects began to wane.

"Biology wasn't taken into account when the chemical era got under way," explains Mark Fulford, an independent soil and crop consultant who also farms organically in Monroe, Maine. "Because it became the industry standard to view things in terms of just chemistry, the value of living and complex topsoil was somewhat overlooked. And products made available on the market also were somewhat simplistically formulated, so they focused mostly on NPK and not a great deal on other things."

Over time, the problems with pesticides and chemical fertilizers started to emerge. "Because at first most of the soils in this country were relatively healthy, there was a huge response in crop productivity when the first chemical wave came through," Fulford says. "The soil was still a storehouse of minerals and humus. But it didn't take too many years to use it."

The web of life in the soil—water-retaining humus made from carbon, the earthworms that aerate and fertilize, microbes that help feed plants— began breaking down. Yields began dropping, bugs converged on weakened crops, and farmers responded with more pesticides and chemical fertilizers. The nutritional value of the food grown in those soils plummeted. Fertilizers washed off of fields with the topsoil entered lakes and rivers, causing pollution in the form of unwanted growth of aquatic plants that suck the oxygen out of the water.

The chemicals running into waterways weren't just fertilizers; many of them were poisons. In 2001, the U.S. Public Interest Research Group reported that many commercial fertilizers contain high levels of toxins including arsenic, lead, mercury, and dioxin. In two thirds of the cases studied, levels were so high that the fertilizer could not legally be sent to a public landfill.

Chemical pesticide use continues to rise—climbing from 900 million pounds in 1992 to 940 million pounds in 2000—even as the area of treated cropland decreases, according to the U.S. General Accounting Office. Even though use of the riskiest pesticides is waning, the GAO reported, they still account for more than 40 percent of those used in U.S. agriculture. Pesticides have been implicated in cancers, lowered fertility, and other reproductive changes in humans and wildlife. They also are ubiquitous: a February 2000 study published by the Environmental Illness Society of Canada found pesticides in the amniotic fluid in one third of human pregnancies in the United States and Canada.

Pesticides ultimately work against controlling pests. Some bugs eat human crops, while others eat the bugs that eat the human crops (see sidebar on page 220). By killing off the predators as well as the prey, any new infestation of unwanted bugs can munch away unimpeded. Further, because pesticides don't kill every bug in a field, those that survive breed more resistant offspring, setting farmers on a toxic downward spiral. The late Dartmouth Professor Donella Meadows wrote in the September/October 2000 edition of *Organic Gardening* magazine that "In the past 50 years, more than 500 insect pests, 230 crop diseases and 220 weeds have become resistant to pesticides and herbicides."

Farmers, gardeners, and consumers began looking for alternatives. The most famous promoter was J. I. Rodale, who founded the Rodale Institute (and *Organic Gardening* magazine) to research and report on advances in old-style, natural agriculture. Urbanites going "back to the land" in the 1960s and 1970s began shifting to those methods. In the 1970s and 1980s, local groups sprang up to define and certify organic production, giving consumers a chance to help farmers who didn't use chemicals get more money for the crops.

As the organics market blossomed, interest grew in having one uniform national standard within the United States. After years of work by farmers and bureaucrats around the country, the 1990 federal Farm Bill included the Organic Foods Production Act, which established the National Organic Program of the U.S. Department of Agriculture. According to the Organic Trade Association, "Organic growers use biological and cultural practices as their first line of defense against pests. Methods include crop rotation, the selection of resistant varieties, nutrient and water management, the provision of habitat for the natural enemies of pests, and release of beneficial organisms to protect crops from damage. The only pesticides allowed in organic agriculture must be on an approved list, with restricted use." The rules went into full effect in January 2003.

Organic agriculture makes a difference. According to the Canadian Parliament, organic farming reduces soil erosion, helps retain soil nutrients, and protects the health of groundwater. The effects on water are so pronounced that several German utilities pay farmers to go organic because doing so is less expensive than removing farm chemicals from the water supply. A review of forty-one published studies in *The Journal of Alternative and Complementary Medicine* found that organic crops contain up to 30 percent more nutrients such as vitamin C, iron, and magnesium, and have substantially fewer harmful nitrates than conventional foods.

The Food and Agriculture Organization of the United Nations says that going organic even improves biological diversity. In the United Kingdom, a 2000 study found that organic farms had 25 percent more birds at the edge of their fields, 44 percent more in the field during fall and winter, three times more "non-pest" butterflies, up to five times more bug-eating spiders, and significantly fewer crop-eating aphids.

"We're not farming organically by default now," Fulford says. "We're trying to farm ecologically or organically by intent. That's a huge difference. It requires people waking up" and recognizing that dependence on chemical fertilizers and large quantities of pesticides is a sign that the soil is suffering—and so, too, is the quality of the food.

It's All About the Soil

Talk to any organic grower and she or he will tell you the same thing: It's all about the soil. "When you begin to grow a garden, it starts with a healthy soil," says Allison Blount, who grows organic flowers on her farm in the

Green Lawns

Perfect, weed-free lawns use tons of plant-killing herbicides each year, some of which have been linked to health problems in children and adults. Keeping lawns green uses as much as half of all the fresh water used in urban areas each year, according to the U.S. Environmental Protection Agency. Older gas lawnmowers emit as much pollution in an hour as an average car driving 18.7 miles. Rains can carry pesticides and fertilizers off lawns and into nearby rivers or lakes, harming the webs of life in those waterways.

But living green doesn't have to mean giving up your lawn. Changing a few strategies—and expectations—can bring your yard into greater harmony with nature.

- **Longer grass is healthier.** If you wait a little longer than usual between mowings, your lawn will need less water and food. Try a push lawnmower instead of a gas- or electric-powered one. With sharp blades you won't end up making much more work for yourself and you'll be keeping pollutants out of the air. They're available everywhere, from Wal-Mart and Sears to the Dallas-based Clean Air Gardening, and cost about $200.

- **Aerator sandals** improve the health of your lawn. Pins at the bottom of the strap-on sandals poke holes into the ground, helping water and nutrients reach to the roots of your grass. They cost less than $15 and are available through Gardener's Supply Company and others online.

- **Feed your grass naturally.** Lawn clippings are full of nitrogen, which promotes lush, green growth. Fallen leaves make terrific soil conditioners. Using them on your lawn is a perfect way to recycle rather than add to the local landfill. Or use organic fertilizers carefully; even they need to stay out of waterways to keep those ecosystems healthy.

chilly Oregon coastal mountains. "That builds healthy plants that can take the barrage of insects and disease and anything else the environment throws at them."

In the same way that a well-nourished child does better in school, plants grown in rich soils are better able to withstand pests, diseases, competing weeds, and environmental factors such as pollution or drought. When plants grow better, so too do the things that depend on them for life, including birds, butterflies, bees, and humans.

According to a fifteen-year study by the Rodale Institute published in 1999, organically managed soils also do a better job of holding water and may even help curtail global warming by keeping more carbon in the

What's a Weed?

The pesticide industry has made a fortune convincing homeowners to kill every unfamiliar bit of green on sight. But just because something grows without being planted doesn't necessarily make it a bad thing. Some "weeds" provide food and shelter for beneficial insects that help pollinate garden plants and keep down critters that compete for a gardener's food or flowers. Others are edible, including pigweed, chickweed, and dandelion. And "weeds" have been used for centuries as medicine. Many make great soil-building, water-conserving mulches or add nutrients to the compost heap.

Author and gardening activist Heather Coburn cites tenacious yellow dock as an example of how the benefits of weeds get overlooked. "Yellow dock's big taproot goes deep into the soil and gathers up trace minerals and other essential nutrients and draws them up to the topsoil to make them available for your vegetables," she explains. "The same plant can be harvested and made into medicine, including a blood purifier. The seeds are spicy and edible. And it's one of the most common weeds that people pull without even knowing what it is."

Coburn's rule of thumb is to never pull a weed she doesn't recognize: "If I don't know what it is, how do I know it's not going to produce a big beautiful purple flower, attract a rare butterfly or cure some disease I have?"

ground than conventionally managed soils. Researchers have found that one teaspoon of organic soils rich in compost can contain as many as one billion helpful soil bacteria, while the same amount of chemically treated soil contain as few as one hundred.

How to grow these miracle soils? Feed the soil—and the microbes and fungi in it—not the plant. Soil needs carbon for structure, which comes from substances including straw, dried leaves, and most importantly, from compost. But it also needs minerals. Many gardeners know lime lowers soil acidity, but it has an even more important function: adding calcium, which is used in the cell walls of everything in the plant kingdom.

"The more diverse the system is, the better," explains Patrick Ironwood, director of landscaping and architecture with the Sequatchie Valley Institute at Moonshadow in rural Tennessee. More kinds of microorganisms mean a greater percentage will survive in any given condition. For instance, he says, a rich soil will have a better chance in a world of changing weather because among the microorganisms will be individuals that thrive under the new conditions and breed more like themselves.

WHAT YOU CAN DO

- **Compost!** In the same way that you close the loop by recycling old newspapers and glass bottles, reuse or recycle the things that would normally go in the trash. Grass clippings and fall leaves, old flowers, spent plants—from unsprayed sources, of course—or kitchen scraps take a turn at feeding your garden soil. Use them as mulch around the base of other plants to keep moisture and soil in place and promote healthy soil life. Or put them into the compost bin or onto the compost pile and let the magical, bacterial processes turn them into top-notch fertilizing soil conditioner. Then turn around and use that compost to feed your soil. If you don't have room for an outside compost pile, try a box and a batch of worms inside.

- **Water at night during summer hot spells.** Hot sun speeds evaporation, so your water bill goes up and your plants get less water. The most efficient systems use drip or soaker hoses to take water directly to plant roots where it's most needed.

- **Green your lawn.** Or better still, replace your grass entirely. You can mimic lawn with low-growing perennials such as chamomile, which smells great, or white Dutch clover, which feeds the soil. Turn your yard into a native prairie by growing local or other regionally adapted wildflowers that need no mowing and will host beneficial insects. Or plant a garden of food for yourself and your family and reduce your trips to the supermarket! (See sidebar on page 209 on green lawns.)

- **Grow plants that have a variety of purposes.** For instance, try plants that feed humans and birds or beneficial insects. (See sidebar on page 223 on the edible landscape.)

- **Choose heirloom, rare, traditional, or unusual plant varieties.** By keeping up demand for old varieties or building interest in new ones your garden can help grow history, promote genetic diversity, and give incentive to seed companies to maintain or even increase their offerings. (See sidebar on page 213 on planting diversity.)

- Whatever you choose, remember to **pick the right plant for the right place.** Disease-resistant varieties and those adapted to the local climate will need less pampering, meaning reduced watering, and fewer problems with pests and disease.

- **Get your garden certified**. The national organic standards were intended for farm produce that makes its way to markets, not really for home gardeners. But a unique program through Oregon Tilth, one of the official organic certifiers, allows gardeners to get in on the action. Join the organization as a gardening member and staff will send you the organic rules. After reading the regulations, you can sign a pledge to abide by them and call yourself organic. That doesn't mean you can turn around and sell your extra zucchini with an organic label, but it is another way of voting with your actions for a cleaner world.

GREEN PRODUCTS

Because gardening is so popular, going organic can make a big difference. The venerable *Economist* magazine has called gardening "the world's favorite leisure pursuit," and the National Gardening Association says that 84 million households—that's eight out of ten in the United States—tended a lawn or garden in 2003. Those people feed a huge gardening industry, spending $38.4 billion that year.

That's good news for people who want to help create a more sustainable world. You can vote with your landscape and your checkbook to increase the availability of ecological gardening supplies including seeds, plants, compost and composting systems, rain-catching barrels, human-powered lawnmowers, fertilizers, pest controls, magazines, and books.

Twenty percent of the households in the National Gardening Association's survey already have. By adding to the roughly 11 million households that bought organic fertilizers or natural pest controls in 2003, you can help make the environment around you cleaner, safer, and healthier.

"Even one little patch of improved soil is going to make a difference," says Heather Coburn, author and founder of the Eugene-based group Food Not Lawns. "If you're using chemicals to garden, you're contributing to environmental degradation, plus you're poisoning yourself. But if you're gardening organically, you're part of the solution."

"Somebody once told me that the knowledge of how to live on the

Planting Diversity

Purple potatoes. Orange eggplants. Sweet, white tomatoes. If you haven't heard of them, you're not alone.

Biological diversity is being lost around the planet at an alarming rate. But those losses aren't happening only in sensitive ecosystems; they've been happening for generations on grocery store shelves. Yes, cabbage comes in green and purple. But how often have you seen red brussels sprouts, purple carrots, or striped tomatoes?

Our food choices have been shrinking steadily for decades. According to the Seed Savers Exchange in Decorah, Iowa, Americans grew 7,000 named apple varieties at the turn of the last century; only 10 percent of those are available today, and total named apples are down to about 1,900. The old varieties are important because they may include important genes from their wild ancestors, or because they were saved over decades because of unique characteristics, reliability under stressful growing conditions, or just because they were the yummiest varieties around.

The good news is that the decline is slowing. Home gardeners can help by joining a growing movement to preserve our planet's edible heritage.

"Heirloom" or traditional varieties are being offered by dozens of small and midsized seed companies around the country, many of which specialize in varieties well suited for the growing conditions of their regions. Others specialize in introducing varieties or even new species from places like the Andes, Russia and Eastern Europe, or Southeast Asia. (Be cautious about relying on a catalog's stated dates to maturity for anything but relative season requirements; the numbers vary based on where the plants are grown and may not be relevant to your backyard.) Organic seed is increasingly available, and companies selling such seed always clearly label it as such. But even if the seed isn't organic, you can still grow it using organic methods.

Despite the progress, seed companies are still dropping old varieties from their rosters and many time-tested varieties are on the verge of winking out of production entirely.

Earth sustainably is free and available to anyone who puts their hands in the soil," Coburn said. "This is our birthright as humans, to live in paradise. And it's only by conscious choice that we're going to get back to paradise."

Gardening Supplies

Sources of Fertilizer, Tools, Composting Equipment, Beneficial Insects, Season Extenders, and More

A.M. Leonard. "Tools that work" since 1885. 241 Fox Drive, Piqua, OH 45356-0816, (800)433-0633, www.amleo.com.

Beneficial Insects. www.A-1Unique.com or www.insectary.com.

Clean Air Gardening. Offers push mowers, composting supplies, and more. 5802 Penrose Avenue, Dallas, TX 75206, (214)370-0530, www.cleanairgardening.com.

Common Sense Landscape and Garden Care. P.O. Box 812, Arcadia, FL 34266, (877)877-0257, www.commonsensecare.com.

ComposTumbler. 160 Koser Road, Lititz, PA 17543, (800)880-2345, www.compostumbler.com.

Country Home Products. Offers a bounty of lawn and garden equipment, including the Newton Mower, a clean air-friendly cordless electric model. Meigs Road, P.O. Box 25, Vergennes, VT 05491, www.countryhomeproducts.com.

Dripworks. A leading seller of drip-irrigation supplies. 190 Sanhedrin Circle, Willits, CA 95490, (800)522-3747, www.dripworksusa.com.

Extremely Green Gardening Company. Specializes in organic fertilizers, pest and weed control. 49 Lincoln Boulevard, PMB 113, Abington, MA 02351, www.extremelygreen.com.

FEDCO. A Maine-based cooperative serving gardeners and farmers alike, FEDCO is closely allied with the Maine Organic Farmers and Gardeners Association. FEDCO offers tools, fertilizers, seeds, trees, and a wide variety of other grower's supplies. P.O. Box 520, Waterville, ME 04903, (207)873-7333, www.fedcoseeds.com.

What Is Mulch?

It's a simple idea: Put some organic stuff—straw (not hay, which has seeds), grass clippings, fall leaves—at the base of your plants, and that "mulch" will help retain water, suppress weeds, and slowly decompose and feed the underlying soil.

What can you use? Almost anything that isn't toxic and that won't start growing unintentionally. Thinnings and spent plants can make great mulch. Many weeds accumulate nutrients from deep in the soil. Take advantage of their prolific presence and hard work by putting their leaves (not their seeds) around the base of your plants. But beware of invasive plants. Wild morning glory, also known as bindweed, can root from even the smallest bit of itself, as many gardeners learn the hard way. And be sure to get your materials from areas that haven't been sprayed!

Other mulches include shredded paper, straw, cocoa shells (which smell like chocolate), oyster shell (which adds calcium), or most coarse wood products. If you get bark dust or wood chips, ask about the source. Some cities chip and sell all the accumulated wood waste, including materials treated with the toxic heavy metals arsenic and chromium.

Gardener's Supply Company. 128 Intervale Road, Burlington, VT 05401, (800)863-1700, (888)833-1412, www.gardeners.com.

Gardens Alive. Sells a wide variety of organic supplies including fertilizers, weed-suppressors, beneficial insects, and composting equipment. 5100 Schenley Place, Lawrenceburg, IN 47025, (513)354-1482, www.gardensalive.com.

Happy D Ranch. Down-to-earth ideas for a better environment, including worm bins and water filters. (888)989-1558, www.happydranch.com.

Hida Tool and Hardware. Specializes in excellent Japanese tools. 1333 San Pablo Avenue, Berkeley, CA 94702, (510)524-3700, www.hidatool.com.

NaturaLawn of America. 1 East Church Street, Frederick, MD 21701, (301)694-5440, www.nl-amer.com.

Organic Gardening **Magazine.** www.organicgardening.com.

Peaceful Valley Farm Supply. Offers the full range of organic growing supplies, from fertilizers and tools to composters and seeds. P.O. Box 2209, Grass Valley, CA 95945, (888)784-1722, www.groworganic.com.

Planet Natural. 1612 Gold Avenue, Bozeman, MT 59715, (406)587-5891, www.planetnatural.com.

Rabbit Hill Farm. Run by gardeners for gardeners, the farm offers composting worms as well as books, fertilizers, and worm-composting supplies. 288 SW CR 0020, Corsicana, TX 75110, (903)872-4289, www.aogc.org/pages/rhf.

Real Goods Trading. One of the groundbreaking suppliers of all manner of tools for ecological living, the garden offerings include compost bins and aerators, barrels for storing rainwater, and push (human-powered) lawnmowers. Route 101, Hopland, CA 95449, (800)762-7325, www.real goods.com.

Smith and Hawken. Renowned for high-end gardening tools, furniture, and ornaments. P.O. Box 8690, Pueblo, CO 81008-9998, (800)776-3336, www.smithandhawken.com.

Soil Soup. 305 9th Avenue North, Seattle, WA 98109, (877)711-7687, www.soilsoup.com.

Wormman's Worm Farm. Sells a variety of worms for composting as well as beneficial insects and other gardening supplies. P.O. Box 6947, Monroe Township, NJ 08831, (732)656-0369, www.wormman.com.

Worms.com. Offers a variety of worm-composting supplies, online discussion, and a daily digest of related news from around the world. 24 Leon Avenue, Norwood, PA 19074, (800)COMPOST (266-7678), www.worms.com.

Worm Woman. This is the website of Mary Appelhof, who literally wrote the book on worm composting. It offers advice as well as supplies. 10332 Shaver Road, Kalamazoo, MI 49024, (269)327-0108, www.wormwoman.com.

Plants and Seeds

Where to Find Heirloom and Unusual Plant Varieties

- At the epicenter of the movement to preserving our edible heritage is the **Seed Savers Exchange.** The membership organization publishes the definitive listings of where specific varieties are available (including catalogs and nurseries), tracks the growth and loss of varieties, and now includes a catalog with many unusual offerings. 3076 North Winn Road, Decorah, IA 52101, (563)382-5990, www.seedsavers.org.

- Looking for something specific, or wondering what experience others have had with a small company? The **Garden Watchdog** website (http://gardenwatchdog.com) lets you search for specific product types (e.g., organic seeds), see customer reviews, and link to company websites. You can even search by zip code for companies near you. Find specific plants online at www.plantsources.com.

- Around the United States, the Department of Agriculture runs several **National Germplasm Repositories** (www.ars-grin.gov/npgs/holdings.html), from which home gardeners as well as commercial operations can get seeds or cuttings at little or no cost.

- **Seed of Diversity Canada.** Not a seed company, but a nonprofit group of gardeners throughout Canada who save seed from rare and unusual garden plants in order to preserve the varieties. Members of the "living gene bank" grow 675 varieties of tomatoes, 275 varieties of beans, 37 varieties of eggplant, squash and peas, and about 300 more vegetables, fruit, flowers, and herbs. P.O. Box 36, Station Q, Toronto, Ontario M4T 2L7, Canada, (905)623-0353, www.seeds.ca.

- Ask at **farmers' markets** (see www.localharvest.org or www.ams.usda .gov/farmersmarkets), or check out the organizations or catalogs below.

- Check with your local cooperative extension for listings.

Abundant Life Seed. (360)385-5660, www.abundantlifeseeds.com.

Baker Creek Heirloom Seeds. 2278 Baker Creek Road, Mansfield, MO 65704, (417)924-8917, www.rareseeds.com.

Botanical Interests. Offers a good selection of unusual seed, including some organic seeds. 660 Compton Street, Broomfield, CO 80020, (800)486-2647, www.botanicalinterests.com.

Bountiful Gardens. 18001 Shafer Ranch Road, Willits, CA 95490-9626, (707)459-6410, www.bountifulgardens.org.

Filaree Farm. A huge selection of organic garlic varieties. (509)422-6940, www.filareefarm.com.

Golden Harvest Organics. 404 North Impala Drive, Fort Collins, CO 80521, (970)224-4679, www.ghorganics.com.

Heirloom Gardening **(newsletter).** 60 Howard Avenue, East Norwalk, CT 06855, (203)354-8756, www.heirloomgardening.com.

Heirloom Seeds. Sells very old varieties, some more than a century old! P.O. Box 245, West Elizabeth, PA 15088, (412)384-0852, www.heirloomseeds.com.

High-Altitude Gardens. Specializes in varieties adapted to harsh mountain climates, including many Russian tomato varieties. P.O. Box 1048, Hailey, ID 83333, (208)788-4363, www.seedsave.org.

JL Hudson, Seedsman. The huge catalog lists flowers, herbs, and vegetables by Latin name first, and so is not the most user-friendly, but still offers a wide variety of otherwise rare seeds. Star Route 2, Box 337, La Honda, CA 94020, http://catalog@jlhudsonseeds.net.

Johnny's Selected Seeds. All seeds and accessories are thoroughly tested at the company's certified organic farm in Maine. 955 Benton Avenue, Winslow, ME 04901, (207)437-9294, www.johnnyseeds.com.

Landreth Seed. The oldest seed company in the nation, it started operations in 1784. P.O. Box 16380, Baltimore, MD 21210-2229, (800)654-2407, www.landrethseeds.com.

Native Seeds/SEARCH. Company focuses on seeds adapted to the Southwest, with a huge selection of beans, corn, peppers, and other traditional Native American crops. 526 North 4th Avenue, Tucson, AZ 85705-8450, (520)622-5561, www.nativeseeds.org.

Peace Seeds. 2385 SE Thompson Street, Corvallis, OR 97333, (541)752-0421.

Prairie Garden Seeds. Box 118, Cochin, SK, Canada S0M 0L0, (306)386-2737, www.prseeds.ca.

Seeds of Change. The first of the big catalogs featuring organic heirloom seeds is now owned by M&M/Mars. The company offers a wide variety of rare and unusual seeds, including many vegetables you'll never see in the supermarket, and some organic food and gardening products. 3209 Richards Lane, Santa Fe, NM 87507, (888)762-4240, www.seedsofchange.com.

Southern Exposure Seed Exchange. Offers a growing selection of organic seed, working with independent growers on heirloom varieties that thrive in mid-Atlantic states. P.O. Box 460, Mineral, VA 23117, (540)894-9480, www.southernexposure.com.

Territorial Seed Company. Founded with the goal of offering seeds that grow in the maritime Northwest, Territorial offers a growing selection of organic seeds and plants. P.O. Box 158, Cottage Grove, OR 97424-0061, (888)657-3131, www.territorial-seed.com.

Thomas Jefferson Center for Historic Plants. P.O. Box 316, Charlottesville, VA 22902, (804)984-9821, www.monticello.org.

Good and Bad Bugs

Gardeners these days are remembering that a garden is more than just the plants within it. What you grow can also attract a variety of welcome wildlife, including bees, birds, and butterflies. Do so and you'll be rewarded not only with wildlife to watch, but critters that help improve the bounty of your fruits, flowers, and vegetables.

Patrick Ironwood gardens in a mountainside cove in Whitwell, Tennessee. The five acres he tends for research, education, and his family's food see some of the most chaotic weather on the continent. Hot humid summers and variable winters mean that when it comes to bugs, he never quite knows how many he's going to get.

Every gardener has favorite recipes for keeping bad bugs away. Some use sprays made with garlic or pepper. Others sprinkle coarse-ground oyster shell around new seedlings to discourage slugs. A strong stream of water from the garden hose will wash away aphids. Sheets of thinly spun plastics, known as floating row covers, can literally lock out pests. Ask other gardeners or check with your local nursery, extension office, or farmers' market for ideas that suit your region.

But Ironwood's favored approach is what's known as "integrated pest management," a practice that uses pesticides only as a last resort.

As director of landscaping and architecture for the Sequatchie Valley Institute at Moonshadow, Ironwood works to encourage predatory bugs including parasitic wasps, praying mantises, assassin beetles, ladybugs, and spiders. The predators feed on everything from aphids to grubs and caterpillars.

His primary aim is to increase the diversity of bugs on his bit of tended land, putting into practice the notion that a critical mass of lots of bugs will keep itself in check.

Some ideas for attracting beneficial insects, and protecting plants from bad ones:

- What you plant matters: Stick with **plant varieties that thrive in your environment**. In the same way that wild wolves pick on the slowest or sickest deer in the herd, bugs in your garden can tell which plants aren't thriving. If you choose well-adapted plant varieties, they'll have a better chance of growing faster than the bugs can eat them. (Good soil, once again, is also key.)

- **Don't give bad bugs a roadmap to their favorite foods.** Plant your broccoli in different places each year. Or spread individual tomato plants around the garden, rather than all in one spot, so bugs that find one won't find them all.

- Try **growing herbs and flowers in among your food crops** to attract beneficial predator bugs and confuse those that would share your harvest. Ironwood recommends interplanting with herbs including basil, sage, cilantro, garlic, chives, catnip, and yarrow. You can cut the herbs back and mulch with whatever you don't use in the kitchen. Other choices include anise hyssop, lavender, cosmos, and sweet alyssum, which all provide lots of beneficial-friendly nectar.

- **Import predators you don't have enough of.** Many companies now sell predatory insects such as lacewings, praying mantises, and even ladybugs. Once you bring them to your garden, though, make sure you have the bugs and plants they like so they'll stick around.

- **Keep some water around** so bugs can both breed and drink. Ironwood says a small drip—every five to ten seconds, not enough to add much to your water bill—creates a wet spot and special glint and tinkle that seem to attract beneficial birds and bugs.

- **Build or buy condos for native Mason bees**, which help pollinate crops. The most common at-home method is to drill holes three to five inches into scrap wood with a 5/16-inch drill bit. But you can also use a bundle of drinking straws or pencil-thick, hollow bamboo or reeds, and put the bundle inside a piece of plastic pipe to hold it all together. Put the apartment complex on a south-facing structure to keep it warm; or in a protected place such as under an eave. Make awnings over the holes with chicken wire or hardware cloth to protect the bees from hungry, nosy birds.

But perhaps the best way to keep good bugs in your garden, Ironwood says, is simply not to kill them. "Be open to them as not that creepy or dangerous, but just a normal part of a healthy system," he says.

Mail-Order Plant Nurseries

More and more nurseries are offering organically grown garden plants. But some of the more unusual varieties may be available only by mail order, where organic pickings are relatively few. The companies below sell plants that may not be strictly organic—their growers haven't gone through the official certification process but may still use organic practices—or may not be organic at all. But if diversity interests you, consider buying them anyway and growing them organically once they reach your garden.

Burnt Ridge Nursery and Orchards. Has a very good selection of fruit and nut trees, Northwest native plants, berries, and some unusual plants, all at excellent prices. 432 Burnt Ridge Road, Onalaska, WA 98570, (360)985-2873, http://landru.myhome.net/burntridge.

Cross Country Nurseries. A huge selection of hot peppers (with heat index), sweet peppers, and tomatoes. The website offers growing advice and a handy guide to tell you when it's safe to plant them in your area. P.O. Box 170, 199 Ringwood-Locktown Road, Rosemont, NJ 08556-0170, (908)996-4646, www.chileplants.com.

Edible Landscaping. 361 Spirit Ridge Lane, Afton, VA 22920, (434)361-9134, www.eat-it.com.

Forestfarm. One of the largest selections anywhere of "ornamental and useful plants from around the world." 990 Tetherow Road, Williams, OR 97544-9599, (541)846-7269, www.forestfarm.com.

Hidden Springs Nursery. Family-run nursery featuring "organically grown edible landscape plants for people and wildlife." Extensive offerings and reasonable prices. 170 Hidden Springs Lane, Cookeville, TN 38501-9178, (931)268-2592.

High Country Gardens. Specializes in plants suited for low-water gardening (known as xeriscaping). The catalog even shows garden plans. www.highcountrygardens.com.

Johnson Nursery. Outstanding selection of fruit trees. 1352 Big Creek Road, Ellijay, GA 30540, (888)276-3187, www.johnsonnursery.com.

Nolin River Nut Tree Nursery. Highly recommended, offering a good selection of named varieties of nut trees, persimmons, and paw paws. 797 Port Wooden Road, Upton, KY 42784, (270)369-8551, www.nolinnursery.com.

One Green World. An excellent selection of fruit and nut trees, berries, and unusual edible plants from around the world. 28696 South Cramer Road, Molalla, OR 97038, (503)651-3005, www.onegreenworld.com.

Oregon Exotics Nursery. Calls itself the world's largest source of rare and exotic useful plants, and very well may be. Their offerings include subzero citrus, ancient nuts, medicinal plants from the Amazon, and new USDA re-

The Edible Landscape

Growing native plants is catching on like wildfire, and for good reason. Because natives are adapted to local soils and weather patterns, they often need less attention to special watering or careful soil management. Many natives hold the soil in place—a handy trick if a portion of your garden includes a steep slope.

Natives often attract pollinators such as bees and butterflies, helping boost their diversity in your environment while helping nearby food plants make more fruit. More birds may also come to visit, keeping down garden bug pests, scratching up the soil in their search, and leaving behind fertilizer in the form of their droppings.

But despite the best of intentions, mimicking a native landscape in an isolated urban yard doesn't do all that much to make up for lost habitat. So what's the most ecological use of your garden space? At or near the top of the list is gardening for your own food.

There's no reason that what you plant for birds, butterflies, and bees can't also feed you and your family. Sunflowers are often called "nature's bird feeders," but you can plant enough to share the oil-rich seeds. Many fruit trees (including small ones that will fit even in urban backyards) can feed both birds and you. Bee balm, also known as Monarda or Oswego tea, not only attracts hummingbirds; it was used by members of the Boston Tea Party and other rebel Americans as a caffeine-free alternative to paying tea taxes to England.

Other edibles that attract wildlife are herbs and vegetables in the carrot family, including parsley, dill, fennel, coriander (cilantro), parsnips, and carrots. Most flowers will attract some beneficial insects (see the sidebar on page 220 on "good bugs"). Edible food crops may be passing their prime for human consumption when they start to flower, but they'll provide nectar for a variety of beneficial insects that will make your garden—and the birds you've attracted—thrive.

leases. 1065 Messinger Road, Grants Pass, OR 97527, (541)846-7578, www.exoticfruit.com.

Raintree Nursery. An excellent selection of fruit and nut trees, berries, and unusual edible plants from around the world. 391 Butts Road, Morton, WA 98356, (360)496-6400, www.raintreenursery.com.

Southmeadow Fruit Gardens. P.O. Box 211, 10603 Cleveland Avenue, Baroda, MI 49101, (269)422-2411, www.southmeadowfruitgardens.com.

California Rare Fruit Growers. Fullerton Arboretum, California State University, Fullerton, CA 92634, www.crfg.org. Membership is $30.

Home Orchard Society. A nonprofit educational organization dedicated to assisting both novice and expert growers and promoting the science, culture, and pleasure of growing fruit. Founded in 1975 in Portland, Oregon, Home Orchard Society operates worldwide. Membership is $15. P.O. Box 230192, Tigard, OR 97281, www.homeorchardsociety.org.

Maine Organic Farmers and Gardeners' Association. The oldest organic organization in the United States, MOFGA certifies organic farms and is a clearinghouse of information and political updates on organic issues. Membership is $25. P.O. Box 170, Unity, ME 04988, (207)568-4142, www.mofga.org.

North American Fruit Explorers. RR1 Box 94, Chapin, IL 62628, www.nafex.org. Membership is $13.

Oregon Tilth. A nonprofit research and education organization certifying organic farmers, processors, retailers, and handlers internationally. 470 Lancaster NE, Salem, OR 97301, (503)378-0690, www.tilth.org. Membership is $25.

Sequatchie Valley Institute at Moonshadow. Offers residential classes and internships in sustainable building, community, and permaculture. Website includes terrific resource lists. Route One, Box 304, Whitwell, TN 37397, (423)949-5922, www.svionline.org.

Southern Sustainable Agriculture Working Group. Its mission is "to empower and inspire farmers, individuals, and communities in the South to create an agricultural system that is ecologically sound, economically viable, socially just, and humane." P.O. Box 1138, Huntsville, AR 72740, www.ssawg.org.

Agrobotanicals. Website offers reference materials on pest and disease controls. www.agrobotanicals.com.

Appropriate Technology Transfer for Rural Areas. A terrific online resource for every aspect of organic growing, including composting, soil biology and science, pest management, fertilizing, and more. Includes an exhaustive listing of opportunities to intern or apprentice in sustainable agriculture. P.O. Box 3657, Fayetteville, AR 72702, (800)346-9140, http://attra.ncat.org.

Eco-Gardening.com (service of Green Culture). 23192 Verdugo Drive, Suite D, Laguna Hills, CA 92653, (877)204-7336, www.eco-gardening.com.

Food Not Lawns! P.O. Box 42174, Eugene, OR 97404, www.foodnotlawns.com.

National Organics Program (U.S. Department of Agriculture). www.ams.usda.gov/nop/indexNet.htm.

The National Wildlife Federation's Backyard Wildlife Gardening. The page helps you develop a wildlife garden and register your yard with plants that attract the birds and the bees. www.nwf.org/backyardwildlifehabitat.

Organic Gardening. This is the mother and the motherload of organic gardening resources. Offers books, magazine subscriptions, basic information, and advice, and links to suppliers of many organic products. www.organicgardening.com.

Organic Materials Review Institute (OMRI). Maintains the list of products certified for use in organic agriculture. If you're uncertain as to whether something is organic or not, this is where to look. P.O. Box 11558, Eugene, OR 97440, (541)343-7600, www.omri.org.

Composting Information

Clean Air Gardening. 5802 Penrose Avenue, Dallas, TX 75206, (214)370-0530, www.cleanairgardening.com.

Urban Options. East Lansing, MI, (517)337-0422, www.urbanoptions .org/pages/composting.htm.

U.S. Environmental Protection Agency. www.epa.gov/epaoswer/ non-hw/compost/index.htm.

WormDigest. Subscriptions to the thirty-two-page quarterly newsletter are $12. P.O. Box 544, Eugene, OR 97440.

Lawn Care

Environmental Protection Agency. www.epa.gov/epahome/home.htm.

Local extension agents. www.reeusda.gov.

Native plant organizations in your region. http://dir.gardenweb.com/ directory/nph-ind.cgi.

Magazines

Birds & Blooms. Although not about organic gardening per se, this magazine is a good resource for those interested in attracting birds to their gardens. 5400 South 60th Street, Greendale, WI 53129, (414)423-0100, www.birdsandblooms.com.

E/The Environmental Magazine. A national magazine about environmental issues, *E* is one of the few of its kind to include how-to information for green-minded homeowners on subjects including gardening. $20 for six issues, free trial subscription through the website. 28 Knight Street, Norwalk, CT 06851, (203)854-5559, www.emagazine.com.

Mother Earth News. Bimonthly magazine covers subjects ranging from gardening to natural health, with an emphasis on "blending old-fashioned values with modern ingenuity." 1503 SW 42nd Street, Topeka, KS 66609-1265, (800)234-3368, www.motherearthnews.com.

Organic Gardening. Bimonthly put out by the Rodale Institute; founder J. I. Rodale is the father of the modern organic movement. Also produce *Organic Style* and the online magazine *Newfarm.com*. www.organicgardening.com.

Permaculture Activist. Permaculture, roughly defined, is a system of garden planning and design that aims to make gardens as self-sustaining as possible. *Permaculture Activist* is one of the best resources for learning about these ideas and staying updated about the latest successes in its implementation. www.permacultureactivist.net.

Books

Because of its popularity, the general subject of gardening has produced an endless stream of books covering a staggeringly broad universe of subjects. Even the books that deal with organic gardens could fill a tall shelf. What follows are some selected resources, many of which include bibliographies for further reading.

Appelhof, Mary. *Worms Eat My Garbage*. Flower Press, 1997. The classic book on worm composting, from how to do it to how to use it.

Bubel, Nancy. *The New Seed Starter's Handbook*. Rodale Press, 1988. Very helpful for people learning to start plants from seeds.

Coburn, Heather. *Food Not Lawns: How to Turn Your Yard into a Garden and Your Neighborhood into a Community*. Chelsea Green, 2005. Author Heather Coburn is experienced, hugely knowledgeable, a true believer in the notion that gardening can change the world—and a terrific writer.

Coleman, Eliot. *The New Organic Grower: A Master's Manual of Tools and Techniques for the Home and Market Grower*. Chelsea Green, 1995. This book is one of the classic introductions to organic gardening, with clear instructions for beginners and good reference information for more seasoned growers.

Creasy, Rosalind. *The Complete Book of Edible Landscaping: Home Landscaping with Food-Bearing Plants and Resource-Saving Techniques.* Sierra Club Books, 1982. Very good in terms of getting started in your yard, with a focus on planting and caring for classic fruit trees.

Ellis, Barbara, and Fern Marshall Bradley. *The Organic Gardener's Handbook of Natural Insect and Disease Control: A Complete Problem-Solving Guide to Keeping Your Garden and Yard Healthy Without Chemicals.* Rodale Press, 1996.

Garrett, J. Howard. *The Dirt Doctor's Guide to Organic Gardening: Essays on the Natural Way.* University of Texas Press, 1995. Offers many recipes and tricks.

Hemenway, Toby. *Gaia's Garden: A Guide to Home-Scale Permaculture.* Chelsea Green, 2001. After you've learned the basics of organic gardening, this may be one of the best books around to take you to the next level. Permaculture, or "permanent agriculture," is about designing self-sustaining gardens that require little by way of outside fertilizers, water, or work by the gardener. Hemenway does a masterful job of pulling together all of the components of gardening—water, soil, bugs, and a huge variety of plants—and showing readers how to turn their back yards into functioning, edible ecosystems.

Jeavons, John, and Carol Cox. *The Sustainable Vegetable Garden: A Backyard Guide to Healthy Soil and Higher Yields.* Ten Speed Press, 1999. A beginner's book on growing intensively and organically. Jeavons is also the author of the classic *How to Grow More Vegetables.* Ten Speed Press, updated in 2002.

Kourik, Robert. *Designing and Maintaining Your Edible Landscape Naturally.* Metamorphic Press, 1986.

Ogden, Shepherd. *Straight-Ahead Organic: A Step-by-Step Guide to Growing Great Vegetables in a Less Than Perfect World.* Chelsea Green, 1999. This book covers all the basics on organic growing for beginners, and offers good reference information for those with more experience.

Peavy, William S., and Warren Peary. *Super Nutrition Gardening: How to Grow Your Own Power-Charged Foods.* Avery Penguin Putnam, 1992. Instructions for home gardeners on raising the nutritional content of fruits and vegetables.

Riotte, Louise. *Roses Love Garlic: Companion Planting and Other Secrets of Flowers.* Storey Press, 1998.

Seymour, John. *The Self-Sufficient Gardener: A Complete Guide to Growing and Preserving All Your Own Food.* Doubleday, 1979. A classic book by an author who has maintained old-time skills.

Van Nostrand, Jillian, et al. *Wild Woman's Garden: Seven Radical Weeds for Women Over 40.* Radical Weeds, 1998.

chapter eleven

Power for the People

Renewable Energy and Smart Conservation

Photo by Warren Gretz/DOE/NREL

When Curry Caputo and his wife, Andrea Lani, set out to build their first home in the small town of Whitefield, Maine, they hadn't planned on generating their own electricity. But after their local utility told them it would cost about $9,000 to connect power lines to their five-acre plot, the self-described environmentalists decided to consider all their options. Instead of spending their money setting up a conventional electrical system, they chose to make a bold foray into a brave new energy world.

The couple designed the house to take advantage of passive solar heating with large south-facing windows. Caputo and Lani also laid out about $17,000 for eight rooftop photovoltaic solar panels, twenty deep-cycle batteries and a computer control system. The "power" couple also invested in energy-efficient appliances and a backup generator. Caputo takes issue with anyone who says solar power isn't a viable option now, and he says he and his wife have only had to make minor modifications in how they live. Caputo expects the energy investments to pay for themselves within fifteen years.

The reality, however, is that Caputo and Lani are hardly typical energy users. The average U.S. household spends $1,338 on home energy a year, according to the Energy Information Administration (EIA). Across the country, nearly $1 million worth of energy is consumed every minute, and its generation represents the single most polluting industry in the nation. Globally, the United States accounts for about 26 percent of the world's energy use, despite comprising less than 5 percent of the human population. The Department of Energy predicts American residential energy use will increase by about 20 percent by 2020.

Much of the concern over energy use centers around its likely impacts on global warming, through the release of so-called greenhouse gases. Since the Industrial Revolution, reports the EIA, atmospheric concentrations of the primary greenhouse gas carbon dioxide (CO_2) have risen 30 percent. This increase is largely due to the combustion of fossil fuels for energy as well as transportation.

As the United States continues to grow in population, wealth, and power, CO_2 emissions continue to rise, and now make up about 25 percent of the world's total output. U.S. energy-related CO_2 emissions grew 16 percent between 1990 and 2002, according to the EIA. The average U.S. household is responsible for the emission of around 60 tons of CO_2 annually. This is a similar impact to driving nearly 133,000 miles in a year.

Americans continue to demand more energy-guzzling products, and a greater spectrum of products are becoming wired, from electric screwdrivers, nose clippers, and weed trimmers to digital displays on everything from toasters to automatic massagers. As the Worldwatch Institute reports, the average size of refrigerators in U.S. households increased by 10 percent between 1972 and 2001, and the number per home rose as well.

Still, there are many actions people, governments, and organizations can take to reduce future impact. Some, like Caputo and Lani, are taking personal action to generate their own energy from renewable sources, while others are heavily involved in conservation.

According to the U.S. Department of Energy, by 1992 energy-efficiency measures were saving Americans $150 billion every year, and were reducing carbon emissions by 300 million metric tons—the equivalent of 168 coal-fired power plants. But since then individual energy use has gone relentlessly up, partly because of fuel-hungry SUVs, and partly because of ever-larger homes (to accommodate all those big refrigerators). A University of Michigan study estimated that the average American household could reduce its energy bills by 65 percent simply by maximizing energy efficiency. And who doesn't want to save money?

The American way of life is heavily dependent on fossil fuels. The United States produces about 52 percent of its electricity by burning coal, 20 percent by nuclear power, 16 percent by combusting natural gas, 7 percent through hydropower, 3 percent by burning oil, and only about 2 percent through other renewable sources, according to Department of Energy data. These renewable technologies include solar, wind, and geothermal energy, as well as the burning of biomass (rotting plant material, wood waste, and vegetable oils). Despite their relatively low deployment rate in the United States, wind and solar power are among the fastest-growing sources of energy, both domestically and around the world.

The environmental group Natural Resources Defense Council (NRDC) argues, "America's swelling thirst for oil is one of our leading economic and national security problems." The group points out that the United States uses a quarter of the world's petroleum, while only controlling three percent of known reserves. "We're importing more than half the oil we use each day from some of the most unstable regions of the world, including spending more than $20 billion each year on Persian Gulf oil alone," writes NRDC.

A growing number of environmentalists, as well as such national leaders as John Kerry, Al Gore, and Robert F. Kennedy Jr., have argued that energy conservation and renewable technologies instead offer a practical, affordable light at the end of the dark tunnel of fossil-fuel dependence, oil-driven foreign policy, and pollution. Further, windmills and acres of solar panels represent much less favorable targets to terrorists than massive oil supertankers and sprawling fuel storage facilities. And unlike fossil fuels, the wind and sun are in no danger of running out within the next few centuries. *Business Week* magazine, not known as a major friend of the environment, recently recommended more use of renewable energy to help break America's "addiction to oil."

In 2001, Vice President Dick Cheney famously dismissed conservation as "a sign of personal virtue that is not a sufficient basis for a sound, comprehensive energy policy." Not surprisingly, his ties to the oil industry run as deep as Texas wells. Cheney served as CEO of oil services provider Halliburton before his election. As vice president, Cheney's industry-dominated energy task force excluded environmentalists and met behind closed doors, triggering a Supreme Court showdown. Just months after leaving the White House, Cheney's executive director of the National Energy Policy Development Group became a lobbyist on behalf of energy companies.

The Cheney-Bush administration not only proposed to cut incentives for energy efficiency, but also endorsed a plan built around dangerous, unpopular nuclear power, dubious and unproven fusion energy, and more oil and coal extraction, including from wilderness areas. The administration's first proposed federal energy bill included more than $14 billion in tax incentives and subsidies for these environmentally harmful industries. In contrast, Hal Harvey, executive director of The Energy Foundation, argues that it would probably only take a few billion dollars in federal investment to help make renewable technologies truly price-competitive.

Leading up to the summer of 2001, experts predicted that California was headed for a serious energy crisis, complete with rolling blackouts. Then the state government mobilized a $730 million conservation campaign that included "kill-a-watt" TV and radio ads, tougher efficiency standards for new construction, and financial incentives for conservation. What Cheney and other skeptics hadn't predicted was that these methods helped decrease total energy demand by up to 12 percent during peak times. As a result, the Golden State ended up with a *surplus* of energy by the end of the summer. In fact, NRDC points out that since 1980, conservation measures in California have equaled the output of eleven new power plants.

GREEN PRODUCTS

One great way eco-conscious consumers can cut their personal power drain is to let the sun do the work. The same technology that energizes satellites and powers hand-held calculators is now being used in an intriguing and diverse array of products.

For example, the California-based company Real Goods (which merged with natural products giant Gaiam of Colorado in 2001) offers a line of portable solar-powered radios, some of which can also be charged by an efficient dynamo hand crank (thirty seconds of cranking provides thirty minutes of listening).

Other popular solar-powered devices include lawnmowers ($750 from Real Goods), mosquito guards that emit high-frequency sounds to deter biting insects, water fountain pumps, small appliances such as the milk frother from German company Solarc, and a range of efficient battery chargers. Solarc's Scotty product uses small solar cells to charge almost any small electronic device, from batteries to cell phones and CD players. Some "portable power packs" generate enough electricity from the sun to run laptops, bringing new meaning to the idea of the mobile office. Swiss LeJour solar watches ($155) charge in either bright sunlight or ambient lighting, and can function for about a month in complete darkness.

Although the very idea of solar-powered lights might sound like a joke or con, a little invention called batteries has made the idea work surprisingly efficiently, turning even some of the harshest skeptics into true believers. For example, a number of parks and private landowners have now invested in solar sign and flag lighting kits. Solar-powered security lamps are also gaining popularity.

In late 1998, Maui's Keopuolani Park opened a solar-illuminated jogging trail to the public. Nineteen solar lights made by Heinz Solar (now owned by Solar Outdoor Lighting, Inc.) shine for about six hours a night. The wind and vandal-resistant units each consist of one 110-watt, single crystal photovoltaic panel, two 95 amp hour gel cell batteries (which have a four-day reserve capability), and four thirteen-watt compact fluorescent lamps. The installation cost of $77,000 was actually $15,400 *cheaper* than the estimated cost of $92,400 for conventional lighting, since the extension of nearby electrical lines would have been necessary. The county estimates the solar lights also save about $400 per year in electrical costs.

For smaller lighting jobs, the latest solar flood and decorative lamps now fit the bill. The attractive pagoda-style, four-watt fluorescent light ($60) from Solite, for example, uses a solar cell and a NiCad battery to provide about six hours of light per night. It switches on automatically at dusk. Similar lights, in a wide variety of attractive designs, are available from Alpan (formerly Siemens) and Soltek, among others.

Improving safety and adding cheerful ambience to driveways, paths, and lawns across the world is a growing array of solar-powered accent lights. Since they require very minimal to no wiring, these affordable lights are usually far easier to install and maintain than traditional models.

Many solar-powered accent lights take advantage of efficient LED (light-emitting diode) technology. Most of the power supplied to an LED is converted into light, with minimal waste heat, making it extremely efficient compared with conventional bulbs. So not only do LEDs remain cool to the touch, but they also use a fraction of the energy consumed by standard bulbs. An LED can last for decades, providing 100,000 to 200,000 hours of operation, and they are so compact that they are commonly used as backlighting behind the liquid crystal displays of notebook computers. For years, a drawback of the technology was that it couldn't produce very bright light, which has thus far limited its range of applications. However, new high-intensity LEDs are now pushing the envelope.

A string of seventy LED holiday lights ($15) uses only four cents in energy costs after running six hours a day for a month. Compact solar LED "candle" or "carriage-style" lanterns provide portability and flexibility without plugs or open flames. Particularly striking are LED-lighted stepping stones, which can provide warm, soft illuminations for walkways and driveways. These appealing faux stones are typically made from fiberglass and resin, and require no wiring or maintenance. In Alpan's $140 model, a single-crystal solar cell charges the built-in AA NiCad battery during the day.

Seeing the Light

As the ubiquitous screwing-in-a-lightbulb jokes make clear, those iconic pieces of glowing hardware never seem to last as long as they should. Despite the fact that some of Thomas Edison's original incandescent bulbs still burn in museums, contemporary bulbs often last only a few months.

The tungsten filament incandescent bulb has remained the standard for so long because it is cheap, and because it is so well-known. But the bulb has a darker side. An incandescent light has a short lifespan and is expensive (and therefore usually more polluting) to operate. According to the U.S. Department of Energy, only 10 percent of the electricity an incandescent light consumes is actually used to generate light. The other 90 percent becomes heat, which is simply wasted.

Halogen bulbs are actually modified incandescents. The outer bulb is made of quartz or special glass, and the technology uses the reactive properties of a halogen gas to increase performance of the filament. Halogen bulbs produce bright light and have the advantage of small size, which makes them especially suited for vehicles and trendy track lighting. They typically last two to three times as long as ordinary bulbs, and are 10 to 40 percent more efficient.

Halogen bulbs have some serious drawbacks, however. There is a relatively high risk of the quartz or glass shattering violently, and the bulbs are expensive. The California Energy Commission estimates there are between 30 and 40 million halogen torchieres in the United States, and they have sparked a firestorm of criticism. These lamps usually take 300- or 500-watt

Forget the Folk Wisdom: Turn It Off

Many people grow up being told that it is better to leave lights on for extended periods than to turn them off and on again. This belief arose in the 1940s when energy was cheap and technologies were inefficient. But these days, leaving the lights on in an attempt to save energy is not a bright idea.

Modern fluorescent lamps use much less starting energy than historic models. Researchers at the U.S. Naval Civil Engineering Laboratory and elsewhere have discovered that turning off a contemporary fluorescent fixture for only one to five seconds saves the energy required to turn it back on. And just one extra hour a day of unnecessary lighting can increase electricity costs by 5 to 10 percent per month.

Bill Prindle of the Alliance to Save Energy explains, "The energy savings from turning a light off for a brief period of time greatly outweigh any minuscule reduction in the bulb's life span." In fact, many experts argue that turning lights off can actually help them last longer. The Vermont Agency of Natural Resources reports that a standard fluorescent lamp can run for 34,000 hours if left on round-the-clock, which amounts to 3.9 years. "However, by turning the lamp off for 12 hours a day," reports the agency, "it increases the overall longevity of the lamp to 6.8 years."

The Northwest Energy Efficiency Alliance suggests that for most fluorescent fixtures, it is a good idea to turn the lights off if they won't be used for fifteen to twenty minutes or longer. Turning off an incandescent lightbulb starts saving energy after three seconds; halogen lights, after five minutes.

Similarly, leaving your home or office computer on all the time may not be the smartest decision. According to the Energy Star program, powering down unused computers and monitors actually increases their longevity because it generates less heat, collects less dust, and reduces mechanical stress. Over one year, concludes Energy Star, turning off a typical computer when not in use can save an estimated $186 in home electricity and prevent the release of one and a half tons of carbon dioxide into the air.

It also helps to set your computer to go into "sleep mode" when not in use, rather than using graphical screensavers, which take energy to run. It is a simple adjustment on most modern computers, and it usually only takes a few seconds for your system to "wake up" when you need to use it again. Some computers can also be set to have their hard drives power down when not needed, saving even more electricity.

halogen bulbs, which "waste energy by creating four times more heat than the average incandescent bulb," explains the California Commission. A 500-watt halogen reaches temperatures of more than 1,200 degrees, which can ignite many fabrics on contact.

After several widely publicized fires started by halogen bulbs, many instituions banned the torchieres. Further, halogen lamps add considerable heat to indoor air, which can result in people running fans or air conditioners more than otherwise needed. The California Energy Commission argues, "Halogen torchieres are an example of low-price technology that proves to be costly in the long run. Using a [300-watt halogen] lamp for two hours a day will consume nearly 220 kilowatt-hours of electricity in a year, at an average cost of $18." This annual price tag is more than what most of the lamps cost.

Another contemporary take on the old-fashioned lightbulb is the so-called EnergyMiser or Supersaver bulb. These are specialized incandescents that use 5 to 13 percent less electricity than standard bulbs. Such models cost a little more, but yield substantial energy savings. Buyer beware, however: EnergyMiser bulbs are not the same as regular "longlife" incandescents, which gain lifespan by sacrificing energy efficiency.

In a twist that is surprising to many environmentalists, the jewel in the eco-smart lighting universe is actually a bulb that usually contains one of the Earth's most toxic pollutants: mercury. Today's compact fluorescent lights (CFL), which are being widely adopted by greens around the world, actually got their start as the mercury vapor lights patented by Peter Cooper Hewitt in 1901. Nowadays fluorescent bulbs contain only tiny amounts of mercury, which can be safely remediated by qualified recyclers. The key is to dispose of spent bulbs properly.

The new generation of CFL bulbs combine the Earth-friendly benefits of fluorescent technology with the design features people have come to expect from incandescents. CFLs now come in a wide assortment of colors and shapes, and can be engineered to give off a warm, attractive glow without harsh glare. Contemporary fluorescent ballasts have eliminated the flickering and audible buzz that turned many people off to those white tubes in the past. Many CFLs can now be used with dimmer switches, and most can be screwed easily into existing light fixtures (perhaps spawning a whole new class of jokes).

Fluorescent bulbs last ten to fifteen times longer than incandescents. This means they reduce the amount of trash going to landfills. Yet to produce the same amount of light, fluorescents use only one-quarter to one-

Greening Your Castle Naturally

Not everyone has the resources and the ability to generate their own electricity from the sun, wind, or Earth. But there are many other ways people can improve the environmental footprint of their homes, as well as save money.

For instance, well-designed daylighting can slash the energy needed for illumination by 50 to 80 percent, according to the U.S. Green Building Council. Large, well-placed windows and skylights will obviously let the light in. But many home layouts only allow so much light penetration. That's why many people are discovering the benefits of high-tech skylights such as the SunPipe, Solatube, and Sun Tunnel Skylight, which trap light and channel it down through a tube mounted in your roof. These devices can be located on one section of your roof and direct light to another, providing tremendous flexibility. Fiber-optic systems that provide even more natural illumination are also in development.

In colder climates, tips to a greener home include using Mexican tiles that hold and radiate heat, putting in south-facing windows, using energy-absorbent paints on exterior walls and roofs, making sure your dwelling is sealed from drafts, and sinking rooms below ground. Another tip is to build or buy only the square footage that you really need, so you don't have to waste energy on unused space. New houses in the United States were 38 percent bigger in 2000 than in 1975, despite the fact that the average household included fewer people.

Many homes also benefit from so-called green roofs, which are covered in plants to reduce the heat island effect of solid surfaces. More ambitious home designers may want to investigate such alternative materials as straw bale and rammed earth construction.

third of the energy. As the Californa Energy Commission points out, this means that a 20-watt CFL used in place of a 75-watt incandescent will save around 550 kilowatt-hours over its lifetime, while providing an equivalent amount of illumination. At a coal-fired power plant, those 550 kilowatt-hours would have required about 500 pounds of the black stuff, which would have released 1,300 pounds of carbon dioxide and twenty pounds of sulfur dioxide into the atmosphere.

Nationwide, the United States devotes 25 percent of its total energy consumption to lighting. A typical household uses about 2,000 kilowatt-hours per year, which usually works out to 10 to 15 percent of the family's energy expenditure and costs around $110. Commercial establishments tend to spend 20 to 30 percent of their total energy budgets on lighting. If every

American household switched from incandescents to CFLs, it would cut power demand for lighting in half.

Since light output is actually measured in lumens and not in watts, a good way to save energy is to select the bulb with the lumens you need, and then choose the one rated to the lowest watts. While a CFL may cost $10 compared to 75 cents for a traditional bulb, consumers who leave their lights on for four hours a day will realize a $5.85 savings after the second year, according to the American Council for an Energy-Efficient Economy (ACEEE).

One 18-watt CFL bulb will replace ten 75-watt incandescents and save $45 in electricity costs over its lifetime. In fact, electricity accounts for a whopping 88 percent of the total cost of producing light, while bulbs only comprise 4 percent and labor comprises 8 percent, according to the Energy Efficient Lighting Association.

The more people use CFLs, the more bulbs are produced, driving the price per unit down. Global sales of CFLs increased nearly thirteenfold between 1990 and 2001. Major manufacturers include GE, Panasonic, Osram, Sylvania, Philips, MaxLite, and SunPark. There are even good alternatives to torchiere styles. Further reducing the cost of CFLs, many utilities offer rebates on the technology.

Other tips for reducing energy use for lighting include making sure to turn off lights when you leave the room, and installing timers, occupancy sensors, and dimmers. Another bright idea is to use task lighting to illuminate only specific areas at a time. People can also maximize daylight by using light colors for walls and curtains.

Keeping Cool and Staying Warm

Most households spend 50 to 70 percent of their energy budgets on temperature control. The percent rises to two-thirds in colder regions. U.S. heating systems release a billion tons of carbon dioxide a year, so reducing energy use for heating may be the single most effective way to reduce your home's contribution to global environmental problems, as well as keep more money in your pocket.

The good news is there are many practical steps homeowners can take to maximize efficiency. The Department of Energy suggests, "If your heating system or air conditioner is old or inefficient, it may also be cost effective to replace it with a newer high-efficiency design." In fact, most heating equip-

Watch Those Windows

Senior Scientist Rob Watson of the Natural Resources Defense Council says windows should also be airtight and double-glazed. Triple glazing may even make sense in the coldest climates. Other advances that significantly raise a window's R-value, and therefore make it a better insulator, include gas or vacuum fills, interpane barriers, and insulating frames. Casement windows are generally the most efficient type, followed by awning and sliding windows. Double-hung styles are least efficient. Also, choose Energy Star–rated windows.

Another window feature that should pay for itself in energy savings over time is a "low-e film," which is a very thin metal oxide or semiconductor film that reduces incoming heat while retaining visibility. The technology works in reverse for greenhouses. Future green homes will likely take advantage of next-generation "smart" windows, which will adjust light filtering either at the push of a button or automatically based on temperature.

ment is only designed to last about twenty years. If 40 million households upgraded their 70 percent efficiency furnaces to those rated at 90 percent, it would reduce output of CO_2 by 45 million tons. If you have electric heat, consider switching to more efficient natural gas.

Even easier actions, simple to put in place in the short term, include the regular maintenance and changing of air filters and turning down the thermostat (which can be done automatically with an inexpensive electronically programmable model). Turning down the heat at night and using timers to reduce usage when occupants are away can save tremendous amounts of energy. Also, in hot weather, running big heat generators such as washers, dryers, and ovens in the morning or evening can reduce the need for cooling. So can planting shade trees.

And don't forget the power of insulation. *The Consumer Guide to Home Energy Savings* estimates that a third of a home's heat loss is through poorly sealed windows and doors, which translates to a national waste equaling all the oil carried by the Alaska pipeline. Weather stripping and caulking are easy remedies. Natural fibers such as cellulose and cotton, as well as so-called radiant barriers, can provide excellent insulation without the possible health effects of traditional fiberglass. Make sure your attic, in particular, is well insulated.

Another important piece of the energy efficiency puzzle is ductwork. Senior scientist Rob Watson of NRDC says inadequately sealed ductwork can cause higher energy bills and release dust back into the home. In a 1990 Florida study, 85 percent of homes surveyed had leaky ducts. Consumers may also want to invest in Heat Recovery Ventilators, which introduce fresh air and reuse heat, thereby lowering energy bills while increasing air quality. Similarly, such devices as solar-powered fans (around $195) keep homes cool by pushing hot, stagnant air out of the attic in summer.

Keeping cool also need not be such a heated topic. The Energy Efficiency and Renewable Energy Network recommends that room air-conditioners should have an Energy Efficiency Ratio of at least 9.0 and above 10.0 for hot climates. Central air-conditioners are ranked according to their Seasonal Energy Efficiency Ratio, which should be a minimum of 10.0, although the best units are rated at nearly 17. Also, don't forget to limit use of bath and kitchen fans while the air-conditioner is on.

The Future of Appliances

Household appliances use substantial amounts of energy. To see for yourself, buy or borrow an inexpensive digital power meter, which can be plugged between the appliance and a wall socket to track energy usage.

To reduce impact on the environment, buy only appliances that have high efficiency ratings from the Environmental Protection Agency (EPA)'s Energy Star program. The program posts Energy Guide ratings, usually in the form of yellow stickers, on appliances listing annual operating costs and consumption. A substantial number of products in more than forty categories now carry the Energy Star label, from home electronics to office and commercial equipment (as well as CFLs). If all Americans switched to these labeled products over the next fifteen years, energy costs would be reduced by an estimated $100 billion, and the savings in greenhouse gas emissions would equal taking 17 million cars off the road.

Another tip is to plug electronics devices into power strips (particularly if they're not Energy Star–rated) and turn those off when not in use, or simply unplug the products directly, thereby preventing the "energy vampire" effect. According to the EPA, this phenomenon means that half of the power drain by home electronics occurs when the products are turned off.

There is also ample opportunity to green up the laundry room. Eco-minded consumers have begun to do what their grandparents did: Dry clothes on a clothesline or rack. Dryers use a large amount of energy, and they really aren't necessary to keep a clean household. Ambitious environmentalists may want to forego electric washers as well, and instead try the efficient hand-cranked models that are advertised in back-to-the-land catalogs (about $50). Particularly for delicates and small loads, these devices may also make sense as supplemental appliances.

For the typical consumer who doesn't have the time or interest to adopt old-fashioned techniques, new technology has bestowed impressive gains in energy (and water) efficiency on select models of electric washers and dryers, as well as dishwashers. Companies such as homegrown Staber, Sweden's Asko, and Germany's Miele have excelled in this arena, although efficient models are also being introduced by such mainstream brands as Kenmore, Maytag, and Whirlpool. Spinning dryers that remove water from clothes by centrifugal force use much less energy than conventional models, since they don't produce heat and take much less time.

Regardless of the machine, try to wash your clothes in warm or cold water instead of hot. Additionally, make sure your dishwasher or washing machine is full when you run it, and use energy-saving settings. Disabling the heat in the drying cycle can save 20 percent of your dishwasher's total electricity use.

Further, make sure your refrigerator and freezer have tight seals and are set to optimum temperatures (normally thirty-seven and three degrees, respectively). Sun Frost and other manufacturers also offer highly efficient models.

Pool owners can improve their eco-footprint by investing in sun-powered pool systems, which are time-tested and extremely efficient. Albuquerque, New Mexico–based AAA Solar offers a setup that keeps outdoor pools clean and heated ($1,075 to $2,490). Helicol installed the solar systems that heated the swimming pools of the Atlanta 1996 and Athens 2004 summer Olympics games, and is well established in the private and public market.

WHAT YOU CAN DO

There are many ways each of us can reduce our energy footprint. Often the first step is to assess personal energy needs and actual consumption. A good way to begin this process is to type in your zip code at Energy Star's Home Energy Saver website (http://hes.lbl.gov/hes). The site estimates the annual energy bill for an average house in your area, and then suggests practical ways to reduce costs. The next step is to bring in an expert to do a home energy audit. Many utilities provide the valuable service free or at a low cost to their customers.

Another step is to consider how your home energy is produced. While critics such as Public Citizen have warned about the risks of deregulation to consumers, and the media widely blames the process for California's 2001 energy woes, eco-conscious consumers can use the system to their advantage when applicable and choose to buy power produced from renewable sources.

For example, energy customers in Florida, New Jersey, New York, Pennsylvania, Ohio, Oregon, and Texas can choose to buy their electricity from Green Mountain Energy, the nation's largest retail provider of cleaner power. The switch is extremely easy, because there is no rewiring or interruption of service. Power is still routed through your local utility. Green Mountain says a Texas household buying their 100 percent wind-generated power for a year could offset more than 17,000 pounds of CO_2, which is the equivalent of taking a car off the road for a year.

Homeowners who really want to make a difference may consider generating their own electricity. People need not necessarily join Caputo and Lani and the estimated 150,000 other Americans who have completely severed ties with power companies. Getting off the grid costs between $20,000 and $50,000, says Dave Hollister of Sundance Power Systems in Mars Hill, North Carolina.

A much easier option for the typical household is to start with a smaller installation to supplement existing grid electricity. A majority of states have net metering laws, which means utilities are required to allow independent power producers to plug into the grid. In these states, utilities must buy any excess energy. This means many families get the thrill of watching their meter run backward when they don't use all the power they generate, and the money they earn can help pay for the system.

Depending on the three rules of real estate—location, location, location—homeowners may be able to take advantage of small-scale hydroelectric or geothermal generating capabilities. For those who live near running water or tidal zones, one small water turbine can be enough to generate a household's power needs. Care can be taken to minimize impact on aquatic life. Manufacturers include Ampair, Harris Hydroelectric, and Energy Systems and Design. Small hydro systems work particularly well with solar installations, since they both can charge the same batteries.

Geothermal energy need not require a location with steam coming to the surface, as is famously the case in Iceland and New Zealand. Today's geothermal heat pumps can be placed in the ground in many locales, and take advantage of the natural warmth of the Earth to heat water and mitigate home temperature. No greenhouse gases are emitted, and there are no flames, fumes, odors, or threats of carbon monoxide release. Home units from Indiana-based WaterFurnace can help families save up to 60 percent of their annual energy bills.

Wind energy has grown 30 percent annually over the past five years. According to the catalog *Creative Energy Technologies* (CET), "Wind power can be cost effective if the average wind speed is nine miles per hour (mph) or more at the location of the wind generator. If you are using wind in combination with photovoltaic power, it may be cost effective if you have good wind only during part of the year." However, because of turbulence, a wind turbine should be mounted at least twenty feet higher than any obstruction within 300 feet.

Affordable 1,000- and 3,000-watt wind power systems will offset 20 and 60 percent of a typical home's electric bill, respectively. CET explains that as wind speed doubles, the power delivered is eight times as great.

Go Solar

For a variety of reasons, including ease of placement and low maintenance, solar is the renewable of choice for many homeowners. Between 1990 and 1999, the solar power industry around the world grew at an annual rate of 16 percent. A large part of the growth can be attributed to the developing world, where the technology makes especially good economic sense because of remote locations. But the homegrown market is maturing.

On a bright sunny day, the sun shines approximately 1,000 watts of energy per square meter onto the Earth's surface. This plentiful, natural energy can be harvested in a number of different ways, and is not an option reserved only for those in hot, sunny climates. Solar thermal systems use the sun's heat directly, and are either passive, in which the energy transfers itself, or active, in which mechanical devices collect and pump heat. Photovoltaic (PV) systems make electricity directly from sunlight, and are exemplified by the iconic blue or black panels adorning rooftops around the world.

In 2004, the price per watt of solar-generated electricity was $5.85, which is still more expensive than fossil-fuel power, but cheaper than nuclear. The price of the power has dropped dramatically in the last twenty years, and

In Hot Water

Many people would probably be surprised to learn that, behind heating and cooling, the hot water heater is the home's largest energy user. As Jay Burch of the National Renewable Energy Laboratory explains, "Running the electric water heater of a single-family home for one year creates more emissions than driving an automobile 12,000 miles."

Conventional water heaters run all the time to keep hot water on tap twenty-four hours a day, which means a sizable amount of heat is lost to the outside air. A tankless water heater, on the other hand, heats water only as needed by passing it through a gas burner or electric element. The supply of hot water never runs out and no energy is wasted keeping it warm. A disadvantage is a limited flow rate, which can be overcome with multiple heaters. Another option is the heat pump unit, which takes heat from the surrounding air and transfers it to the water in the tank—meaning it works like a refrigerator in reverse. Such units use half the electricity of conventional heaters, although they don't work well in cold temperatures.

The sun's rays can also be used to heat water, either directly or through an intermediate heat-transfer fluid. Collectors are typically mounted on a roof. These systems are often best for preheating water for another method. Similarly, homeowners can install systems that take advantage of the home's larger heating system, such as a tankless coil heater hooked up to a boiler. A variety of alternative water heaters are available from such companies as Get Tankless and Super Supreme.

For those who need to get a few more years out of their current water heaters, there are a few simple steps that can be taken to increase energy efficiency. Turning the temperature down to 120 degrees from the common 150 degrees can save up to 15 percent of energy a month. Insulating the tank and piping also makes a big difference. Low-flow showerheads can reduce consumption of hot water.

many experts predict that it may become the cheapest form of energy within the next decade and a half or so. The top five producers of solar cells in 2001 were Sharp, BP Solar, Kyocera, Siemens Solar, and AstroPower (since acquired by GE). Real Goods has "solarized" more than 60,000 U.S. homes and businesses during its long history.

PV cells produce no air pollution, hazardous waste, or noise, and they produce considerably more energy in their long life (typically thirty years or so) than is needed to produce them. But when the sun isn't shining, they require batteries. For large installations, a number of electronic components are also needed. PV cells can be of the traditional panel design, or thin-film wafers, which are less efficient but can be integrated into building materials. United Solar Systems of Michigan is one company that offers solar roofing shingles, which function well as roofing material and blend seamlessly into contemporary architecture. Such PV devices cost a little more than large panels (the shingles sell for about $139 each), but are attractive.

A variety of financing options can help make solar technology fiscally feasible for a range of budgets—not just the ultra-rich. Government incentives are usually a key part of the equation, because the technology is still relatively young, and it must compete with the relatively enormous subsidies still in place for fossil fuels.

The Bush administration's first proposed federal energy bill was slated to include a 15 percent solar residential tax credit (capped at $2,000) for the installation of photovoltaic or solar thermal systems. But given the blockage of the bill, the only help Uncle Sam lends to renewable energy projects is President Clinton's Million Solar Roofs program, which was conceived to get solar energy systems on one million U.S. commercial and residential buildings by 2010. Consumers may qualify for financial and technical help from the program.

More than twenty states and territories also offer personal tax breaks for renewable energy projects, including Alabama, Arizona, California, Colorado, Georgia, Hawaii, Idaho, Kansas, Louisiana, Maryland, Massachusetts, Montana, New York, North Carolina, North Dakota, Ohio, Oklahoma, Oregon, Rhode Island, Utah, West Virginia, and Puerto Rico. Barry Hopkins, a policy analyst with the Council of State Governments, says such programs also help generate revenue and create jobs in deploying new technology. Local governments and utilities sometimes have programs in place as well. The nonprofit Interstate Renewable Energy Council maintains a searchable Database of State Incentives for Renewable Energy (online at www.dsireusa.org).

As Caputo and Lani found out the hard way, conventional banks tend to view loans for renewable energy projects skeptically. However, a number of progressive lending institutions—including Wainwright Bank and Trust of Boston and Permaculture Credit Union of New Mexico—do offer excellent interest rates for investment in the technology. Homeowners may also finance renewable energy set-ups with home-equity loans, which can make payments tax-deductible.

Alliance to Save Energy. Promotes energy efficiency through research, policy advocacy, education, public-private partnerships, technology deployment, and communications. 1200 18th Street NW, Suite 900, Washington, DC 20036, (202)530-2231, www.ase.org.

American Council for an Energy-Efficient Economy. Provides a wealth of consumer resources on saving energy, including posting ratings of energy-efficient appliances. 1001 Connecticut Avenue, NW, Suite 801, Washington, DC 20036, (202)429-8873, www.aceee.org.

The Big Frog Mountain Corporation. Suppliers of alternative and renewable energy equipment. 100 Cherokee Boulevard, Suite 321, Chattanooga, TN 37405, (423)265-0307, www.bigfrogmountain.com.

EcoBuild Companies. Experts in green architecture. 5 Jean Road, Arlington, MA 02478, (781)646-6165, www.ecobuild.com.

Efficient Windows Collaborative. Provides useful information on efficient windows. 1200 18th Street NW, Suite 900, Washington, DC 20036, (202)530-2231, www.efficientwindows.org.

EPA Energy Star Program. Government program that sponsors green initiatives and rates a broad spectrum of products on energy efficiency. 1200 Pennsylvania Avenue NW, Washington, DC 20460, (888)STAR-YES, www.energystar.gov.

Fully Independent Residential Solar Technology (FIRST) Inc. Independent nonprofit set up to teach people how to heat and power their own homes with solar energy. 66 Snydertown Road, Hopewell, NJ 08525, (609)466-4495, www.solarhome.org.

Green Mountain Energy Company. Retailer of renewable electricity to residential, business, institutional and governmental customers in a growing number of states. P.O. Box 42349, Austin, TX 78704, (800)286-5856, www.greenmountain.com.

Home Power **Magazine.** This journal of homemade energy is packed with articles, charts, system schematics, pricing tables, and availability information. $22.50 per year for six issues. P.O. Box 520, Ashland, OR 97520, (800)707-6585, www.homepower.com.

JC Solar Homes. This company serves as a source of information and plans for solar installations. 890 Bruce Drive, Wantagh, NY 11793, (516) 785-6947, www.jc-solarhomes.com.

Native Energy. The company offers ways to offset greenhouse gas emissions from your home or business with 100 percent wind energy, much of which is produced on Native American land. P.O. Box 22, North Ferrisburgh, VT 05473, (800)924-6826, www.nativeenergy.com.

Positive Energy Conservation Products. This company produces *The Green Builder's Catalog* in print and online, which is an excellent place to shop for a wide range of renewable and energy-efficiency technology. P.O. Box 7568, Boulder, CO 80306, (800)488-4340, www.positive-energy.com.

Real Goods Solar Living Institute. This nonprofit organization is dedicated to promoting sustainable living through environmental education. The group is a spin-off from renewable energy product giant **Real Goods**, which can be contacted at (800)762-7325, www.realgoods.com. The Institute: P.O. Box 835, Hopland, CA 95449, (707)744-2017, www.solarliving.org.

Solar Energy Industries Association (SEIA). Trade association for the solar industry. 1616 H Street NW, 8th Floor, Washington, DC 20006, (202)628-7745, www.seia.org.

Southwest Windpower. The world's top seller of small wind turbines. 2131 North First Street, Flagstaff, AZ 86004, (928)779-9463, www.windenergy.com.

Sun Frost. Leader in ultra-efficient refrigerators. P.O. Box 1101, Arcata, CA 95518, (707)822-9095, www.sunfrost.com.

U.S. Department of Energy program on **Energy Efficiency and Renewable Energy.** Provides information and support. Info Center: (877)337-3463, eereic@ee.doe.gov, www.eere.energy.gov.

WaterFurnace International. Sells a range of geothermal heating and cooling systems for residential, commercial and institutional applications. 9000 Conservation Way, Fort Wayne, IN 46809, (800)GEO-SAVE, www.waterfurnace.com.

Books

Power with Nature: Solar and Wind Energy Demystified ($24.95, PixyJack Press, 2003) by Rex A. Ewing is a practical, highly readable book written by someone who actually lives off the grid. The book explains the essential concepts of renewable energy in plain language and includes lucid diagrams, tables, and worksheets.

The Complete Idiot's Guide to Solar Power for Your Home ($19.95, Alpha Books, 2002) by Dan Ramsey is filled with real-world tips and know-how to help anyone get started in the exciting world of home power generation.

The Real Goods Solar Living Sourcebook: The Complete Guide to Renewable Energy Technologies and Sustainable Living ($30, Real Goods, 2001) is an invaluable resource from the Real Goods team that is filled with detailed explanations, sensible advice and technical data. Now in its eleventh edition, the book is edited by Douglas M. Pratt and John Schaeffer.

The Return of the Solar Cat Book ($14.95, Patty Paw Press, 2003) by Jim Augustyn is a delightful update of the 1979 cult classic, which used unique line drawings and hilarious feline humor to teach basic concepts of solar energy. The new edition includes most of the original's brilliant material plus new information.

The Solar House: Passive Heating and Cooling ($29.95, Chelsea Green, 2002) by Daniel D. Chiras is a tremendously useful guide for do-it-yourselfers and anyone interested in maximizing the efficiency of the built environment.

Wind Power: Renewable Energy for Home, Farm, and Business ($50, Chelsea Green, 2004) by Paul Gipe, also a new edition, is an authoritative resource packed with color photos, diagrams, data charts, and explanations of this emerging technology. For a slimmer, less expensive option, consider Gipe's 1999 *Wind Energy Basics: A Guide to Small and Micro Wind Systems* ($19.95, Chelsea Green).

Going Green
Ecotravel Comes of Age

Photo by Inga Spence/Index Stock

*A*t a 7,000-foot elevation in the Southern Sierra Madre de Chiapas Mountains in Mexico you'll encounter the magical 300,000-acre El Triunfo Biosphere Reserve. This cloud forest is home to the elusive tapir and jaguar, as well as one of nature's most beautiful birds, the resplendent quetzal.

Or journey by train to the northern reaches of India, where buses carry you 7,000 feet up a perilous road to Mussourie, a former hill station in the days of the British raj near the Nepalese border. Although there's been some deforestation in the region, the mountain air is still relatively clear, and the hills (dotted with silver oaks, horse chestnut trees, long-needle pines, deodars [Himalayan cedars] and rhododendrons) also abound with monkeys and rare birds. A great place for walkers, one trek leads to Nag Tibba at an altitude of 10,000 feet, amidst pine forests, mountain brooks, and slate-roofed villages. On clear days you can see K2, the second highest mountain in the world.

The lure of such incredible beauty, flora, and fauna attracts ecotourists by the thousands to these still-unspoiled corners, and there's no shortage of tour operators to ease your way.

Recent studies indicate that a full 4 to 7 percent of all tourism worldwide now operates under a green label. By 1992, according to one survey, eight million U.S. travelers had taken at least one ecotourist holiday, and by 1994, 77 percent of American travelers had taken a trip involving nature and the outdoors. In some areas, like the Asia-Pacific region, ecotourism accounts for 20 percent of all travel. In South Africa, where most visitors travel to nature reserves and game parks, the figure is even higher. The Kenya Wildlife Service estimates that 80 percent of visitors come to see wildlife. And The International Ecotourism Society (TIES) says that 20 to 40 percent of all American tourists can be classified as "wildlife-related."

Travel and tourism are one of the world's biggest industries, generating more than $4.4 trillion in economic activity annually. The travel industry represents more than 11 percent of the world's gross domestic product, and it employs 8.2 percent of the world's workforce—some 207 million people. For 83 percent of countries worldwide, tourism is one of the top five sources of foreign currency. In the Caribbean, tourism provides half of the total gross domestic product.

CURRENT EVENTS/LEGISLATIVE/POLITICAL

Without a generally accepted set of guidelines, hotel operators who practice business-as-usual are free to ride on the goodwill created by genuine ecotourism. Will your trip be arranged by a fast-buck artist who maximizes his own profits while exploiting the local community, or will you go with a dedicated, conservation-minded tour operator such as Boulder-based Emerald Planet? The tragic fact is that you're more likely to hear about the high-volume commercial services, because they advertise widely.

The year 2002 was celebrated as the International Year of Ecotourism, and it was an opportunity to begin to define green travel. According to TIES, the concept can be summed up in a single sentence: "Ecotourism is responsible travel to natural areas that conserves the environment and sustains the well-being of local people." But in reality, the term "ecotourism" has been applied to a wide range of travel options, some far more green than others. A beachfront hotel tower built of imported materials with absentee owners and no local employees is not an eco-resort, even if it does offer its guests the option of not washing their towels.

According to the United Nations, successful ecotourism needs to include all of these elements:

- Its **main motivation** is "the observation and appreciation of nature as well as the traditional cultures prevailing in natural areas";

- It **contains** "educational and interpretation features";

- It is **organized** "for small groups by specialized and small, locally owned businesses";

- It **minimizes** negative impacts "upon the natural and sociocultural environment";

- It **supports** the protection of natural areas by 1) generating income for host communities; 2) providing alternative employment and income opportunities; 3) increasing awareness of the need for conservation of natural and cultural assets.

Ecotourism: Hope and Reality

Tourism offers huge—and in many cases, indispensable—benefits to local economies, but it also causes unforeseen consequences. According to Sue Wheat, editor of the British organization Tourism Concern's quarterly magazine *In Focus*, "Evidence of the downside of tourism—culturally, environmentally, and economically—is now such that tourism has become a dirty word among many communities, environmental groups, and human rights campaigners." Although there are now many shining lights of holistic ecotourism, Tourism Concern cites such negative examples as "ecological hotels" around Lake Titicaca in Bolivia that dump untreated wastewater into the lake and "ecotourism" operations in Botswana's Central Kalahari desert that have pushed the remaining few hundred San people off the land they've inhabited for centuries. The Botswanan government has stated that tourists will not want to see "primitive" people.

Ironically, the huge biodiversity that still exists in many parts of the world is both a draw for tourists and is to some degree threatened by them. The World Tourism Organization (WTO) notes that between 1980 and 1998, visitors to seven ecotourism destination countries with high levels of biodiversity—Brazil, Indonesia, Malaysia, Mexico, the Philippines, South Africa, and Thailand—rose 242 percent. But these are some of the same countries experiencing massive biodiversity loss, partly because of the increase of tourism.

As the second-largest tourism destination in Africa (behind South

Choosing an Ecotour

Let's say you want to go to Mexico. Simple enough, right? You buy a guidebook, go to Google and type in "Mexico" and "ecotour." The problem is that a whole range of options come up, and they all claim to be the last word in sustainable tourism.

OK, then, you say, I'll choose a tour that's been "certified" or "eco-labeled." But there are more than one hundred certifiers out there, with widely divergent standards and criteria. All the certification systems are voluntary. According to The International Ecotourism Society (TIES), they measure three things: health and safety; quality and service, the focus of traditional certifiers like the American Automobile Association (AAA); and, the newest part of the triangle, sustainability.

Traditional certifiers focus on hotels and resorts, but green certification adds tourism operators. According to Martha Honey of TIES, certifiers are looking at tour operators (Certification for Sustainable Tourism, or CST, in Costa Rica), naturalist guides (The Nature and Ecotourism Accreditation Program, or NEAP, in Australia), beaches (Blue Flag in Europe, South Africa, and the Caribbean), parks (Protected Area Network, or PAN, in Europe), golf courses (Committed to Green in Great Britain), and boats (Smart Voyager in the Galapapos).

Given all this, it pays to be an Internet detective. If you want a certified trip, visit the online directories at www.planeta.com, www.GoNOMAD.com or TIES at www.ecotourism.org. That will connect you with likely operators, but you'll have to do more research to find the perfect trip. Ron Mader of Planeta.com, the online journal of practical ecotourism, recommends posting queries in relevant newsgroups, such as rec-travel.latin-america or regional bulletin boards and forums. Then, he adds, "Ask potential tour operators questions, but don't drill them needlessly. What are their conservation projects? How do they encourage or use community participation? How do they sustain themselves? Many of these travel operators and local services are very proud of their dedication to environmental conservation and community development and will send details via e-mail or direct you to a section of their website that explains their programs in detail."

Deborah McLaren, author of *Rethinking Tourism and Ecotravel*, points out, "Recommending a responsible ecotour can be difficult when so many operators are marketing themselves simply as 'green.' Good operators will have a history of responsible travel and offer small group tours that support quality conservation efforts designed by local communities. They will also make sure that the host community directly benefits from the profits of the tour."

TIES adds that you should also ask if ecotour operators employ locally trained naturalists and staff, and if they encourage travelers to make a personal commitment. The best operators offer direct support. One tour company, Natural Selections, says, for instance, that its expedition members have helped fund a Masai school and an indigenous community in Kenya, a sea turtle recovery project in Mexico and a butterfly conservation project in Ecuador.

Responsible ecotour operators employ local people in all aspects of their operations, use local materials and building methods in constructing lodges and other buildings, and adopt stringent waste management policies, using recycled and biodegradable materials whenever possible, encouraging travelers to minimize the disposable products they take with them and carry out everything they carry in.

Try to find out the ratio of travelers to paid staff, and make sure participant limits are observed. Try to find out all you can about your expedition leader. Many tour companies can furnish a biography.

If the tour includes watching wildlife, the best operators go to great lengths to minimize impact on them, including rules of behavior and encroachment distances.

Remember, even the sleaziest tour operators have learned to make ample use of phrases like "ecotourism," "sustainable," and "certified." So be suspicious if you can't find much evidence to back up their claims. Victor Emanuel of the Texas-based Victor Emanuel Nature Tours urges travelers to ask prospective tour operators what they've specifically done for the environment. "These kinds of questions are going to put moral and ethical pressures on people to do better," he says.

Africa), Kenya receives 700,000 visitors annually. Though the money they spend is vital to Kenya's economy, *The Christian Science Monitor* reports that the tourists take a toll through the vehicles that wreck vegetation and pollute the air in national parks and game reserves, in the sewage that seeps into rivers from tourist camps, in the trees that are cut down for firewood, and the interference with the natural rhythms of wildlife, which in some cases has led to changes in hunting habits.

Wangari Maathai, who founded Kenya's Green Belt Movement, and was imprisoned for campaigning against deforestation (but who now serves in the Kenyan government), notes with some heat that many of the country's ecotourists never interact with Kenyans. "They fly to Nairobi, then fly to the animal reserves without seeing or interacting with the people of the country to whom this rich and wonderful heritage should belong," she says. "The government gets the tourist's dollar and uses it to enrich itself. But if the people benefited from tourism, they would attach more value to the animals."

But there's been some improvement, however incremental. Judy Gona, executive director of the Ecotourism Society of Kenya (ESOK), says, "The future of Kenyan tourism is green." ESOK has eighty members, the majority of which call themselves ecotourism destinations. Most of the new operators are locally owned, small, and secluded, catering to no more than twenty visitors at a time. They are built with indigenous materials, use alternative energy sources, serve locally grown food, and are careful about disposing of their waste. Most support community projects.

Martha Honey, president of TIES, says the Galapagos Islands and Costa Rica are good examples of destinations that have taken a positive approach to ecotourism. "Costa Rica got the right stakeholders together, developed good guidelines and certified fifty hotels," she says. "Now they're working on certifying tour operators and guides. You need a strong national park system and a good infrastructure to serve as a backbone to sustainable travel."

Honey identifies three emerging trends. "There is authentic ecotourism, 'ecotourism lite,' and greenwashing," she says. "Authentic ecotourism incorporates seven or eight of the principles. Ecotourism lite refers to businesses that make only a few cosmetic and cost-saving changes, like not laundering the sheets every day. And greenwashing occurs when big resorts label themselves as ecotourism destinations but reject core principles."

GREEN PRODUCTS

Obviously, it would be ideal on one level if we could all just stay home and leave the polluting airplanes on the ground and the forest paths untrampled. But that's ignoring the considerable value in exposing people to nature in all its complex diversity, to other cultures and to other lifestyles, not to mention the economic boon that tourism in general and ecotourism in particular provides for many subsistence-level economies.

People *will* travel, and they will want to see wildlife in a pristine state, so it becomes the environmentalist's burden to help define responsible ecotourism and to ensure—as much as possible—adherence to that definition.

The British Tourism Concern worries that undefined ecotourism falls prey to "greenwash" marketing. "There is no internationally accepted definition of ecotourism," it points out, "and there is no certification system to abide by, or international monitoring body."

There may be no *universally accepted* certification program, but there certainly are a host of certification schemes and guidelines, including TIES's

Guidelines for Nature Tour Operators. There are as many as one hundred "green" certification and eco-labeling programs around the world (see sidebar on page 254), creating a good degree of confusion. Certification is widely accepted in some countries, and practically unknown in others, including most of Asia.

Based on audits, certification programs award logos or seals to those businesses and attractions that meet or exceed agreed-upon standards. All these certification programs are voluntary and dependent on consumer awareness and willingness to follow their dictates.

It's impossible to boil down the best ecotourism destinations into a short list—there are far too many wonderful places for that—but here's a listing of just a few of the ecotourism operations that are making outstanding efforts to walk the talk. These places are intent on leaving a small footprint and ensuring that protected areas will remain protected.

Global hot spots for travel include:

- **Lindblad Expeditions.** Lars-Eric Lindblad opened up such then-exotic destinations as Antarctica, the Galapagos, and the Amazon to tourism beginning in 1958. His son, Sven-Olof, founded Lindblad Expeditions, which added a green tinge to the adventure touring. The shipboard tours allow visitors to listen to the songs of whales on hydrophones or watch live undersea video from a remotely operated camera. Away from the ship, tourists get close to nature in Zodiac landing craft, and are guided by naturalists and experts in local culture. "We seek to travel in an environmentally responsible way," says Lindblad, "leaving the places we visit as we found them, and working with local governments and individuals to preserve them for others." For many operators, that's just boilerplate, but Lindblad practices what it preaches. 720 5th Avenue, 6th Floor, New York, NY 10019, (800)EXPEDITION, www.expeditions.com.

- **Tropical Nature Travel, South America.** The U.S. arm of the Tropical Nature system of conservation organizations in Peru (InkaNatura, Selva Sur, and Peru Verde), Brazil (Bio-Brasil Foundation), and Ecuador (Eco-Ecuador), Tropical Nature Travel conducts birding, cultural, and natural history tours to its own Amazon rainforest lodges. In a trip to Peru's Manu Biosphere Reserve, for instance, guests stay in screened tents. There are hot showers and flush toilets, but it's not exactly luxury touring. Instead of indulging themselves, conservation-minded visitors look for the ten species of local monkeys and take in the sights at a parrot and macaw lick. (The birds dine on cliffside clay.). P.O. Box 5276, Gainesville, FL, 32627-5276, (888)287-7186, www.tropicalnaturetravel.com.

- **Victor Emanuel Nature Tours, USA.** Victor Emanuel's company, known as VENT, specializes in birding tours, with 100 to 140 destinations annually. Founded in 1974 when birding tours were in their infancy, VENT's early guides included nature writer Peter Matthiessen and bird authority Roger Tory Peterson. VENT arranges tours for such environmental groups as the Nature Conservancy, the World Wildlife Fund, and the National Audubon Society. The company has worked to protect Mexico's El Triunfo Cloud Forest Reserve, and it donates profits to local green groups. 2525 Wallingwood Drive, Suite 1003, Austin, TX 78746, (800)328-8368, www.ventbird.com.

- **Sierra Club Outings Department.** The Sierra Club specializes in membership-based wilderness trips, which are nonprofit and reasonably priced. A recent featured trip is a week-long, rim-to-rim family backpack around the Grand Canyon ($875 for adults). Kids over twelve are invited for $775, but they can't be complete couch potatoes. If that doesn't appeal, consider five days of rafting down the Colorado River's last undammed tributary, the Yampa, with the opportunity to see bighorn sheep and eagles ($795 for adults). The Club also conducts special group trips and nature tours for inner-city kids, and it operates a network of lodges and huts, including the Clair Tappaan Lodge at the Donner Pass (503-426-3632) and other places in California. 85 Second Avenue, 2nd Floor, San Francisco, CA 94105, (415)977-5522, www.sierraclub.org/outings.

- **Turtle Island, Fiji.** How close to paradise can you get? Turtle Island, purchased by American businessperson Richard Evanson in 1972, was at first only a way for one man to get away from it all. In 1980, it began its transformation into an exclusive eco-resort (rates start at $1,090 per couple per day), with room for 28 guests, 160 staff, and an approximate beach-to-visitor ratio of one to two. According to investor Andrew Fairley, Turtle Island is working to raise the standard of living of local people on the 500-acre island, in part by using them as building work crews and staff. It is also helping to publicize locally owned tourist facilities in the region. Cataracts and diabetes are rampant among the native population, and Turtle Island brings in teams of international doctors to stay free while treating patients. Turtle Island also works with Coral Cay Conservation, which organized the Fiji Reef Conservation Project, and has undertaken multiyear efforts to create reef reserves on Fiji. Another eminently worthy operation is **Rivers Fiji**, which operates kayak-based tours on the main island, employing local people as guides and paying a users' fee to native land owners. Rivers Fiji, c/o Travel Outdoors, P.O. Box 581, Angels Camp, CA 95222, (800)446-2411, www.riversfiji.com; Turtle Island, 10906 NE 39th Street, Quad 205, Suite A-1, Vancouver, WA 98682-6789, (877)2-TURTLE, www.turtlefiji.com.

- **Maho Bay Camps, St. John, Virgin Islands.** Hardly an upstart, Maho Bay is instead a pioneer in small-scale, tent-based ecotourism. As with Tropical Nature Travel, sixteen-foot square canvas cottages adjoin facilities with modern plumbing and a state-of-the-art graywater recycling system. Many of the 114 tents ($75 a night in the low season, $108 in the high season) offer sweeping views of a jewel-like Caribbean cove, which boasts kayaking, snorkeling, and diving. Vegetarian food is available in the outdoor restaurant. Slightly more upscale accommodations are just a short distance away at **Harmony Studios** ($110/$185), which is built from recycled materials and gets its electricity from a passive solar installation. P.O. Box 310, Cruz Bay, Saint John, VI 00830, (800)392-9004, www.maho.org.

- **Binna Burra Mountain Lodge, Australia.** One of Australia's first nature-based resorts, the Green Globe- and Nature and Ecotourism Accreditation Program (NEAP)–certified Binna Burra was opened in Southeast Queensland in 1933. The resort offers easy access to a treasured World Heritage site, Lamington National Park, with its subtropical rainforest featuring ancient Antarctic Beech trees and mountain streams. The lodge itself employs energy-efficient compact fluorescent lights, recycles waste (and operates a worm farm to break down kitchen and paper materials), conserves water as much as possible, and employs environmentally friendly cleaners. A native plant nursery regenerates local flora. Guests stay in homey, hand-cut log cabins, with accommodations for 115. Activities include guided bushwalks and picnics. For kids, there's the Discovery Forest, an environmental playground. Prices range from $167 to $198 (Australian) a night. Beechmont, Queensland, 4211 Australia, www.binnaburra lodge.com.au.

- **La Milpa Field Station, Belize.** Only three miles from ancient Mayan tombs, the La Milpa Field Station is home to two archaeological projects, run by Boston University and the University of Texas, that aim to help solve the mysteries of the highly evolved civilization's collapse. But you don't have to be interested in archaeology to visit La Milpa. Northwestern Belize teems with life, including hundreds of bird species (featuring multicolored toucans and many varieties of hummingbirds), Belize's famous howler monkeys, peccaries, coatimundis, jaguars, and many more. There are nine nature trails, three of them interpreted. Guests stay in private thatched-roof cabanas or a unique solar-powered dormitory with composting toilets and graywater recycling. Rates are $76 per person per day in the dormitory (includes meals and guided activities) and $92 per day in the cabanas. The field station is a project of the locally run Programme for Belize, which works to preserve the 260,000-acre Rio Bravo Conservation and Management Area (some 4 percent of Belize's total land area that would otherwise have been cleared for development). The Programme also helps Belizeans sell their handicrafts, and it runs environmental education initiatives for local teachers and students. 1 Eyre Street, P.O. Box 749, Belize City, Belize, Central America, (501)2-75616, www.pfbelize.org.

- **Phinda, South Africa.** It's impossible to see all of South Africa in one trip, but the Phinda eco-resort in KwaZulu-Natal Province is a good place to start. The Mountain and Forest Lodges offer a unique opportunity to explore several distinct ecosystems, from scuba diving on the world's most southern coral reefs to touring colorful palm savannah and enjoying the vistas from the Ubombo Mountains. Phinda Mountain Lodge offers split-level accommodations in rock chalets with decks overlooking the bushveld. Phinda Forest Lodge's glass chalets were hand-built by people from the Zulu community. Rates, which include meals and guided tours, are $340 to $590 per day, depending on season and accommodations. The resort is owned by Conservation Corporation (CC) Africa, which also owns the 42,000-acre Phinda Private Game Reserve, where populations of elephant, rhino, and cheetah have been established. CC Africa runs twenty-seven lodges and

Green Hotels: Beyond Good Hospitality

Until recently, Philadelphia's Sheraton Rittenhouse Square didn't even have smoke-free rooms. Now it has air that's swept clean of such pollutants as mold, pollen, and bacteria every thirty-four minutes. What's more, the cut-glass front desk is 100 percent recycled, there's a stand of oxygenating palms in the atrium lobby, the bedding is organic cotton, the paint is volatile organic compound–free, and the wallpaper is made of recycled fibers.

These days, a hotel has to do more than not wash its towels every day to be considered environmentally correct. The Texas-based Green Hotels Association, for instance, has 200 members representing 17,000 rooms in the United States. Hoteliers like Janet Byrd of the Colony Hotel in Kennebunkport, Maine (where kitchen waste is composted, recycled paper is used for all office operations, and the grounds are certified as a wildlife habitat by the National Wildlife Federation) say that eco-awareness is good business: Bookings increased 25 percent after the green marketing campaign began.

The leading global body is the International Hotel Environment Initiative (IHEI), a nonprofit group founded in 1993 that now represents 11,000 hotels on five continents. It's difficult, given differences in cultures and attitudes, to develop guidelines that work for such a diverse range of accommodations, but IHEI has published handbooks, purchasing manuals, and user-friendly action packs, as well as *Green Hotelier* magazine.

The model of the foreign-owned tourist skyscraper, exporting its profits and operating with zero input from the local community, may be fading, but that's not to say that victory has been achieved. "A lot of the larger hotels are making efforts to be more sustainable from the environmental side," says Costas Christ, senior director for ecotourism at Conservation International. "They are using less detergents in the laundry, and going beyond that to reform their wastewater treatment. But they haven't yet approached the side of the equation that addresses local people's needs and benefits. Do they buy local produce? Do they hire local people for construction jobs and as staff?"

A model, Christ points out, could be the ecolodge developed as a collaboration between the nomadic Shampole Maasai people of Kenya's Rift Valley (used as a set for the movie *Out of Africa*) and the Africa Conservation Centre. More than one hundred local community members were involved in building the lodge, and their expertise is behind the marketing and managing of it. The Shampole Maasai own 30 percent of the ecolodge, a stake that will eventually grow to 80 percent. Meanwhile, the ecolodge is a linchpin in the preservation of a 25,000-acre conservation area, which supports lions, cheetahs, elephants, and even the highly endangered African wild dog.

While large hotel chains are unlikely to ever be as conscientious as this, they can certainly start paying far more attention to the communities whose hospitality they enjoy and whose resources they profit from.

camps in six African countries. P.O. Box 16336, Vlaberg 8018, Cape Town, South Africa, (011)+27-21-425-0222, www.ccafrica.com.

- **Kuyima, Mexico.** An outfitter in San Ignacio Lagoon in Baja California Sur, Mexico, Kuyima is owned and operated by local people within the El Vizcaino Biosphere Reserve to promote sustainable economic development. By creating jobs for underemployed fishermen, promoting environmental education and assisting the reserve staff, as well as providing outstanding local-guided whale-watching tours, Kuyima shows how tourist development and conservation can work hand in hand. Rates for the adventure package are $150 per person per day, including food, camping and a boat trip to see the whales. When Mitsubishi wanted to build one of the world's largest salt factories in the heart of this World Heritage site—which is also one of the world's last birthing grounds for the Eastern Pacific Gray Whale—Kuyima staff helped lead local efforts to explain that ecotourism offers far more to local people than factory jobs. In the end, its vision prevailed, and Mitsubishi canceled its project in 2000. Beth Trask of the RARE Center says, "RARE is proud to have played a role in Kuyima's success by training most of its staff through our intensive three-month program that prepares primarily rural adults with limited education to become English-speaking interpretative nature guides. RARE has trained more than fifty local guides in southern Baja, and more than 200 total through targeted programs in Mexico, Honduras, and Costa Rica." Morelos #23, corner of Miguel Hidalgo, Zona Centro, San Ignacio, BCS, Mexico, (011)52-615-154-00-70, www.kuyima.com.

- **Saint Lucia, Caribbean.** Located in the eastern Caribbean, Saint Lucia has created nature trails that are the foundation of a strategy to protect forest reserves by creating economic incentives for local people. With support from the U.S. Fish and Wildlife Service and tour company Lindblad Expeditions, RARE and the Forestry Department opened the Des Cartier Trail in the mountainous rainforests of the Central Forest Reserve in 1996. The Des Cartier and En Bas Saut trails are not only profitable but generate more than $500,000 for the local economy each year. Before the trails were built, the island's tourism market was entirely dominated by foreign-owned beachfront resorts. The trails lure sunbathing tourists away from the beaches for a day, and their visits are supported by a network of Saint Lucians—including tour operators, taxi drivers, guides, and the cooks who prepare box lunches. The day trips average more than six hundred visitors a month. Similar trails have since been developed all around the Caribbean, in Nevis, Grand Cayman, the Turks and Caicos, Jamaica, and Monserrat. And there are similar programs in Palau, Belize, Mexico, and Honduras. P.O. Box 221, Sureline Building, Vide Bouteille, Castries, Saint Lucia, (011)758-450-2231, www.stlucia.org.

WHAT YOU CAN DO

There's no question that ecotourism is wildly popular, but that in itself is not enough. As more and more of the world's tour operators are beginning to acknowledge, ecotourism has to live up to its green claims.

If you've ever wanted to try an ecotour, now is the time to get up and get out. Never has there been a better opportunity to see nature up-close and personal while also giving something back to the communities you visit.

The responsibility for the impact of your travel rests with you. Be an activist—traveling the world as a dedicated ecotourist is not a spectator sport. If you choose an organized ecotour, ask about the trip fee. Besides responsibly sourced food and lodging, it can also help defray the cost of field-work, support local education or health programs, and leave economic dividends with the host community. (Often, if paid to a nonprofit organization, the fees for service trips are also partially tax-deductible.) Ask whether you'll be visiting a place during the most heavily traversed time of year, contributing to overcrowding, and whether you'll be using mass transportation (to reduce pollution), and eating regional cuisine (to support local markets).

Here are some basic guidelines for going green, as developed by the Union of Concerned Scientists:

In nature spots:

- Leave only footprints (no littering).

- Take only photographs (no "souvenirs" from the wild).

- Stay on trails.

- Don't disturb wildlife or natural habitats.

- Don't introduce foreign plants or animals.

- Don't pollute water bodies with soap or detergents.

In all places:

- Don't buy things made from endangered animals (like products containing ivory or tortoise shell).

- Don't waste water.

- Turn off lights and air-conditioning when you leave your room.

- When possible, walk—it's the best way to see the sights anyway. When you can't, use the most environmental methods of transportation you can.

- Patronize hotels, airlines, and tour operators that employ environmental practices, such as energy conservation and recycling.

- Support locally owned businesses and follow local regulations.

These organizations can provide a wealth of information about going green. They suggest destinations, offer places to stay and issue codes of conduct:

Conservation International. Ecotourism is one project area for this wide-ranging group whose mission is to conserve the Earth's natural resources and preserve global biodiversity. 1919 M Street NW, Suite 600, Washington, DC 20036, (202)912-1000, www.conservation.org (with its Ecotravel Center at www.ecotour.org).

Earth Routes. Makes reservations and provides travel research "with respect for the Earth's resources and inhabitants." Pierce Pond Road, Box 22-B, Penobscot, ME 04476, (207)326-8635, www.earthroutes.net.

Green Earth Travel. A one-stop shop for vegetarian travel needs. 7 Froude Circle, Cabin John, MD 20818, (888)246-VEGE, www.vegtravel.com.

Green Hotels Association. A trade organization for creating environmentally friendly lodging. P.O. Box 420212, Houston, TX 77242, (713)789-8889, www.greenhotels.com.

Hostelling International-USA. This is the website for the largest network of U.S.-based hostels, and its website links to international hostels. 8401 Colesville Road, Suite 600, Silver Spring, MD 20910, (301)495-1240, www.hiayh.org.

The International Ecotourism Society. TIES, founded in 1990, is the largest and oldest group dedicated to ecotourism information. It has members in more than seventy countries. 733 15th Street NW, Suite 1000, Washington, DC 20005, (202)347-9203, www.ecotourism.org.

International Tourism Partnership. Creator of the International Hotels Environment Initiative, founded in 1992 by chief executives at a dozen multinational hotel chains. 15-16 Cornwall Terrace, Regent's Park, London NW1 4QPU, England, (011)+44(0)20-7467-3620, www.internationaltourismpartnership.org.

Rainforest Alliance Sustainable Tourism Program. Information about responsible ecotourism and certification programs. (212)677-1900, X205, www.rainforest-alliance.org/programs/sv/index.html.

RARE Center. Provides training, technical support and resources for conservationists around the world, including ecotourism guides. RARE is the parent group of the Central America–based Mesoamerican Ecotourism Alliance (described in the "Global Hot Spots" section above). 1840 Wilson Boulevard, Suite 204, Arlington, VA 22201, (703)522-5070, www.rarecenter.org.

Tourism Concern. Campaigns for fair and "ethically traded" tourism in Great Britain. Its aim is to reduce social, economic, cultural, and environmental problems associated with ecotravel. Stapleton House, 277-281 Holloway Road, London N7 8HN, England, (011)020-7133-3330, www.tourismconcern.org.uk.

Books

Ecotourism by David Weaver ($71, John Wiley & Sons). An overview of world ecotourism with information on how indigenous communities can benefit.

Ecotourism and Sustainable Development: Who Owns Paradise? by Martha Honey ($28, Island Press). Offers a prescription for a strong international certification program.

Healthy Highways: The Traveler's Guide to Healthy Eating ($18.95, Ceres Press). Offers consumers vegetarian and health-oriented eating places keyed to roadmaps, with local driving instructions plus interesting attractions.

Rethinking Tourism and Ecotravel by Deborah McLaren ($23.95, Kumarian Press). An exposé of business as usual in the world travel industry, with a blueprint for change.

The Business of Ecotourism: A Complete Guide for Nature and Cultural-Based Tourism Operators by Carol Patterson ($29.95, Explorer's Guide Publishing). Provides a blueprint for "staying in business without sacrificing your ethics."

chapter thirteen

Getting There

Planet-Friendly Cars, Trying Transit, and Dusting Off That Bicycle

Photo by National Railroad Passenger Corp/Amtrak

As a nation, we *love* our cars. America invented the drive-through restaurant and the drive-through bank. NASCAR racing is one of the fastest growing spectator sports in the United States, and car magazines have millions of subscribers. We love our cars so much, that we actually have more of them than we do drivers. For a total population of 292 million, there are 191 million drivers with a staggering 204 million vehicles parked outside their homes.

We also love *big* cars, and are buying as many light trucks (the category that includes sport-utility vehicles, or SUVs) as we are passenger automobiles. The result is that the United States is the largest per-capita consumer of oil (using up eight million barrels of it a day) and the largest per-capita producer of carbon dioxide (CO2), the leading global warming gas.

While the United States leads the world in car ownership, other countries are catching up. Visitors to China used to talk about all the bicycles. Now they talk about the increasingly smoggy cities as China's auto industry grows at the fastest rate in the world. The Chinese obviously have the same right to drive alone to work as the rest of the world, but if they do, the environmental consequences will be devastating, especially in terms of global warming. But, hands down, when it comes to auto dependence, the United States leads the way.

The kind of car you drive *does* matter. If every new vehicle averaged forty miles per gallon, we would save more oil than we now import from the Persian Gulf. What's more, it would save you a lot of money—as much as $2,200 over the lifetime of your car or truck, says the Sierra Club.

Fortunately, even as SUVs seem to be gaining the upper hand, cleaner, greener vehicles are finally available. These include cleaner versions of popular models (known as partial zero-emission vehicles, or PZEVs), and hybrid cars with both gas and electric motors to optimize fuel economy and tailpipe pollution. Consumers have a real choice for the first time since the early 1900s, when the gasoline car had real competition from battery electrics and steam cars.

Hybrids (which have both an electric and a gasoline engine) were first developed in Japan, where a wide variety of hybrid models are now on sale. Despite the common misconception, hybrids *do not* need to be plugged in. Ever. The Toyota Prius (which starts out in electric mode, then switches on the gas engine when more power is needed) and the Honda Insight (whose electric motor acts as a supercharger for a small gas engine) first appeared on the U.S. market in 2000. American manufacturers were latecomers to the hybrid market.

The first American hybrid to appear was the thirty-five-mile-per-gallon Ford Escape SUV, which debuted in the summer of 2004. U.S. carmakers, noting that SUVs account for 25 percent of all American vehicle sales, are likely to concentrate their hybrid plans on that market segment.

Quite a few Hollywood celebrities own and champion hybrids. Actor Ed Begley Jr. has long been one of the biggest proponents of clean cars and electric vehicles, along with actors Cameron Diaz, Leonardo DiCaprio, Danny DeVito, Ted Danson, Robin Williams, and Alexandra Paul. Some environmental groups have even provided Toyota Priuses for celebrities to use in attending film premieres. (The 10-mile-per-gallon GM Hummers favored by other personalities send an opposite message.)

Hybrid sales have risen consistently in the United States, from 9,350 cars in 2000 to 20,287 in 2001, 35,000 in 2002 and 47,525 in 2003. The future outlook for hybrids is bright. Automotive analyst J.D. Power and Associates foresees annual sales totaling 350,000 by 2008, accounting for 2 percent of all car sales. The 2004 Prius, an all-new design, had received 10,000 orders before it was delivered, and waiting lists stretched six months or more. It's not a huge number, but when contrasted with the roughly 1,500 battery-electrics sold in America from 1980 to 2000, it's a promising start.

Beyond the hybrid and the PZEV, the long-term solution is likely to be the fuel-cell vehicle, which runs on hydrogen gas, the most abundant element in the universe. The fuel cell has the potential to eventually replace the internal-combustion engine, because it's far more than just the best environmental choice. The reason the auto industry is spending billions of dollars on fuel cells is because it sees the potential for a much better car than internal combustion can deliver, with improved performance, fuel economy, range, and emissions, too.

There are good reasons to believe we will be driving fuel-cell cars by 2015 or 2020, though skeptics such as Joseph Romm, author of *The Hype About Hydrogen* (Island Press), think it might take longer. Fuel-cell research for the automobile is quite advanced in the United States, Japan, and Europe. The fuel cell itself goes all the way back to 1839, when Sir William Robert Grove, a British barrister who moonlighted as a scientist, first discovered that you could get electricity from hydrogen, and the by-product would be water—drinkable water at that. The first practical use for Grove's invention was in the U.S. space program, where it provided electricity and drinking water for astronauts in flight.

Hydrogen does not have to be coupled to a fuel cell; it can be burned with relatively satisfying results in an internal-combustion engine. California Governor Arnold Schwarzenegger converted one of his many Hummers to burn hydrogen, and some automakers (including Ford and BMW) have experimented with the process. But producing electricity from hydrogen through a chemical reaction is the cleanest process.

There is a growing consensus that the world will eventually have a hydrogen energy economy. Environmentalists such as Amory Lovins, head of the Rocky Mountain Institute, have long predicted it, but in recent years the chorus has grown to include many people at high levels of government and industry. A hydrogen economy will abandon internal-combustion engines completely, and it will also eventually replace the electric grid to your house, and even your flashlight and computer batteries.

Although transit ridership was bolstered when some frequent fliers switched to trains after the airplane hijackings of September 11, 2001, and was already rising faster than automobile use, it is still only a tiny niche in the American transportation picture. More than 90 percent of all travel in the United States is by automobile, and only 4 percent is by all forms of public transit. What's more, the number of transit rides has actually gone down as population has gone up. In 2000, in what was described as a victory for public transportation, Americans took 9.4 billion transit trips (up 3.5 percent from 1999). But in 1946, as we emerged from the shortages of World War II (including a ban on new car production), conserving Americans recorded 23.4 billion transit trips. The United States had 141 million people in 1946, half the current number.

The plain fact is that highways and car culture are supported by what is arguably the most powerful lobby in the United States, and there's nothing comparable to stand up for public transportation. The highway lobby is an alliance of road builders and automakers, and it exerts heavy influence on both transportation and energy policy. Associated General Contractors of America, for instance, contributed $4,111,210 to federal candidates between 1987 and 1997. In the same period, the American Trucking Association contributed $2,660,064, and the International Union of Operating Engineers $4,591,595, according to Common Cause. The construction sector poured $33 million into the 1997/1998 federal election cycle (two thirds of it going to Republicans), and celebrated when nine out of ten top cash recipients were victorious in their U.S. House races. In just one state, Michigan, the highway lobby outspent mass transit and rail interests by ten to one on state legislative races between 1994 and 1998, reports the Michigan Environmental Council.

The pressure to rebuild the thriving mass-transit infrastructure the United States had before World War II is coming almost entirely from the states, mirroring state action (particularly in smoggy California) to increase emissions and fuel-efficiency standards.

California's tough air-quality standards, set by its pioneering Air Resources Board, have also been adopted by several Northeastern states, including New York, Massachusetts, Maine, and Vermont. In early 2004, New Jersey and Connecticut became the fifth and sixth states endorsing the standards.

The PZEV (which costs car manufacturers a premium of $300 to $500 per vehicle) would never exist were it not for California's emissions regulations. Rich Varenchik, spokesperson for the state Air Resources Board, says that PZEVs help manufacturers satisfy California quotas for the production of environmentally friendly vehicles.

PZEVs, now sold by at least a dozen manufacturers, emit 90 percent less pollution than standard models, and are even cleaner in some cases than hybrids. "These cars have fewer emissions while being driven than your average car puts out while sitting still," says Violette Roberts, spokesperson for California's Mojave Desert Air Quality Management District.

To be called a PZEV, a vehicle has to have extremely low tailpipe emissions, as well as next-to-no evaporative emissions (the gasoline vapor that leaks out through gas caps or imperfectly sealed engine systems). And those emissions standards have to be guaranteed for fifteen years or 150,000 miles.

The Hidden Costs of Owning a Car

Why worry so much about cars, which have, after all, given us unprecedented mobility and convenience? The fact is we may no longer be able to afford them, since cars and trucks consume more than half the oil we use, much of it imported at great expense from hot spots like the Middle East. According to researchers at the University of California at Davis, air pollution costs the United States $200 billion per year. State and federal governments pour an incredible $71 billion annually into building and maintaining roads. Gridlock impacts the economy to the tune of $140 billion, and expenses related to auto accidents add another $350 billion to the bottom line. The average family spends more on transportation every year than they do on food.

Urban sprawl drives up transportation costs. *Driven to Spend*, a report by the Surface Transportation Policy Project and the Center for Neighborhood Technology, found that the average American family living in a highly "sprawled" area can pay thousands of dollars more per year for transportation than families without that kind of congestion. In sprawling Houston, for example, twenty-two cents of every dollar consumers spend goes to transportation, or $8,840 annually to get around—$2,528 more than the national average.

While most Americans believe that fuel economy is improving, the average fuel economy for passenger vehicles has been declining steadily since

1988 because of vastly higher percentages of gas-guzzling SUVs on the road today. What's more, the Bluewater Network reports that actual fuel economy may be as much as 34 percent worse than published EPA figures, because of antiquated testing methods.

What's the real bottom line on car ownership, when all the hidden costs are factored in? In 2002, the American Automobile Association estimated the total cost of a year's driving as $7,533, including gas, oil, tires, maintenance, insurance, licensing, registration, depreciation, and financing. The association put the per-mile cost at 50.2 cents, though gasoline prices have increased considerably since then.

That's bad enough, but Americans might be startled to learn that their cars actually cost them much more. A variety of hidden costs drive the actual price higher than it would first appear. The International Center for Technology Assessment estimates that if these hidden costs (ranging from oil subsidies to health impacts) were added in, gas would cost as much as $15.14 per gallon, and operating a car for a year could cost $14,848.

Obviously, all these costs are aggravated by today's sport utility gas guzzlers. Driven by escalating fuel costs and environmental considerations, a backlash against the SUV has started. Spearheading the fight are Arianna Huffington's Detroit Project and Keith Bradsher's groundbreaking book *High and Mighty* (which showed convincingly that SUVs are not safer than cars, when the rollover risk is factored in). The Clean Car Pledge, signed by more than 100,000 people, is helping convince Detroit that Americans really will buy smaller vehicles.

The Fuel Cell and Hydrogen Economy

Assuming that the automobile will remain the main means of transportation in the United States, is the zero-emissions vehicle championed by the Bush administration anywhere near reality? Fuel-cell cars are already on the road, mostly in California, because the government/industry working group known as the California Fuel-Cell Partnership is a magnet for manufacturers' test vehicles. The latest research shows that you can get an almost 300-mile range out of a fuel-cell car running on hydrogen gas. That's comparable to the range of most cars today.

But it will take until 2020 at the earliest to actually get the first fuel-cell cars on the road, and some critics believe it will never happen. Big hurdles remain, many of them related to the "infrastructure"—the network of hy-

Powered by . . . Biodiesel

One of the quickest and cheapest ways to get behind the wheel of a cleaner car is to convert it to run on biodiesel, which is made from natural, renewable sources such as used vegetable oil from fast-food fryers or (perish the thought if you're a vegetarian) animal fats.

Cars built since 1994 that are equipped with diesel engines can run even 100 percent biodiesel with minor modifications. Some work will be needed to run on pure vegetable oil, which gets a bit sludgy when it's cold. (You'll need an extra fuel tank connected to the car's coolant system, so the oil can be heated and thinned before it's burned.) Older diesel vehicles will run well on blends of 20 percent biodiesel and 80 percent conventional diesel fuel, but the environmental benefit is obviously less.

Filling your car with biodiesel cuts down on emissions of unburned hydrocarbons, carbon monoxide, sulfates, and the nastiest of all diesel by-products—particulate matter. Biodiesel is a particular favorite of musicians such as touring singer-songwriter Jaia Suri, who runs her truck on nothing but used kitchen grease collected on her travels. "I've learned a lot more about diesel engines and the many colorful variations of kitchen grease pits than I'd ever wanted to," she says. "Now I'm researching potato chip and French fry companies, trying to find an easier, cleaner way to get fuel."

The "Bio-Beetle" is a biodiesel-powered Volkswagen running on 100 percent vegetable oil that can be rented for $199 a week by tourists visiting the Hawaiian island of Maui. Get the details at http://mauigreenenergy.org/Bio-Beetle.htm.

A $795 kit to convert your diesel vehicle to biodiesel operation is available from Greasecar, P.O. Box 60508, Florence, MA 01062. Information at (413)586-2432 or by visiting www.greasecar.com.

---

drogen fueling stations we'd need to replace the nation's 180,000 gasoline stations.

The big question is how to produce the hydrogen. Unfortunately, hydrogen is not freely available, but must be extracted from hydrogen-rich sources such as fossil fuels or water. The process is totally clean if the energy comes from renewable sources like wind, solar, biomass, or geothermal power, but hydrogen can also be produced from coal or (the Bush administration's favored method) nuclear power.

For now, hybrids and PZEVs remain the best choice for the environment. The battery-powered electric car, which had a significant share of the market in the early years of the automobile, enjoyed an Earth Day–sponsored revival between 1970 and 2000. Despite do-it-yourselfer enthusiasm, however, the battery car has not taken off in the marketplace. Some environmentalists cite a lack of advertising and marketing as the problem, while others point to the one-hundred-mile range limit of most electric vehicles.

Transit Options

Cleaning up car exhaust is not the only hurdle we face. General Motors executives like to say that the fuel-cell car "will take the automobile out of the environmental equation," when really it will only solve the tailpipe problem. Cars will still take up space, create gridlock, and drive development decisions.

Many of us have seen old photographs of the comprehensive trolley and railroad lines that used to serve even the smallest American community, and wondered whether we've really made "progress" since then. Though the commuter of 1912 lacked an interstate highway system, he or she could walk out the front door, hop a trolley, then connect to an efficient national rail network with 300,000 miles of track.

Our shrunken, financially imperiled Amtrak system is a ghost of the network we tore up in search of modernity and the personal freedom afforded by automobiles. Cities are beginning to rebuild the lost infrastructure, turning to light-rail systems, fast ferryboats, and dedicated bus corridors, among other new approaches.

The American Public Transportation Association (APTA) is full of relatively happy news:

- Fourteen million Americans ride on public transportation each weekday.

- Americans took more than 9.5 billion public transportation trips in 2001.

- Transit usage is at an all-time high and increased by 6.4 percent in the decade from 1990 to 2000.

Some sixty-two American cities now have or plan to build light-rail systems. APTA reports that there are now 651 light-rail stations around the country, operated by twenty-six transit agencies. Commuter rail agencies add another 1,153 stations. Funded proposals will add 131 new stations in coming years. Despite transit critics who charge that light rail offers "limousine-priced" rides to people who would otherwise have taken the bus, there's ample evidence that transit is cost-effective (especially when the cost of gridlock is taken into account), and ridership is increasing from people who would otherwise have taken their cars. When the St. Louis light rail opened in 1993, according to the *Milwaukee Journal*, not only did the number of passengers far exceed expectations but bus ridership also increased 20 percent. In Toronto, Canada, transit carries 77 percent of all downtown-bound commuters during rush hours. Portland, Oregon's, Tri-Met light-rail system eliminates 187,000 car trips every day, or 58 million for a year.

The Federal Transit Agency reports, "Americans lose more than 1.6 million hours a day stuck in traffic. Without transit, the nation's $40 billion in annual traffic congestion losses would be $15 billion higher. In fact, if all the Americans who take transit to work decided to drive, their cars would circle the Earth with a line of traffic 23,000 miles long."

Long-distance trains, so-called heavy rail, are also making a comeback, despite setbacks. Amtrak as a whole has lost about $25 billion since it was created in 1971, a staggering sum until you consider the $40 billion annually spent on highways. States are banding together in high-speed train "compacts" designed to provide ultra-fast and competitive rail service for such regions as the Midwest, Florida, the Northwest, and California.

The model is Amtrak's Acela train between Boston and Washington, D.C., which travels at speeds of up to 150 miles per hour. That's slower than European trains, but it's fast enough to be competitive with flying, especially when the time consumed in getting to airports and checking through new security procedures is factored in. (The part of Amtrak that loses money is the long-distance cross-country routes, because it's much quicker and cheaper to fly, but these routes are protected by pork-barrel political interests.)

Rapid-transit ferries can compete with cars in commuting times. The city of Sydney, Australia, for instance, makes major use of ferryboat commuting, as do Hong Kong; Seattle; and Vancouver, British Columbia. There are some environmental problems and some cost issues with ferries, but, overall, when you have feasible water routes, it's a great mode of transport.

Biking is also gaining in popularity, for health, for its environmental benefits, and to eliminate auto-related costs. Remember how much it costs to own a car for a year, more than $7,000? According to the League of American Bicyclists, operating a bicycle for a year weighs in at $120. Many insurance companies also reduce rates for commuters who bicycle to work rather than drive. The 1995 National Personal Transportation Survey found that approximately 40 percent of all trips are less than two miles in length—which represents a ten-minute bike ride or a thirty-minute walk. Fifty-four percent of all commuters live within ten miles of their worksite—making their commute time by bike or car just about the same.

Employers also benefit, because studies show that people who bike to work are more productive and take less time off for illness. Bikers cut down on an employer's need to subsidize employee parking, and exercise tends to make workers more alert.

If bicycling seems too strenuous for you, there are a range of electric-assisted bicycles (with a top speed of about fifteen miles per hour and a twenty-mile range) available that give you a motorized push up hills and other obstacles. You can motorize a bike yourself with an affordable kit, or pay $500 to $3,000 for a ready-made unit. Santa Cruz County, California, gives $375 rebates for electric bike purchases. And, of course, there's always the Segway gyroscopic scooter, though they remain rather expensive novelties and not the transportation revolution that founder Dean Kamen envisioned.

Our transportation choices obviously have a major impact on the environment, so what can we do to lessen our impact on the planet and reduce our dependence on foreign oil? If we could prepare for the coming hydrogen-based energy economy by promoting interim clean-car technologies and a national public transportation network, we'd certainly be making major progress!

Life Without Cars?

The Europeans and South Americans are far ahead of the car-dependent United States in taking back the streets. The English anti-roads movement actually stopped construction of some highway bypasses after activists blocked traffic. In the United States, anti-car activism is largely restricted to bicycle advocacy, with groups such as Critical Mass and Transportation Alternatives occasionally blocking traffic and demonstrating for better bike access.

European car-free zones have become very successful. Sixty cities have declared that they're going to make their centers car-free. Britain has developed a car-free day, which is supported by 75 percent of the British public. Similar ideas have spread to Central and South America. In some places, such as Athens or Singapore, because of pollution problems, you can drive only every other day (license plates ending in an odd number one day, even the next), and London now is charging cars a hefty fee to enter the city center. In Copenhagen, Denmark, 30 to 40 percent of commuters get to work by bicycle.

GREEN PRODUCTS

Fuel-efficient, low-emission hybrid cars are on the market today, with Japanese manufacturers leading the way. Although somewhat more expensive, the Honda Civic Hybrid looks nearly identical to the standard Honda Civic, and it performs in much the same way. The hybrid's big advantage is its fifty-mile-per-gallon fuel economy, with a range of more than 600 miles. Its gas-electric drivetrain is more complicated and expensive to build, however, which explains its $20,000 sticker price. The alternative is the Toyota Prius hybrid, also $20,000, which has been on the American market since 2000. American carmakers have repeatedly delayed the introduction of their own hybrid cars. That began to change in 2004, when Ford's Escape hybrid first appeared. Ford's hybrid uses some technology from the Prius, but it has the distinction of being the first American hybrid, and the world's first hybrid SUV.

General Motors, which also dragged its wheels on hybrids, hit the market with full-sized "mild" hybrid pickup trucks (with a 10 to 15 percent fuel-economy benefit from their electric assists) in 2004. And in 2007, GM will produce a hybrid version of the Saturn Vue SUV, as well as big SUV hybrids based on such vehicles as the Chevrolet Suburban and the Cadillac Escalade. These will enjoy a 35 to 40 percent increase in gas mileage, bringing them to a none-too-impressive twenty-one mpg.

General Motors sold more than 600,000 large SUVs in 2002. The hybrid drivetrains will be options, and hybrid-equipped versions will probably not sell in high volumes. Activist groups, including the Union of Concerned Scientists, the Sierra Club, and the Michigan-based Ecology Center, continue to protest (even attempting to disrupt the launch of the Ford hybrid Escape in New York) because Detroit companies haven't applied the best fuel-saving technology (including direct-injection engines, variable valve timing, integrated starter-generators, and lightweight body structures) to their entire fleets.

The greenest cars, then, are offered mostly by Japanese manufacturers. German companies make fuel-efficient cars, too, but don't necessarily export them to the United States. Volkswagen, for instance, never sold the seventy-seven-mpg Lupo 3L TDI in the United States, partly because it believes Americans won't buy small cars, and partly because it's convinced we won't buy diesels.

Automakers obviously could be doing more to "green" their fleets, but there are nonetheless some new-model cars that get both excellent gas mileage and low emissions. Here are five choices:

Chevrolet Aveo

American carmakers have largely farmed out their small-car designs, but that's not always a bad thing. The Chevy Aveo, designed by the legendary Giorgetto Giugiaro's Italdesign in Turin and built by Daewoo in Korea, was new for 2004, available as a four-door sedan and a five-door hatchback. It's really teeny, just thirteen feet long and weighing only 2,369 pounds. Parked next to a Suburban, it looks like a kiddy car.

The Aveo gets exactly two times the fuel economy of giants like the Nissan Pathfinder Armada, twenty-eight mpg in the city instead of fourteen. It rates an EPA "green score" on emissions of seven out of ten. Despite its tiny size, it has a reasonable amount of room in the five-door version. The back seats offer adequate legroom, and with the rear seats folded down there is forty-two cubic feet of storage space.

The revelation about the Aveo (with pricing starting at $10,000 for the stripped Special Value model) is its nifty handling. It can be great fun to pilot a very small car around a city, zipping around obstacles and nosing into parking spaces larger cars just passed over. Another good small-car choice is the Toyota ECHO, discontinued in 2005.

Ford Focus PZEV

The Ford Focus PZEV has achieved California's strict certification as a partial zero-emissions vehicle, even though, unlike the Civic Hybrid, it is solely powered by a gasoline engine. The feat was achieved by moving the catalytic converters closer to the exhaust manifold, allowing quicker warm-up times, and improved recirculation of exhaust gas to ensure more complete combustion. "It emits fewer smog-causing hydrocarbons per day than a small pine tree," claims *Electrifying Times*. The PZEV powertrain, built around a fuel-efficient 2.3-liter, four-cylinder engine, became available nationally in 2004. Focus cars begin at $12,820. Fuel-economy specifications for the PZEV manual transmission model are twenty-five mpg in the city, thirty-three mpg on the highway (for the automatic, 24/30 mpg).

Ford Escape Hybrid

The Escape is the first U.S.-made hybrid and the first hybrid SUV on the market. It's a Partial Zero Emission Vehicle (PZEV), which means it's as clean as the Prius in tailpipe terms. Ford actually purchased the rights to the Prius technology for the Escape, which combines a 300-volt nickel-metal hydride battery pack (under the cargo floor) with a more efficient version of the vehicle's standard two-liter engine (which shuts off at traffic lights, thanks to an Integrated Starter Generator). Also part of the package is a 65-kilowatt electric assist motor, plus a 28-kilowatt generator. The Escape has a range of 500 miles. Ford's green Escape is a full hybrid, which means it can go as fast as twenty-five miles per hour on battery power alone. The brakes are regenerative, feeding the battery when in use, and allowing accessories like the CD player and climate control to run on battery power alone. Ford is expanding its hybrid technology to other vehicles, including a midsized sedan.

Honda Civic Hybrid

The Civic Hybrid impresses with its sheer ordinariness. It's *not* special, or weird, or for purists only. It's just like any other Civic, except it's a Super Ultra-Low Emission Vehicle, gets fifty-two miles per gallon and has a range of 600 miles. If there's a sacrifice, it's in the $20,000 purchase price. But even that can be offset with federal income tax credits, as well as state incentives if they apply.

To get ninety-three horsepower out of a 1.3-liter engine requires some wizardry, and under the hood is the Integrated Motor Assist system from the two-passenger Insight, plus a continuously variable transmission (CVT).

Toyota Prius

An improved version of the Prius, which first appeared in the United States in 2000, was introduced in 2004. The wheelbase on the second-generation Prius is stretched six inches, but the car still achieves a combined miles-per-gallon rating in the mid-fifties, while also accelerating as well as a late-model Toyota Camry and winning certification as a Super Ultra-Low Emission Vehicle. Jason Mark of the Union of Concerned Scientists' Clean Vehicle Program describes the car as "a shining example of the gains possible with advanced technology." Roland Hwang of the Natural Resources Defense Council adds that "drivers get half the pollution and half the gasoline bill." Unlike the much-hyped Segway scooter, the 2004 deserves the advance praise it's getting.

Actor Leonardo DiCaprio is vocal about his Prius: "It's a step in the right direction," he says. "I fill it up at the gas pump and it performs like any other car. But I fill it up about once every three weeks. We have the technology to make every car produced in America today just as clean, cheap, and efficient."

WHAT YOU CAN DO

Driving

To read about the greenest vehicles on the market today, check out the American Council for the Energy-Efficient Economy's *ACEEE's Green Book*. Incidentally, the top six scorers are all Hondas and Toyotas. For the federal government's automotive gas-mileage database (which also has information on fuel cells and hybrids), visit www.fueleconomy.gov.

One of the best things consumers can do is to lobby their state legislators to adopt California's strict emissions standards. New York, Maine, Vermont, New Jersey, Connecticut, and Massachusetts have already made that choice, but in other states it has become a high-stakes battle, defeated repeatedly by lawmakers who hear more from paid auto industry lobbyists than they do from their air-breathing constituents.

If you simply want to get better fuel economy out of your existing car, here are some quick ways to do that:

Slow Down! The Environmental Protection Agency (EPA) and the Oak Ridge National Laboratory report that a car or truck loses about 1 percent in fuel economy for each one mile per hour above fifty-five mph. A car that averaged thirty mpg at fifty-five would get only 25.5 mpg at seventy. "Today's cars and trucks are really designed to operate most efficiently at fifty-five," says Jim Kliesch of ACEEE. "Above that, economy drops off rather quickly."

Steady As She Goes. You can get a 5 to 10 percent fuel savings by using your cruise control to maintain a constant speed on uncrowded highways. Cut out the "jackrabbit" starts, and the EPA says you'll see a 20 percent fuel savings. "Gentle and steady acceleration can improve mileage by up to twelve percent," says the Maryland Energy Administration.

Idle Time. Unnecessary idling costs you money and pollutes the air. The Department of Energy estimates that 145 million automobiles idling for five minutes each wastes four million gallons of gasoline. Twenty-four million tons of carbon dioxide emissions could be avoided every year if all American drivers cut their idle time by ten minutes a day. If your wait will be thirty seconds or longer, turn that engine off. Cold weather "warm ups" waste gas, too, and don't do your car any favors either.

Hot Tip. Whatever happened to the vent window? Auto air conditioners (installed on 90 percent of all new cars) may provide relief on a hot day, but using one kills fuel economy by up to 21 percent. Driving with the windows open will increase your car's aerodynamic drag, but it's a small effect compared to the drain of that AC unit.

Stay in Tune. The Department of Energy says a badly tuned engine will cost you a 20 percent fuel penalty. AutoZone, a car repair chain, estimates that replacing a bad oxygen sensor alone can improve mileage by 15 percent. Also check tire pressure. It's quite common for tires to be under-inflated by eight pounds, which increases rolling resistance by 5 percent. Translate that to $2.30 a month in fuel bills. Wheels that are even a quarter inch out of balance will add 2 percent to your rolling resistance.

Transit, Walking, and Biking

How about leaving the car at home, at least part of the time? Let's face it, some of us hop in our cars just to go around the block. It's like we've forgotten how to walk or pedal. Between 1980 and 1990, the Federal Highway Administration reports that the percentage of commuting trips made by bicycling and walking fell from a combined 6.7 percent to 4.4 percent.

Since a fourth of all American car trips are only a mile or less, it would be no great hardship to convert them to walking or biking. A good place to start is getting to know the transit agencies in your area. Is there light rail in the vicinity, or an Amtrak station? Do the bus routes include your neighborhood? How much do rides cost and are discounts available for students or seniors?

Here are a few action items that can help get you started:

- **Start small.** The Pedestrian Transportation Program in Portland, Oregon, advises, "Replace at least one car trip a week with a walk. Encourage family and friends to walk with you."

- **Calm traffic.** You'll be more likely to get out and walk or ride if traffic slows down, and your community will be safer, too. The traffic calming movement—with great success in Europe—encourages such simple-to-implement municipal measures as speed bumps, curb extensions to narrow traffic lanes, roundabouts (a great hit in Seattle!), street closures, bike lanes, and median islands.

- **Advocate for bikes.** Portland, Oregon, is in the forefront here and provides a model for other cities: Buses must be equipped to accommodate bikes, downtown clubs open their showers to bicycle commuters, and new buildings are required to install bike racks. New York City's Transportation Alternatives works closely with city transit agencies to increase bicycle commuting. "Bicycling and mass transit are both antidotes to the congestion and pollution caused by automobile use," the group says. "But for many travelers, neither form of transport alone can compete with the auto's combination of range, flexibility, and convenience. However, if bikes and transit work as a team, they make a formidable alternative."

- **Raise healthy kids.** Nearly three quarters of American schoolchildren (despite being in the throes of an obesity crisis) are driven to school.

Biking Basics

Some 17 million bicycles were sold in the United States in 2001, and the sale of this two-wheeled transport has become a $4.2 billion industry.

According to data from the 2000 census, between 411,000 and 750,000 Americans over the age of sixteen ride bicycles to work in an average week. Others are more optimistic: The Bicycle Institute of America claims 4.9 million ride bikes to work. It's not surprising that California has the largest number of bicycle commuters.

Bicycle lanes benefit all users. A 1989 Texas Transportation Institute study found that bicycle lanes provide nearly $5 in safety benefits for drivers alone for every $1 in costs. A 1995 FHWA study found that bicycle lanes reduce motor vehicle crashes by 49 percent. Presently, only 1 percent of the federal transportation budget is allocated to support projects aimed at improving bike and pedestrian routes, and Congress has proposed cutting even that funding. By comparison, the Netherlands spends fully 10 percent of its road budget on bicycle infrastructure.

The Sierra Club advises bikers to get organized. Among its recommendations:

Join Forces. Is there a bicycle club in your area or, even better, a bicycle-activist organization? Getting together with other cyclists is a good way to learn about routes, improve your skills and technique, and find fellow commuters.

Plan Your Route Carefully. Don't assume that the shortest, most direct route is the best—quality beats brevity. Look for quieter streets that aren't packed with buses and trucks. And stay off sidewalks—it's usually illegal and always dangerous.

Be Aware. Assume that drivers don't see you. Constantly check traffic all around you (a rearview mirror helps) so you can spot trouble before it's too late. Do everything you can to make yourself visible.

Equip Yourself. You've heard it before, but considering how many cyclists continue to tempt fate, wear your helmet, because in an accident, it might keep your skull intact. For shorter commutes, fat, knobby tires are less likely to slip on wet ground or get caught in metal gratings. For night riding, a flashing red light on the back of your bike can get a driver's attention.

A great resource for bikers, including an answer to the question, "How Bikeable Is My Community?" can be found at www.bicyclinginfo.org.

In Britain, according to the book *Divorce Your Car*, the number of seven- and eight-year-old walkers dropped from 80 percent in 1971 to nine percent in 1990. You could try walking your kids to school one or two days a week, or even create a Walking School Bus, as envisioned by British urban activist David Engwicht: Parents, police, local authorities, and teachers collaborate on a plan, and draw a map of children's homes and the safest possible routes. Adult volunteers become Walking Bus Drivers, who walk the routes and collect children along the way.

- **Organize.** Walk Boston provides a vivid model of a community that empowers pedestrians. Weekly walks are held around harbors, historic neighborhoods, and riverside parks. Walk Boston also advocates for traffic-calming installations (including wider sidewalks and bike paths), runs the first Safe Walks to School program in New England, and lobbies for pedestrian-friendly legislation.

Resources

Greening the Automobile

Since environmentalists discovered the connection between tailpipe exhaust and air pollution, they've tried to influence automakers to produce cleaner vehicles. Activists employ both carrots (in the form of praise for hybrid cars or fuel-cell prototypes) and well-sharpened sticks (critical reports, angry press conferences, and the threat of consumer boycotts).

Here are some of the more significant players:

American Council for an Energy-Efficient Economy. The Council publishes *ACEEE's Green Book*, an annually updated environmental guide to cars and trucks. It's $8.95 from ACEEE Publications, 1001 Connecticut Avenue, NW, Suite 801, Washington, DC 20036-5525, or via aceee_publications@aceee.org, (202)429-8873, www.aceee.org.

Clean Car Campaign. This national coalition includes the ACEEE, the Ecology Center of Ann Arbor, Environmental Defense, and the Union of Concerned Scientists. In addition to trying to convince automakers to reduce emissions and increase fuel economy, it also works to reduce or elimi-

Those Wonderful Automobiles

214—Number in millions of cars in the United States.
Source: Earth Policy Institute at www.earth-policy.org/Alerts/Alert12.htm.

1,600—Average annual amount in hours the average American male devotes to his car.
Source: Carbusters.org at www.carbusters.org/freesources/stats.php.

18—Average fuel economy in miles per gallon of U.S. SUVs and pickup trucks.
Source: The Detroit Project at www.thedetroitproject.com/readmore/talkingpoints.htm.

22,802—Miles per year driven by the average family in 1983.
34,459—Miles per year driven by the average family in 1995.
Source: Nationwide Personal Transportation Survey, available online at www.fhwa.dot.gov/ohim/1969/1969page.htm.

19—Percentage of the average American household budget devoted to transportation.
Source: Progress, February 2003, newsletter of the Surface Transportation Policy Project, www.transact.org.

50—Percentage increase in cars and trucks on the road between 1970 and 1990.
Source: Holtz Kay, Jane, *Asphalt Nation: How the Automobile Took Over America and How We Can Take It Back* (New York: Crown), 1997. Page 16. Her website is at: www.jane holtzkay.com.

This excerpt is published with permission from Grist Magazine (www.grist.org). For more environmental news and humor, sign up for Grist's free e-mail dispatches at www.grist.org/signup.

nate use of toxic mercury and PVC plastic in auto manufacturing. The campaign has convinced more than 150,000 people to sign the Clean Car Pledge, a nonbinding agreement to buy "the greenest vehicle available that meets my needs and fits my budget." 117 North Division Street, Ann Arbor, MI 48104, (734)663-2400 or 1875 Connecticut Avenue NW, Washington, DC 20009, (202)387-3500, www.cleancarcampaign.org.

Rocky Mountain Institute. Located in Colorado with a staff of fifty, RMI is headed by the visionary Amory Lovins, whose 1995 *Atlantic Monthly* article "Reinventing the Wheels" predicted today's lightweight hybrids. He is reviled as an impractical utopian by some auto executives, and consulted by others. RMI's latest study, published in the International Journal of Vehicle Design, highlights his virtual design of a projected ninety-nine-mpg mid-sized SUV with a carbon-composite body. 1739 Snowmass Creek Road, Snowmass, CO 81654-9199, (970)927-3851, www.rmi.org.

Got Wheels? How About Sharing Them?

The concept of "car sharing," popular in Europe since the late 1980s, is catching on in the United States. The basic idea: For a small annual fee and a per-use charge, members can have access to a car whenever and wherever they need it—while parking fees, maintenance, insurance, and depreciation are borne by the companies. Vehicles must be reserved in advance and returned to the starting location. Thanks to electronic keys, gas cards, and the Internet, taking advantage of this new public transportation link is becoming increasingly simple.

By the end of 2003, fifteen car-sharing companies had hit the streets in twenty U.S. cities, serving thousands of drivers. Membership doubled between 2002 and 2003, and the enterprise seems to be working best in cities with tight parking, good public transportation, and active "green" communities. Growing demand means growing fleets, say the companies, which helps ensure that the cars will be available when they're needed. They also cite this figure: every shared car equals six others taken off the road.

On the East Coast, drivers have access to the fleets of Zipcar, a private company operating in Boston; New York; Washington, D.C.; and Chapel Hill, North Carolina; Flexcar, a public/private partnership based in the Northwest that has expanded to Maryland, Virginia, and D.C.; and the nonprofit PhillyCarShare, which makes hybrids available in that city. Should you add your name to the rolls?

Besides being kind to your wallet, car sharing cuts down on emissions by reducing both driving time and the number of cars on the road. A recent University of California at Berkeley study followed hundreds of members of City CarShare in San Francisco and found 30 percent of them had sold one or more private cars after joining. Its members were driving 47 percent less than before joining, and using public transit, walking, and biking more.

One of the reasons car sharing is taking off—besides the obvious environmental motivation—is the ease of the Internet. Not only can members join, check availability, and make reservations online, they also use coded wireless-technology cards to unlock their cars. Soon they'll be able to use hand-held devices to locate vehicles, making parking options more flexible. Sharing hasn't looked this good since kindergarten.

Car-Sharing Resources

Flexcar. (202)296-1FLX, www.flexcar.com.
PhillyCarShare. (215)386-0988, www.philly carshare.com.
Zipcar. (617)491-9900, www.zipcar.com.

The Car Sharing Network's resource library is at www.carsharing.net/library.

Sierra Club. The 750,000-member, San Francisco-based Sierra Club regularly engages the auto industry on clean car issues. Dan Becker, its chief global warming campaigner in Washington, is known for issuing funny, Detroit-bashing sound bites that the media find irresistible. "Ford's overall fuel economy is at a twenty-year low," he says. But the club also works behind the scenes, using its considerable membership muscle to pass legislation and influence automaker decisions. 85 Second Street, 2nd Floor, San Francisco, CA 94105, (415)977-5500, www.sierraclub.org.

Union of Concerned Scientists. This nonprofit, based in Cambridge, Massachusetts, issues detailed reports on clean car technology, and works to pass legislation such as the new California law linking auto emissions and greenhouse gasses. "I don't think of our approach as confrontational or non-confrontational," says Research Director David Friedman. "We just try to bring the best technical information to bear." 2 Brattle Square, Cambridge, MA 02238-9105, (617)547-5552, www.ucsusa.org.

Auto Alternatives

Transit groups take many forms, from mainstream advocates for greater rail and bike use to radical anti-car activism. Some organizations excel at compiling statistics, others at direct action. All the groups listed here have done good work.

American Public Transportation Association. APTA pushes for increased public transportation subsidies and publishes an annual guide to U.S. transit habits. 1201 New York Avenue, NW, Washington, DC 20005, (202)898-4084, www.apta.com.

Amtrak Unlimited. A Web resource about the national rail service. www.amtraktrains.com.

Friends of Amtrak. An online resource for passenger rail information, http://trainweb.com.

International Bicycle Fund. A great resource for all things bicycle, including the colorful history of the bike and an index of statistical information.

4887 Columbia Drive South, Seattle, WA 98108-1919, (206)767-0848, www.ibike.org.

National Association of Rail Passengers. This group works for a better deal for the transit consumer. 900 Second Street, NE, Suite 308, Washington, DC 20002, (202)408-8362, www.narprail.org.

Reconnecting America. Headed by Hank Dittmar, founder of the Surface Transportation Policy Project, this philanthropic organization "works toward removing the barriers that prevent our different transportation modes—planes, trains, autos and buses, as well as walking and bicycling—from functioning as one convenient interconnected network." 615 East Lincoln Avenue, Las Vegas, NM 87701, (505)426-8055, www.ReconnectingAmerica.org.

Smart Growth America. Takes on urban sprawl and offers innovative solutions to autocentric development. 1200 18th Street NW, Suite 801, Washington, DC 20036, (202)207-3355, www.smartgrowthamerica.org.

Surface Transportation Policy Project (STTP). A very effective informational resource and lobbying force on behalf of transit and against increased highway construction. 1100 17th Street, NW, Tenth Floor, Washington, DC 20036, (202)466-2636, www.transact.org.

Sustainable Energy Institute (SEI). The head of this ferociously anti-car group, Jan Lundberg, once published the family operated *Lundberg Letter*, a respected source of information on oil industry trends. Now he advocates a car-free America and digs up driveways, opining, "Phasing out massive fossil-fuel use as fast as possible is crucial to saving Earth's climate from total destabilization." SEI publishes *Culture Change* magazine. P.O. Box 4347, Arcata, CA 95578, (215)243-3144, www.culturechange.org.

Books

Asphalt Nation: How the Automobile Took Over America, and How We Can Take It Back by Jane Holtz Kay (Berkeley: University of California Press).

Breaking Gridlock: Moving Toward Transportation That Works by Jim Motavalli (San Francisco: Sierra Club Books).

Divorce Your Car! Ending the Love Affair with the Automobile by Katie Alvord (Gabriola Island, British Columbia: New Society).

Forward Drive: The Race to Build "Clean" Cars for the Future by Jim Motavalli (San Francisco: Sierra Club Books).

High and Mighty: The Dangerous Rise of the SUV by Keith Bradsher (New York: PublicAffairs).

The Hype About Hydrogen by Joseph Romm (Washington, D.C.: Island Press).

chapter fourteen

Second Time Around

The Rewards of Reuse and Recycling

Photo by Paul Meyer/Index Stock

When Ohio University recycling manager Ed Newman wants to see how the campus is recycling he goes right to the heart of the matter—into the Dumpster. Though numbers show that students and faculty are recycling a decent 25 to 30 percent of residence and dining hall trash, Newman finds a different story when he goes on a "Dumpster dive" into one of the university containers. On his last dive, he found that 65 to 70 percent of what was still in the Dumpster was recyclable. While recycling numbers on campus are holding steady, the amount of reusable or recyclable materials still being discarded is growing.

Since the first recycling drop-off centers were established in 1970, community recycling programs have expanded to more than 9,000 curbside programs nationwide. In major U.S. cities, recycling accounts for as much as 50 to 60 percent of the municipal solid waste stream—a number that critics ten years ago said could not be reached. Such cities as Portland (Oregon), Seattle, Chicago, and San Jose showcase recycling success stories and give advocates hope.

But the progress is set against a growing problem: The percentage of traditional solid waste materials such as plastic and aluminum beverage containers being recycled has decreased. According to the National Association of PET Container Resources, the PET plastic bottle recycling rate dropped from 39.7 percent in 1995 to 19.9 percent in 2002. Aluminum can recycling dropped to 49.2 percent—its lowest rate since 1980, according to the Container Recycling Institute.

CURRENT EVENTS/LEGISLATIVE/POLITICAL

"If you don't recycle you can't consider yourself an environmentalist," says Neil Seldman, president of the Washington, D.C.-based Institute for Local Self-Reliance. But while recycling has become established in some cities, the national recycling rate has stagnated at 30 percent since the 1990s. With tough economic times, many recycling programs are among the first on the chopping block—but are often saved by community outcries. Further opposition to recycling comes from the virgin materials industries, including timber and mining, from the waste-hauling industry and other anti-recycling political and corporate groups.

Recycling is also confusing for consumers, according to a study presented at the National Recycling Coalition (NRC) Congress last year by advertising agency DDB Bass & Howes. "We've all been so focused on creating this business that we've not done a good job of listening to customers—Americans at home and at work who want to recycle," says Kate Kreb, executive director of NRC.

In particular, the movement needs to improve education, Kreb says. NRC is working to design standard recycling icons like the familiar circling arrows that will be instantly recognizable.

NRC also is working to dispel many of the myths associated with recycling, such as the idea that it costs more than it can contribute to the economy. In fact, according to an NRC study, recycling is a strong business, larger than either the mining or waste industries in the United States, with jobs that pay more than manufacturing. Another common myth—that materials do not get recycled even when put in the right bins—developed from a few exaggerated incidents.

Whether because of these myths or other factors, we're losing the battle to cope with our growing mountain of waste. One of the main causes of the percentage decrease is the enormous growth of container production, says CRI research director Jenny Gitlitz. PET sales have skyrocketed as the bottled water industry has exploded. Curbside programs are not convenient for the increasing numbers of people consuming these beverages away from home. And current recycling systems cannot hope to match the sheer numbers of products being produced.

Bottle bills, which shift the burden of responsibility for beverage waste from the taxpayer to the producer by forcing manufacturers to design container refund systems of 2.5 to 10 cents, operate in eleven states. Studies have shown that the recycling rates in bottle bill states are much higher than the average.

The best way to address the rising number of containers is to create new bottle bills in states without them, Gitlitz says, and to adjust old bills for inflation. But opponents of bottle bills, including the Connecticut-based Keep America Beautiful, are a major obstacle, Gitlitz says.

Even when materials do manage to avoid the garbage can, other issues arise that may prevent them from being cycled back into new products. Many U.S. cities have adopted single-stream recycling systems using compactor trucks, but the broken and blended materials contaminate other products, particularly paper, since glass shards imbed in paper fibers and reduce or destroy their quality. "The quality of curbside material in single-stream systems has deteriorated significantly," says Tex Corley, president and CEO of the Houston-based glass recycling company Strategic Materials. In the worst cases, as much as 50 percent of the volume of collected glass is actually made up of contaminants.

Recycled glass takes less energy than raw materials to melt. In fact, the demand for recycled glass far exceeds the available supply, Corley says. But low-quality glass is expensive to process, he adds, so more and more contaminated material is "recycled" for use in road construction or as landfill cover.

A new trend in the movement is coalition building toward the ultimate goal of "zero waste." Networks of groups with a broader interest than just solid waste have replaced state recycling associations as the main force of the recycling movement, Seldman says. Such groups as the GrassRoots Recycling Network (GRRN) and the Global Alliance for Incinerator Alternatives connect activists from across the country and around the world.

The zero waste idea is also catching on in the United States, and has been adopted by companies like Minnesota-based personal-care company Aveda and California's Fetzer Vineyards (which hopes to achieve the magic goal by 2009). Xerox's goal is the waste-free factory. "We are using our materials very inefficiently today," says Gary Liss, a zero-waste consultant and pioneer. "We could produce 100 times the products with the same resources if we were looking at the total system on a holistic basis. And it doesn't have to be altruistic."

Bill Sheehan helped found the GRRN in 1995, then left to organize the Georgia-based Product Policy Project. The project focuses on shifting responsibility for product waste from the consumer and communities to the producer. Recycling is not enough, he says, because "the real heart of the matter" lies in the production.

"The makers of products need to take physical or financial responsibility," Sheehan says. "Corporations should be made to adopt a 'cradle-to-cradle' management of their products." Seldman says there has already been considerable progress in this movement with batteries, computers, paints, and building materials, to name a few.

Sheehan would also like to see the United States adopt programs that have worked in European countries. Seldman points out that the developing producer responsibility laws in Europe are causing a revolution, "which will force U.S. companies to comply if they want to sell their products on that continent."

New Zealand launched a national pilot program to achieve "zero waste" in 1999. The group Zero Waste New Zealand Trust is leading the way, and has already achieved significant landfill reduction across the country. One district has cut landfilling from 10,000 tons to 3,500 tons per year. "New Zealand was the first country in the world to give women the vote," says Warren Snow, a Trust leader. "Now it's on its way to become the first zero waste country."

On a local level, recycling programs are finding success in linking up with community sustainability groups, and they benefit from some new laws, such as state tax exemptions on recycling equipment. The combination of all these efforts will give recycling new life and help people realize both immediate and long-term environmental results. "Recycling can be slowed down but it will never be defeated," says Seldman.

WHAT YOU CAN DO

To make the most of the recycling opportunities in your community, it's important to understand the fundamentals. The cryptic symbols on plastic containers and the rules on paper can be confusing. Obviously, regulations vary from community to community, but the everyday items acceptable at local recycling centers or curbside include:

Recyclable Paper

White office paper, corrugated cardboard, newspaper, phonebooks, brown paper bags, magazines, and all mixed paper. (Paper must be uncontaminated—free from plastics, food items, rubber bands, binder clips, tape, and wax. Staples and plastic window envelopes can be recycled, and often paper clips as well.) Normally non-recyclable papers (there are exceptions) include: sanitary paper, tissues, waxed paper (including cartons and cardboards), oil-soaked paper, laminated paper (including fast-food wrappers and pet food bags), stickers, carbon paper, and thermal fax paper.

Recyclable Plastics

Plastics must be separated by type in order to be recycled. Refer to the bottom or back of the container for the designated recycling symbol. This will explain if and how the product can be recycled. Caps, lids, and spray tops are generally molded from a different plastic than the container, but check with your local recycler to see if they need to be removed. Plastic containers (labeled with assigned numbers inscribed in the triangle recycling symbol):

Plastics 1, 2, 4 are . . . Easily recycled curbside or at local recycling centers.
Plastics 3, 5, 7 are . . . non-recyclable in most cases.
Plastic 6 is . . . difficult to recycle (foam packaging as an example); Call local recycling centers for further instruction.

Other Plastics

Recyclable plastics should be labeled with the proper symbol. If nothing is visible, either assume the item is made of multiple plastics and must be discarded or call you local recycling authorities for more directions. Grocery bags (both plastic and paper) can often be returned to grocery stores or reused there.

Recyclable Glass

Unbroken glass bottles. Clear glass bottles (the most valuable) must often be separated from colored glass bottles. Labels do not have to be removed

The Neglected "R": Reuse

Most of us don't think twice about renting videos, borrowing books from the library, patronizing antique stores, donating unwanted clothes to charity, or putting yesterday's newspaper under the pet-food bowl. These seemingly ordinary activities represent "reuse"—the second environmental strategy of the well known three Rs: Reduce, Reuse, and Recycle. What makes reuse so powerful, and worthy of increased attention, is that it couples environmental activity with social needs. In relationship to economic, ecological, and humanitarian concerns, reuse is often more effective—and more rewarding—than recycling.

Reuse is accomplished in many different ways: purchasing durable goods, attending to maintenance and repair, trading in the used marketplace, borrowing or renting, and making or receiving charitable transfers. It can have a huge effect on the environment: By reclaiming parts from 11 million vehicles annually, North American automotive salvage yards save an estimated 85 million barrels of oil that would otherwise be utilized to manufacture new replacement parts.

Exciting inroads in refuse reduction have come from industrial "waste exchanges"—matchmaking services that link businesses discarding potentially usable material with other businesses that can use it. One such program, New Hampshire's WasteCap, diverted more than 1.1 million pounds of waste in 1999. There are an estimated 300 to 500 waste exchanges operating in North America. Beyond Waste, a building deconstruction company in California, salvaged almost fifty tons of reusable material from a single job removing the roof over a city reservoir.

The broad scope of reuse options makes it easy for everyone to participate. An extensive database of reuse opportunities exists at www.iReuse.org. Businesses and charitable organizations (and you, too, if you're an ambitious junk-into-jewels trader) will find a practical reuse website for the exchange of stuff that would otherwise go into landfills at www.throwplace.com. Businesses and organizations can also get help reducing waste on multiple fronts, including reuse, from the EPA's WasteWise Program (www.eps.gov/wastewise or 800-372-9473).

Public libraries make reuse easy, and everyone qualifies for a card. Books, magazines, newspapers, movies, music, and in some places toys and tools are all circulated for free. Catalogs are now online, and in some states you can even locate and check out books in out-of-town libraries.

On an informal level, people can borrow and exchange among family, friends, and neighbors. A related practice is joint ownership. This is most common with expensive tools used only occasionally, but there are examples of people who are the same size sharing their wardrobe in this way.

Despite the fact that people routinely rent videos and cars, few recognize the breadth of this reuse option. There are more than

12,000 rental outlets in North America offering a surprising array of goods from automotive tools to wedding gowns. One way to discover the choices is by consulting the Yellow Pages.

from bottles.) Other glass, from lightbulbs to windows, must typically be recycled separately.

Recyclable Metals

Aluminum cans or foil. "Tin" cans made from steel. (Other household metals are rarely recycled, but larger pieces can usually be recycled at your local junk or scrap metal yard.)

Other Household Items

Rechargeables: nickel cadmium (Ni-Cd), nickel metal hydride (Ni-MH), lithium ion (Li-ion) and small sealed lead (Pb) batteries can be recycled. Call (800)8BATTERY for disposal information.

Automobiles

Tires, oil, and batteries can usually be recycled, and the metal is recovered in junkyards at the end of the car's life. Call your local quick lube shop or auto shop for recommendations.

Toxic Chemicals

Paints, poisons, oils, cleaners, and herbicides should never be thrown away or poured down any drain pipe. Call your local poison control center, garbage or recycling centers for more information on disposal.

A comprehensive and consumer-friendly recycling guide is at www.obviously.com/recycle. Obviously, recycling directions vary considerably from locality to locality and state to state.

Resources

Recycling

Container Recycling Institute. A nonprofit organization dedicated to creating environmental awareness by promoting policies that hold producers, consumers, and manufacturers accountable for any social or environmental impairment. 1911 North Fort Myer Drive, Suite 702, Arlington, VA 22209-1603, (703)276-9800, www.container-recycling.org.

EPA. For a list of waste exchanges, visit the EPA online at www.epa.gov/jtr/comm/exchange.htm. Regional listings are also available at www.epa.gov/jtr/netshare/waste.htm.

Grassroots Recycling Network. The network is compiled of environmental activists who strategize to eliminate the waste of natural and human resources by promoting corporate and governmental responsibility. 210 Bassett Street, Suite 200, Madison, WI 53703, (706)613-7121, www.grrn.org.

Institute for Local Self-Reliance. A small organization that strives to encourage sustainable economic and communal development. 927 15th Street NW, 4th Floor, Washington, DC 20005, (202)898-1610, www.ilsr.org.

National Recycling Coalition. A coalition devoted to maximizing national recycling efforts in the prospect of conserving human and natural resources. 1325 G Street NW, Suite 1025, Washington, DC 20005, (202) 347-0450, www.nrc-recycle.org.

ReDO. Provides information on reuse options and setting up a materials exchange, which channels unwanted equipment from businesses to nonprofit groups, schools, cultural organizations, and community centers. c/o The Loading Dock, 2523 Gwynns Falls Parkway, Baltimore, MD 21216, (410)669-7245, www.redo.org.

Urban Ore. Began as an informal salvage operation at the Berkeley, California, landfill in 1980. Now runs the Urban Ore Eco Park, a showcase for sus-

Routine Reuse

- Use rechargeable batteries wherever possible.

- Carry a refillable mug.

- Donate books you no longer want to local libraries. Or, sell online or to used-book dealers.

- Use cotton towels in the kitchen for cleaning up and hand wiping. Have a good stock and launder often.

- Dry salad greens with a salad spinner rather than using paper towels.

- Clean floors with carpet sweepers, electric brooms, shop vacs, and vacuum cleaners that feature permanent filters or reusable collection bags.

- Bring your own carrier (or several) when buying groceries.

- Carry a handkerchief.

- "Brown" bag in washable cloth sacks or durable lunch boxes. Pack food in resealable plastic containers proportioned to hold salads, sandwiches, beverages, and such. (Rubbermaid makes a good selection.)

- Preserve memories with a standard or digital (rather than single-use) camera.

- Buy recharged computer printer cartridges and return spent cartridges for recharging. There are numerous companies that provide this service, with many listings at www.iReuse.org.

- Donate your old cell phone to a reuse program (www.wirelessfoundation.org, www.collectivegood.com or www.charitablerecycling.com/CR/home.asp).

tainable building materials and design. 2118 Milvia Street, Suite 200, Berkeley, CA 94704, (510)981-7530, www.urbanore.citysearch.com.

For Reuse: National Donation Resource List

American Cancer Society. Upscale Discovery Shops throughout the United States. 1599 Clifton Road NE, Atlanta, GA 30345, (800)227-2345, www.cancer.org.

Practicing Paper Conservation

Simple everyday habits can dramatically reduce paper use.

- Paper waste can be reduced by such reusable products as washable diapers, cloth handkerchiefs and napkins, rags, fabric gift bags, durable shopping bags and lunch boxes, washable air and oil filters, durable dishes, and washable coffee filters and tea infusers rather than their paper-based counterparts.

- When responding to an inquiry letter, answer directly on the original letter.

- Instead of leaving paper notes for household members, institute a message system on a chalkboard or whiteboard.

- Edit and proofread work on the computer before printing.

- Use direct computer faxing and e-mail where possible.

- Borrow books, magazines, and newspapers from libraries.

- Businesses can cut paper use by duplex copying, billing in two-way envelopes, employing e-mail, shipping in round-trip cartons, and outfitting rest rooms with cloth towels.

- Rather than sending separate memos to employees, use a single copy with a routing slip. Post directives on a centrally located message board, or via interoffice software programs.

- Load copying machines and suitable printers with paper used on one side for drafts or file copies.

- Use the clean side of used paper for sending faxes. When sending faxes, avoid using a separate cover sheet.

- Turn scrap paper into notepads.

Association for Retarded Citizens (ARC). Many state and local chapters operate thrift shops. 1010 Wayne Avenue, Suite 650, Silver Spring, MD 20910, (301)562-3842, www.thearc.org.

Gifts in Kind America. Accepts donations of a wide variety of goods from the business sector. 333 North Fairfax Avenue, Alexandria, VA 22314, (703)836-2121, www.giftsinkind.org.

Goodwill Industries International. Operates 1,900 thrift shops, all seeking donated items. 15810 Indianola Drive, Rockville, MD 20855, (301)530-6500, www.goodwill.org.

Salvation Army. The easiest way to find a Salvation Army thrift shop is in the phone book. 615 Slaters Lane, P.O. Box 269, Alexandria, VA 22313, (703)684-5500, www.salvationarmyusa.org.

Society of St. Vincent de Paul. 58 Progress Parkway, St. Louis, MO 63043-3706, (314)576-3993, www.svdpusa.org (click on "stores").

Volunteers of America (VOA). The need for donated items varies widely by location. 1660 Duke Street, Alexandria, VA 22314-3421, (800)899-0089. For a nearby program check www.volunteersofamerica.org/extlocations .cfm.

Waste to Charity.org. Largely manufacturers' and business overstock, but can direct donations from individuals as well. Woodbury Executive Center, 15 East Center Street, Woodbury, NJ 08096, (856)456-4996, www .wastetocharity.org.

Contributors

Brian C. Howard (assisting editor and author of the energy chapter) began his tenure at *E* as an intern and then moved into his current post as managing editor four years ago. He has also written for Britain's *Ergo Living* magazine, Alternet, *Oceana*, the *Green Guide, Glamour, Geological Society of America Abstracts & Programs*, the Appalachian Mountain Club, and Environmental Defense. He has served as an environmental educator and conducted scientific research on wetland birds and invertebrate fossils. Howard holds degrees in geology and biology from Indiana University. He grew up in Michigan and Indiana with a passionate love for the outdoors, and now lives in coastal Connecticut.

Doug Moss is *E*'s publisher and executive editor. Doug cofounded *E* in 1990 with his wife and *E* associate publisher, Deborah Kamlani, and is involved day-to-day in *E*'s editorial planning, its fundraising, circulation and marketing efforts, and in special projects such as this book. Prior to founding *E*, he cofounded *The Animals' Agenda*, a bimonthly animal protection magazine, serving as an editor and its first publisher from 1979 until 1988. He also founded (in 1979) and owns Douglas Forms, a supplier of business forms and other kinds of printing to magazines, nonprofit organizations, and other businesses. Doug has also been involved in numerous community organizing activities, including ballot access efforts for Dr. Barry Commoner's Citizens Party presidential bid in 1980, and a successful nuclear freeze referendum in Norwalk, Connecticut in 1982.

Jim Motavalli (lead editor, and writer on travel and transportation) is the editor of *E* and author or editor of three books, *Forward Drive: The Race to Build "Clean Cars" for the Future* (Sierra Club Books, 2000), *Breaking Gridlock: Moving Toward Transportation That Works* (Sierra Club Books, 2001), and *Feeling the Heat: Dispatches from the Frontlines of Climate Change* (Routledge, 2004). He is a regular featured columnist in both the Environmental Defense newsletter and *AMC Outdoors*, and writes regularly on automotive and environmental subjects for the *New York Times*. He lives in Fairfield, Connecticut, with his wife and two daughters.

Karen Soucy is *E*'s associate publisher and advertising director. She also helps coordinate many of *E*'s partnerships with environmental companies and organizations that promote environmental issues and encourage people to live more lightly with regard to their lifestyle habits and purchasing decisions. Prior to joining *E*, she was publisher of *Wallcoverings, Windows and Interior Fashion*, an international interior fashion trade publication. She has a fifteen-year background in advertising and marketing, including management experience at such publications as *The Village Voice* and Gannett Newspapers. Karen is also a Literacy Volunteers of America volunteer.

Chapter Contributors

Linda Baker (the Internet-only "sick" office chapter) is an award-winning journalist in Portland, Oregon, specializing in family, health, and environmental issues. Her work has been published in the *New York Times, Sierra, E/The Environmental Magazine, Utne, The Christian Science Monitor, Self*, Salon.com and *Vogue*, among other publications.

Sally Deneen (food) has reported extensively on genetic engineering for magazine and book projects. She has won several awards for her environmental reporting in Florida. A freelance writer for more than a decade and previously a staff writer at the *South Florida Sun-Sentinel*, her work has appeared in publications as diverse as *E/The Environmental Magazine, Organic Gardening, U.S. News & World Report, USA Today, Columbia Journalism Review*, and another popular *E Magazine* book project, *Feeling the Heat: Dispatches from the Frontlines of Climate Change* (Routledge, 2004). Her mother grew up on an Indiana farm, and Sally has fond childhood memories of visiting cousins on family farms in Ohio and Indiana. She is passionate about food: A former restaurant reviewer, she and her husband belong to a Community Supported Agriculture program and tend a small organic garden at their home in Seattle.

Kim Erickson (personal care) is a freelance journalist and researcher, and the author of *Drop Dead Gorgeous: Protecting Yourself from the Hidden Dangers of Cosmetics* (Contemporary Books, 2002). Her work has appeared in *E/The En-*

vironmental Magazine, Sierra, Cooking Light, and numerous other magazines. Erickson is on the advisory board of *Delicious Living* and is the former editor of *Health & Longevity*. She makes her home in Las Vegas, Nevada.

Marshall Glickman (socially responsible investing) is the editor/publisher of the environmental journal *Green Living*. He is the author of *The Mindful Money Guide: Creating Harmony Between Your Values and Your Finances* (Ballantine Books). His articles have appeared in many publications, including *The New York Times Magazine, The Washington Post, The Chicago Tribune, E, Natural Home,* and *Mother Earth News*. He lives in Williamsville, Vermont, with his wife and two daughters and, after numerous requests, is considering managing investments for individuals and institutions interested in creating truly balanced socially responsible portfolios.

Nikki and David Goldbeck (recycling and reuse) are authors or coauthors of eleven food, consumer, or environmental books including *Choose to Reuse: An Encyclopedia of Services, Businesses, Tools and Charitable Programs That Foster Reuse* (Ceres Press). David Goldbeck is founder and president of Reuse Opportunities, Inc., a not-for-profit organization dedicated to promoting reuse. www.iReuse.org.

Phoebe Hall (the Internet-only paper chapter), a former *E* intern, has reported for the *Westerly Sun* in Rhode Island and the *Mystic River Press* in Connecticut, and now edits a chain of papers for Connecticut-based Shore Publishing. She has a master's degree in journalism from Northwestern.

Elizabeth Hilts (natural clothing) began her writing career covering fashion for the *Fairfield County Advocate*. Since then she has expanded her scope to include writing about environmental and lifestyle topics for *E/The Environmental Magazine* and other print and online publications and worked as an editor in the alternative press and book publishing. However, Elizabeth is probably best known as the author of *Getting in Touch with Your Inner Bitch*, and *The Inner Bitch Guide to Men, Relationships, Dating, Etc.*

Orna Izakson (gardening) started her first garden in 1994, when friends gave her plants that needed to get back into the soil within twenty-four hours. She's been gardening organically ever since, outside of her working hours as a staffer at newspapers around the country. When she's not hanging out at her local plant nursery in Portland, Oregon, Orna is a freelance environmental journalist whose work has appeared in *E/The Environmental Magazine*, *Utne*, *Pacific Fishing*, and *The Los Angeles Times*.

Melissa Knopper (natural health care) is a Denver-based health and science writer who has written for *E/The Environmental Magazine*, Reuters Health, *CBS HealthWatch*, *The Chicago Tribune*, *The Rocky Mountain News*, *American Health*, *Clinician News*, *CURE Magazine*, *Women's Wear Daily*, and the Robert Wood Johnson Foundation's newsletter, *Advances*. During her five years as a general news reporter for the *Daily Herald* in suburban Chicago, she investigated pollution at O'Hare Airport, chronicled the rise of invasive species in Lake Michigan, and tracked development trends in the fastest-growing county in the nation. She also covered the health and environment beat for the *Register-Citizen* in Torrington, Connecticut, after earning a master's degree in journalism from Columbia University in 1990.

Diane Marty (the baby chapter) is a Colorado-based freelance author specializing in environmental and health topics. She recently gained a special and vested interest in keeping the world safe for children with the birth of her first grandchild. Since then, her house has become a fragrance- and dye-free fortress and her vegetable bins a veritable organic orchard.

Mindy Pennybacker (the healthy home) has been editor since 1996 of *The Green Guide*, a consumer publication of the nonprofit Green Guide Institute. Published in print and online, *The Green Guide* (www.thegreenguide.com) provides practical information on healthier, more ecologically sound products and actions, and reports the latest studies on the links between our personal health and the environment. Home building, renovation and decorating products, energy and water conservation, cleaning products, and least toxic pest control are topics frequently explored in *The Green Guide*. A graduate of Stanford, the University of Iowa Writers Workshop, and the University of California, Davis, law school, she has been a National Endowment for the Arts, Wallace Stegner, MacDowell, and Yaddo writing fellow and a journalism fellow at the Marine Biological Laboratory at Woods Hole. She has published in *The Nation*, *The Atlantic Monthly*, *Sierra*, and the *New York Times*, and is coauthor of *The Mothers & Others Guide to Natural Baby Care* (Wiley, 1999).

Joni Praded (pet care) was the longtime director of *Animals* magazine, which covered wildlife, pets, and the environment. Her articles on emerging environmental issues and international wildife issues have appeared in

Mother Jones, *E/The Environmental Magazine*, *Scientific American Explorations*, *Body & Soul*, *Offspring*, and *Unlimited*. She lives in New Hampshire with her son, a dog, and a hamster.

Starre Vartan (kids chapter) has degrees in geology and English from Syracuse University and is a freelance writer specializing in health, science, and nutrition. Her articles have appeared in *E/The Environmental Magazine*, the *Hartford Advocate*, Friends of Animals' *Action Line*, and Appalachian Mountain Club newsletters. Her regular columns on food and commuting appear in the *Fairfield County Weekly*. She has worked as an environmental educator and as a science writer. Starre grew up in the Hudson River Valley, and its natural areas and unique beauty inspired her to advocate for environmental causes.

Contributing Editors

Katherine Hartley has a degree in communications from the University of Tennessee and has served as an intern at *E Magazine*. She attends the journalism graduate program at the University of Montana.

Becca Manning, a former *E* intern, is a recent graduate of Ohio University, where she studied magazine journalism and environmental studies.

April Reese is a freelance writer and editor based in Santa Fe, New Mexico. She covers environmental topics for various publications, including *High Country News*, the *Santa Fe Reporter*, *E Magazine*, and the *Denver Post*. She holds a master's degree from the Yale School of Forestry and Environmental Studies, and was also an *E* intern.

About *E/The Environmental Magazine*

E/*The Environmental Magazine* debuted in 1990 while the world was celebrating the 20th anniversary of Earth Day, yet reeling from a series of environmental shocks, including the *Exxon Valdez* oil spill, "greenhouse summers," fires in Yellowstone Park, and medical waste washing up on eastern shores. In the time since, *E* has established itself as the leading independent environmental journal.

Edited for the general reader but also in sufficient depth to appeal to the dedicated activist, *E* is a clearinghouse of information, news, commentary, and resources on environmental issues. *E* was founded and is published by Connecticut residents Doug Moss and Deborah Kamlani, and it is edited by Connecticut resident and long-time writer, author, and radio host Jim Motavalli. *E* is a project of the not-for-profit Earth Action Network, Inc., which also owns and manages the environmental website www.emagazine.com, where an extensive archive of *E* stories is maintained. *E* also produces the syndicated question-and-answer column "EarthTalk," which appears weekly in a variety of hometown newspapers around the United States.

E covers everything environmental—from recycling to rainforests, and from the "personal to the political"—and reports on all the key and emerging issues, providing substantial contact information so readers can investigate topics further and/or plug into activist efforts.

E also follows the activities and campaigns of a broad spectrum of environmental organizations, and provides information on a range of lifestyle topics—food, health, travel, "house and home," personal finance, consumer product trends—as they relate to environmental quality.

E has drawn considerable recognition since its launch, garnering a dozen awards and citations for its style and content. In 2003, *E* received three Independent Press Award nominations and won in the category of "Best Science/Environment Coverage." In 1999, The Population Institute awarded *E* a Global Media Award for "Excellence in Population Reporting."

Many *E* articles can be found in mainstream newspapers and such websites as MSNBC.com, TomPaine.com, Environmental News Network (ENN), *Grist*, and others, primarily by arrangement with the Los Angeles Times Syndicate (now Tribune Media), the New York Times Syndicate, and Alternet.

Subscriptions are $19.95 per year (six bimonthly issues) and can be ordered by writing: *E Magazine*, P.O. Box 2047, Marion, OH 43306; by calling: (800)967-6572; or by visiting *E* online at www.emagazine.com.

Green Living readers have exclusive access to even more information about the sustainable lifestyle. Go to http://www.emagazine.com/book on the Internet, type in the keyword "gliving" and the password "chapters," and you'll be taken to a page offering two further chapters of the book. Our chapter "Prescriptions for the Sick Office" will leave you wondering if your work space needs work. And the chapter "Words on Paper: Tree-Free or Recycled?" explores alternatives to tree-based paper.

Index